Wildfire and Power

This book examines disasters as social phenomena. It brings together perspectives from sociology, political science, gender studies and history to produce new ways of analysing and understanding wildfire preparedness and policy in Australia. Drawing on data from many interviews with residents, volunteers and emergency services professionals living and working in wildfire-prone areas, the authors focus on issues of power and inequality, the contested nature of community and the relationship between citizens and the state.

The book questions not only existing policy approaches but also the central concepts on which they are founded. In doing so, the aim is to create a more conceptually robust and academically contextualised discussion about the limitations of current wildfire policy approaches in Australia and provide further evidence of the need for disaster studies to engage with a variety of social science approaches.

Wildfire and Power: Policy and Practice will be of most interest to policy makers, practitioners, researchers and others concerned with disasters and emergency management worldwide as well as debates about policy formulation, implementation and application. It will also provide an opportunity for those in disaster-prone areas to reflect on their experiences and understandings of these events. More generally the book will be of interest to those who seek to understand questions about power and inequality, diversity and participation at a community level and the challenges of gender and household decisions in relation to disaster events.

Peter Fairbrother is Professor of International Employment Relations and Deputy Director, Centre for People, Organisation and Work, RMIT University, Australia.

Meagan Tyler is Senior Lecturer, Centre for People, Organisation and Work, RMIT University, Australia.

Routledge Studies in Employment and Work Relations in Context

Edited by Tony Elger and Peter Fairbrother

The aim of the *Employment and Work Relations in Context Series* is to address questions relating to the evolving patterns and politics of work, employment, management and industrial relations. There is a concern to trace out the ways in which wider policy-making, especially by national governments and transnational corporations, impinges upon specific workplaces, occupations, labour markets, localities and regions. This invites attention to developments at an international level, marking out patterns of globalization, state policy and practices in the context of globalization and the impact of these processes on labour. A particular feature of the series is the consideration of forms of worker and citizen organization and mobilization. The studies address major analytical and policy issues through case study and comparative research.

Reshaping the North American Automobile Industry
Restructuring, Corporatism and Union Democracy in Mexico
John P. Tuman

Work and Employment in the High Performance Workplace
Edited by Gregor Murray, Jacques Belanger, Anthony Giles and Paul-Andre Lapointe

Trade Unions and Global Governance
The Debate on a Social Clause
Gerda van Roozendaal

Wildfire and Power
Policy and Practice
Peter Fairbrother and Meagan Tyler

For more information about this series, please visit: https://www.routledge.com

Wildfire and Power

Policy and Practice

Peter Fairbrother and Meagan Tyler

Routledge
Taylor & Francis Group

NEW YORK AND LONDON

First published 2019
by Routledge
711 Third Avenue, New York, NY 10017

and by Routledge
2 Park Square, Milton Park, Abingdon, Oxon, OX14 4RN

Routledge is an imprint of the Taylor & Francis Group, an informa business

Library of Congress Cataloging-in-Publication Data
Names: Fairbrother, Peter, editor. | Tyler, Meagan, editor.
Title: Wildfire and power : policy and practice / edited by Peter Fairbrother and Meagan Tyler.
Description: New York, NY : Routledge, 2019. |
Series: Routledge studies in employment and work relations in context | Includes bibliographical references and index.
Identifiers: LCCN 2018034641 | ISBN 9781138370203 (hardback) | ISBN 9780429428142 (ebook)
Subjects: LCSH: Fire management—Australia. | Wildfires—Prevention and control—Government policy—Australia. | Wildfire risk—Australia.
Classification: LCC SD421.34.A8 W555 2019 |
DDC 363.37/90994—dc23
LC record available at https://lccn.loc.gov/2018034641

ISBN: 978-1-138-37020-3 (hbk)
ISBN: 978-0-429-42814-2 (ebk)

Typeset in Sabon
by codeMantra

Contents

List of Authors

Yoko Akama: Associate Professor of Communication Design, School of Design, RMIT University

Vanessa Cooper: Professor and Director, Centre for People, Organisation and Work, RMIT University

Peter Fairbrother: Professor of International Employment Relations and Deputy Director, Centre for People, Organisation and Work, RMIT University

Bernard Mees: Associate Professor, School of Business and Economics, University of Tasmania

Richard Phillips: Research Officer, Centre for People, Organisation and Work, RMIT University

Keith Toh: Senior Lecturer, School of Management, RMIT University

Meagan Tyler: Senior Lecturer, Centre for People, Organisation and Work, RMIT University

Acknowledgements

The authors would like to thank all those who contributed to the original research program on which much of this book is based. In particular, we would like to extend our thanks to Dr Susan Chaplin, who conducted numerous interviews across several states, and to Alison Hart and Julie Stratford, who also conducted a number of interviews and cultivated connections in the early stages of the project. A big thank you, as well, to our two research coordinators over the course of the project at the Centre for People, Organisation and Work (CPOW), Amrutha Sakuru and Sam Carroll-Bell.

Particular thanks are due to Professor George Cairns, whose support as Head of the School of Management at RMIT University was essential to the success of the program.

We would also like to thank the professional staff who were part of the Bushfire Cooperative Research Centre (CRC), especially Lyndsey Wright, Richard Thornton and Noreen Krusel, who each made key contributions in seeing the research program through. Thanks must also go to our industry-based adviser, John Schauble, who was unwavering in his support for the project and was always generous with his time and advice.

We wish to express our gratitude to the team at Routledge, and especially to Mary Del Plato for her patience.

Meagan would like to take this opportunity to thank the 20 or so men who walked out of her presentation on gender and bushfire at the Australasian Fire and Emergency Service Authorities Council (AFAC) conference in 2013 for helping to convince her that there is still a lot of work to be done in this area.

Peter would like to thank all of the researchers who have contributed to this project in various ways as well as the CRC academic researchers who engaged in rich and robust debate about bushfire events across Australia.

Finally, all the authors would like to thank the interviewees and participants at workshops, without whose assistance the research program would not have been possible.

1 Wildfire

A Social and Political Perspective

Peter Fairbrother and Meagan Tyler

Disasters are social events. A natural hazard becomes a disaster when it interferes with the lives and well-being of people and communities. How to prepare for, experience and recover from such events is a long-standing challenge and puzzle. Often, the most expedient solution is viewed as a combination of state support and regulation, and the use of technologically based practices to monitor, prepare and deal with the immediate and then ensue recovery. A corollary of this focus is that individuals and their communities require the capabilities to prepare for and address the possibility of disaster events as well as their actual occurrence and aftermath. In this seemingly rounded way, it is claimed that natural disaster can be dealt with in more or less effective and expedient ways (e.g. McLennan and Handmer, 2012). The problem is that these relations bring questions of power into play in stark ways, a feature that is usually overlooked in relation to disaster events. Disaster events therefore require sociological and political analysis.

Increasing attention has been given to the ways in which communities adapt to such events and recover (e.g. Norris *et al.*, 2008; see also McLennan, 2016). In this respect, it is necessary to understand what enables engagement in relation to the prospect and actuality of disaster events as well as the inhibitors of such preparations and arrangements. Specifically, community actors, those living in disaster-prone localities, may not have the capabilities and resources to address these concerns, at least in ways that mitigate and allow adaptations to these types of events. Of course, those in such localities deal with often contested narratives about the dangers and responses that are most appropriate. Further, their resources to deal with such events may be limited. What appears to be a sensible, rational way of addressing such events for one individual, one household or even one locality may not be the same for another.

To understand the exercise of capacities, we argue that it is necessary to reflect on the social relationships that make up the societies in which we live. This focus draws attention to the complex relations between the state, the economy and civil society. These relations can be marked by inclusiveness and closure; they may be structured so some can exercise agency, while others are more constrained, and hence it is important to understand the ways in which societies are organised and structured. In general, in liberal democratic states, questions relating to the exercise of power and the bases of equality are to the fore. Increasingly, these states are structured in terms of inequalities – wealth, social position, gender, race, perceived capacities – and the exercise of power by dominant interests. So, who has capability and who has resources matter. Thus, to understand disaster, and in this case wildfire events (bushfire, grass fire, forest fire),[1] we argue that it is necessary to consider power and inequality, and the ways individuals and collectivities may be enabled or marginalised in relation to their vulnerability to such events. Policymakers often lack comprehensive understandings of the 'vulnerable' (frequently limiting the notion to the elderly and infirm) and do not appreciate the social bases of vulnerability, access to resources or unhelpful administrative and bureaucratic procedures (Wisner and Luce, 1993). More specifically, it is critical to trace out the power relations that define how and under what circumstances different social groupings can exercise agency in relation to disaster events. Such a focus draws attention to those who wield power in society (those who own and control resources), and those who 'control information and ...define agendas' (Wisner and Luce, 1993: 129).

Understanding disasters, therefore, is not just about observing, tracking and documenting 'uncontrolled brute forces' but rather about analysing the 'interaction of hazards and natural events with social structures' (Enarson and Morrow, 1998, p. 1). Over time, disaster studies have shifted to recognise this aspect: from quantitative, military-influenced studies in the 1950s and 1960s to the inclusion of qualitative social sciences and humanities in more recent decades (Reynolds, 2017). This shift has led to a greater acknowledgement of the role of social disasters and the need to better understand how people, in varied contexts, prepare for, react to and recover from disaster events.

We argue, however, that disasters must be situated not only in social contexts but in political contexts as well. As Enarson and Morrow (1998: 2) note, '[d]isasters reveal community, regional and global power structures, as well as power relations within intimate relationships'. That is, disaster events bring power relations to the fore across all levels, from the international and national to the organisational and local to the household and familial. This is one reason why disaster studies can and should focus on inequalities of power. We use this prism to analyse the context of wildfire/bushfire in Australia, where these themes are still significantly under-represented in existing research.

The Problem

Wildfire is one of the most common diaster events in many countires, including Spain, Portugal, the United States, Canada, Russia and Australia. Wildfires are an ongoing threat to society and increasingly so with climate change. The evidence is persuasive that societies across the world can expect an increasing range of disaster events throughout the twenty-first century, and wildfires are part of an increasing frequency and intensity of disasters, including floods, cyclones, hurricanes and other extreme events. It has become especially pressing to consider how and under what circumstances the residents and others in disaster-prone localities can deal with these events in ways that minimise the consequences.

The question becomes how best to address these disaster events for individuals, for families, for communities, for disaster agencies and for states. The impact of disasters will become part of the lives of many, and people across the world, and their governments and related agencies, will seek to prepare, quell, mitigate or adapt to these events. The question is how can these events be addressed in ways that minimise the loss of life and damage to property, infrastructure and livelihoods that are crucial for humane and sustainable societies? Thus, to put the question in the context of wildfire in Australia, it is necessary to review the relationship between the likelihood of the increased incidence and intensity of natural disasters; the preparations and responses taken by agencies and organisations; and the experience and understandings that individuals and groups bring to bear to prepare for, respond to and recover from such events.

Climate Change

There may be debate about the precise sequence and patterns of climate change, but there is no scientific doubt that Earth's surface is warming, with compelling consequences for the incidence and intensity of disaster events (IPPC Synthesis Report, 2014). Of course, in modern society, where some claim that all opinions have value, public irrationalists (euphemistically termed climate sceptics) can have a disproportionate impact on public debate and, in many cases, policy formulation and implementation. Such irrationality has the consequence of clouding understandings about the actual and probable impacts of climate change. But disasters do have a way of clarifying understandings about danger, preparation and response. Hence, for us the first step in the analysis is to understand the context in which there is an increased incidence and intensity in disaster events.

The evidence is clear; climate changes are taking place, and they are principally a consequence of human intervention.

> Human influence on the climate system is clear, and recent anthropogenic emissions of greenhouse gases are the highest in history. Recent climate changes have had widespread impacts on human and natural systems.
>
> (IPCC Synthesis Report, 2014: 36)

The impact is that the Earth's surface is warming. As stated, rather starkly:

> Warming of the climate system is unequivocal, and since the 1950s, many of the observed changes are unprecedented over decades to millennia.
>
> (IPPC Synthesis Report, 2014: 36)

But, of concern and reflected in the incidence and intensity of disaster events, in each of the last three decades, the Earth's surface has been successively warmer 'than any preceding decade since 1850' (IPPC Synthesis Report, 2014: 38).

Scientists express caution in relation to causation:

> Anthropogenic forcing have *likely* [sic] made a substantial contribution to surface temperature increases since the mid-20th century over every continental region except Antarctica.
>
> (IPPC Synthesis Report, 2014: 5)

Nonetheless, these changes play out in rather precise ways. As stated:

> In urban areas, climate change is projected to increase risks for people, assets, economies and ecosystems, including risks from heat stress, storms and extreme precipitation, inland and coastal pollution, drought, water scarcity, sea-level rise, and storm surges (*very high confidence*). These risks are amplified for those lacking essential infrastructure and services or living in exposed areas.
>
> (IPPC Synthesis Report, 2014: 15–16)

And:

> Rural areas are expected to experience major impacts on water availability and supply, food security, infrastructure, and agricultural incomes, including shifts in the production areas of food and non-food crops around the world (*high confidence*).
>
> (IPCC Synthesis Report, 2014: 16)

There has been an observed increase in the incidence and intensity of disaster events, including droughts, wind-storms, fires and pest outbreaks. While not conclusive, it is reasonable to attribute these trajectories in part to climate change, with '*medium confidence*' (IPCC Synthesis Report, 2014: 53). Thus, climate changes are increasing the likelihood of extreme weather events, such as flooding and drought (van Aalst, 2006).

Of importance these impacts are climate-related events, and hence it is necessary to take climate changes into account in relation to disaster events.

Impacts from recent climate-related extremes, such as heat waves, droughts, floods, cyclones, and wildfires, reveal significant vulner-ability and exposure of some ecosystems and many human systems to current climate variability (*very high confidence*). Impacts of such climate-related extremes include alteration of ecosystems, disrup-tion of food production and water supply, damage to infrastructure and settlements, human morbidity and mortality, and consequences for mental health and human well-being. For countries at all levels of development, these impacts are consistent with a significant lack of preparedness for current climate variability in some sectors.

(IPCC Synthesis Report, 2014: 55–56)

Thus, it is reasonable to suppose that disaster events are something that will continue to impact society, and there is a reasonable expectation that they will intensify in incidence and impact.

In relation to policy and preparation a variety of levels of action are necessary. Steps should be taken, and in limited ways are being taken, to address the causes and impacts of climate changes. It is vital that such initiatives are understood as intimately related to research and work to address and mitigate disaster events.

Disaster Events: Wildfire/Bushfire

Wildfires affect approximately 350 million hectares of land a year (FAO, 2010) in the northern and southern hemispheres. Australia, in particular the south-eastern part of the continent, is one of the most wildfire-prone localities in the world. Wildfires account for a significant incidence of injury and death, in the latter case comparable to flood and tropical cyclone (Coates *et al.*, 2014). Other assessments claim that bushfires and grass fires account for nearly half the total death and injury cost from natural hazards (AIC, 2004). Wildfires impact the social, ecological and economic domains. Such fire events affect populations across urban, peri-urban and rural settings.

In Australia it is predicted that there will be an increasing number of high or extreme risk fire days (Hennessy *et al.*, 2006; Climate Council, 2013). Recent wildfires in Australia have caused losses of life, property and livestock as well as environmental damage to large areas of land. For example, in 2013 wildfires in New South Wales burnt over 1.4 mil-lion hectares (RFS, 2013). Just over 200 homes were destroyed in Dunal-ley, Tasmania, in January 2013. Most significantly, the February 2009 bushfires in the State of Victoria killed 173 people and destroyed 2,059 homes (AEMI, n.d.). These have become known as the 'Black Saturday' fires. The subsequent Victorian Bushfires Royal Commission (Teague *et al.*, 2010) drew attention, in part, to how state agencies communicate information and warnings about wildfires to the public.

Background

Wildfire, an increasing threat in Australia, raises specific questions for populations living in localities as well as for governments and agencies tasked with the question of how to ensure the ongoing safety of the communities that constitute these localities. Effective communication is central to the processes of wildfire preparedness and response. Two approaches are possible, one focussing on the modes, forms and content of communication in the event of fire and the other examining the ways in which communication takes place within complex social relationships, involving citizens, residents, workers, protective and service agencies, and governments.

The research that informs this book addressed the latter theme. This research was undertaken by researchers from the then Centre of Sustainable Organisations and Work (now the Centre for People, Organisation and Work) at RMIT University in Melbourne, Australia, for the Bushfire Cooperative Research Centre. The report focussed on the forms, media and processes of communication in relation to bushfire. It identified strengths, shortcomings and complexities in communication and examined the salience of formal and informal relationships, and their dynamics within communities and community networks. Of note, and relevant for this book, the report addressed education and capacity-building strategies. They were assessed in relation to the mode of provision as well as in relation to forms of dissemination. The question was whether people in bushfire-prone localities hear, understand and act.

In the Australian context, the issue of wildfire safety communication can be especially fraught, given that the history and official policy position for fire agencies is not one of mandatory evacuation when a bushfire threatens. The Prepare, Stay and Defend or Leave Early (PSDLE) policy, known colloquially as 'Stay or Go', has significantly shaped bushfire safety practice in Australia and has a long informal history. It is a policy unique to Australia and encourages residents to determine a bushfire safety strategy that involves either 'staying to defend' a property while a fire front passes (often involving extinguishing embers) or self-evacuation well before a fire threatens. This policy stands in contrast to most other bushfire-prone localities around the world, where state-facilitated evacuation is standard (Reynolds, 2017). Although the policy has come under increasing scrutiny in recent years, it is still widely supported and was in place, largely unquestioned by wildfire agencies and staff, at the time our research was conducted.

As wildfire agencies are State-based (rather than national) in Australia, the project comprised focussed case study research within selected communities in four States: New South Wales, Tasmania, Victoria and Western Australia. Many of the participants had actually experienced bushfire or had heard stories from family members. These localities were selected because they are designated as highly vulnerable to bushfire by the respective state fire agencies. Utilising ethnographic-type research techniques, the research focussed on the intersection between authorities, agencies and community groups. Between 2010 and 2013 the research team carried out more than 200 interviews (mostly in person, with some by telephone) with residents and wildfire agency staff across 12 different localities – a mix of rural, urban-rural interface and what are colloquially known as 'sea-change' or 'tree-change' localities – which have experienced a recent influx of former city or urban residents and tourists. Two related work packages took up particular themes, each building on the case study research and utilising methodologies developed in previous research. First, an action research program was initiated to identify ways of building and strengthening social networks that facilitate effective communications. Second, a focussed enquiry was undertaken into the role and place of education and awareness strategies as forms of communication in the process of capacity building and awareness development (see Fairbrother *et al.* 2014).

Thus the project examined and provided an understanding of the social, political and historical bases of community awareness and resilience in bushfire contexts. It focussed on the intersection between community, institutions and organisations in relation to communication. As a broad concept, communication is the process of establishing meaning, encompassing all forms of social interaction from the personal to public announcements. Communication takes on significance at multiple levels within the community, from organisational and operational communications, such as bushfire warnings, to community education programs and the communication of messages and information via public campaigns.

It is also important to note that the original data collection, on which the analysis in this book is based, occurred in the years immediately following 'Black Saturday' (2010–2013). The Black Saturday fires are understood to be one of the worst peacetime disasters of postcolonial Australia. Black Saturday occurred in February (late summer) 2009 and involved a series of fires in the State of Victoria, one of the most wildfire-prone locations on earth. As noted earlier, the fires claimed the lives of 173 people, destroyed 2,059 houses and burned more than 450,000 hectares of land (MacDougall *et al.*, 2014). The fires damaged not only the surrounding infrastructure but also the social fabric of the communities that were affected (Teague *et al.*, 2010). The subsequent Royal Commission into the fires, and the official response to them, brought to the fore significant questions as to the effectiveness of wildfire communication and community preparedness in Australia.[2] Our data collection, therefore, provides an illuminating snapshot of a time when wildfire agencies and residents in wildfire-prone localities were often questioning the established approaches to wildfire safety, community organising and effective communication. In the years during which we conducted this research, we saw significant flux in terms of how agencies were structured, how they related to each other and how they framed their communications. We also saw resistance to new ways of doing things and a reluctance to admit that many of the traditional approaches to wildfire safety in Australia were flawed.

The project therefore offered a unique opportunity to consider approaches to wildfire in the wake of one of the worst wildfire disasters on record, and we developed an innovative approach in applying a robust sociopolitical framework to understand communication strategies and their effectiveness. The use of this perspective provided a significant chance to critique and update existing understandings as well as provide a way of assessing and evaluating preparation and communication strategies. It employed the concept of relational networks to understand the links between social institutions, such as the fire authorities and citizens. Hence the project addressed the social and political context of wildfire via a focus on communication strategies and practices.

The research was also, in many ways, constrained by the relationship with 'end users' – the agencies that helped oversee funding and research outcomes. As is common with the majority of bushfire research in Australia, the work was conducted in close consultation with representatives from wildfire-related agencies and, as such, tailored to the needs of the agencies themselves. At times this presented challenges, for example, when some funding and agency representatives did not welcome the use of a gendered analysis, maintaining that there was no 'gender issue' to be analysed with regard to contemporary wildfire safety. Or when others did not appreciate our attempts at analysing what was meant by 'community' in policy and practice, pushing us to accept this as a given and to get on with the 'real work' of assessing what kinds of communication were most effective. This left many avenues for more critically engaged political and social analysis open to us once the project had concluded.

The next step in the analysis is presented in this book. Starting from the presumption that wildfire is both a natural and a social event, the original research drew attention to the proposition that to understand how those within bushfire-prone localities prepare for the possibility of disaster events and deal with them when they occur. In this book, we extend the analysis more overtly to the exercise of power as central to this process and the way it plays out in a myriad of ways in relation to complex social relationships, involving citizens, residents, workers, protective and service agencies, and governments. Via narrative understandings, through the guidance and advice provided in relation to wildfire events, by the development of procedures and approaches to such events, some actors prevail, and others are marginalised and occasionally are invisible. As became clear over the course of the research those who have capability and resource are of consequence. Without such an understanding it is almost impossible to create the conditions for a democratic and active engagement in relation to these events.

Wildfire events draw attention to three sets of relations. First people are located in localities in wildfire-prone areas. It is in these localities that they plan for and experience such events, occasionally. Second, governments promote policies and procedures to deal with disaster events via agencies, such as fire authorities, related emergency services, the police and a range of voluntary and other support organisations. Third, the ways that agencies and localities work together to address disaster events draw attention to the social relations that define localities, the organisational structures and practices of agencies, and the communicative relations between and involving these two sets of actors. Each is dealt with in turn.

Localities and Communities

The analytic focus in this book is community as a set of power relations. Often community is confused with locality. The concepts of locality and community can be puzzling and misleading, especially when they are used interchangeably. Each has its own meaning. While localities include a range of people, some residents, some travelling to work in the locality, others visiting, and so on, it is important to explore the bases of cohesiveness and disunity within localities. This focus draws attention to the various and contested meanings of the term community: as place, as a sense of belonging or association, and as an ideal in terms of cooperation and engagement. Hence community and locality should not conflated because locality as place is not a necessary condition for community (to be developed later). Nonetheless, it may often be the case that those who are part of a community associate it with place and in such circumstances, the sense of community can become confused with the sense of place, sometimes in exclusionary ways (Brent, 2004). Hence, the task facing us is to distinguish these concepts carefully, and show how they can be used to explain disaster and, in this case wildfire experiences and challenges.

While community is a contested term that is open to overlapping and different understandings, the concept of community attempts to capture the dimensions of social life at a local level (Crow and Allen, 1994; Wellman, 1999; see also Fairbrother *et al.*, 2013). It is also important to draw attention to the way in which understandings are developed in relation to the specificity of localities (Snow *et al.*, 1986; Paton and Jackson, 2002; see also Fairbrother *et al.*, 2013). There are a number of dimensions to take into account. First, there is the question of geography. An increasing number of people belong to geographically dispersed communities of interest rather than forming reciprocal ties among a 'community of place' (i.e. people living in a specific geographical area). Second, there is evidence of a general decline in the level of trust in government and authorities, and the members of a community may be shifting their focus from the public to the private and personal (Robinson, 2003). Third, there is also evidence of 'fragmentation' in some communities of place, with complex relations relating to knowledge, commitment and engagement, for example, involving long-term people and incomers (Bourdieu, 1973; Boyle and Halfacree, 1997). Residents in such places make up permanent households, non-permanent/newly arrived households, holiday home owners and tourists. It is possible that they *lack* strong, reciprocal relationships. Such fragmentation may take other forms and be associated with the shifts in service provision in rural society, involving education, financial and legal support, provisions and leisure. These different aspects provide the context for the study, which is grounded in the ways that communities organise and operate.

One way of developing a theoretical understanding of the social relationships that characterise community and civic participation is derived from social capital theory (Putman, 1993; 2003). Involvement and engagement in community life lay the foundation for social cooperation, civic engagement and trust. These understandings are further developed in relation to the types of social interactions that allow capacity building to take place in the context of community diversity and social inclusiveness (Cooke and Morgan, 1998; Cuthill and Fien, 2005). Such analytic frameworks provide the basis for developing accounts of why there may be variation in the way in which communities respond and develop in reaction to disaster threats. Thus, the basis will be laid for moving beyond the evocative accounts that can be provided about specific communities towards explanations of the barriers to effective forms and aspects of communication and action.

A further related theme is to address the processes surrounding local mobilisation in relation to communication within the context of community networks. This part of the research sought to answer a number of questions: (1) how people develop awareness, (2) who is typically involved and who is not, (3) how people prepare for the possibility of wildfire and organise under the auspices of authorities and agencies, (4) how they utilise educational and awareness practices and (5) how they exchange information and learn from one another and specialists.

In conducting these studies, the initial next step on from social capital theory was to consider the circumstances for, condition and outcomes of community engagement and network building. This step draws attention to the processes of engagement and participation in relation to locally based mobilisation, where there is a process of public calculation and consideration of public concerns that is deliberative in its practice (Wright, 1995; Bohman and Rehg, 1997; Baber and Bartlett, 2007; Nabatchi and Farrar, 2011). The challenge is to incorporate questions relating to power and inequality of capacity (see Mansbridge *et al.*, 2010).

The initial parameters of our study led to this focus being complemented by the study of risk awareness, motivations and capabilities (Marske 1991; Tierney, 1999). There may be different degrees of emphasis in these processes, particularly in relation to the technical aspects of fire and the ways communities prepare and deal with wildfires. The key problem is that it is not clear what the conditions for participation and awareness are or how authorities and agencies, through the messages they promote and disseminate, may facilitate them and engage in mutually appropriate ways. Some of these themes have been addressed in social movement literature focussing on the processes of mobilisation, considering organisation, capacity and purpose (Voss and Sherman, 2003; Lévesque and Murray, 2010; Fairbrother, 2015). These ways of developing awareness and understandings bring into contention the ways of framing, developing and expressing understandings (Melucci, 1996; Obach, 2004). It may be the case that, with appropriate education, awareness sessions, forms of network building and engagement within these contexts, local people, in conjunction with relevant authorities and agencies, could organise, develop capacities and elaborate understandings. Moreover, it became clear that there were a multitude of largely unrecognised barriers and a lack of understanding, beyond the superficial, of differences within communities and the power dynamics between agencies and residents, especially in the context of the white, hegemonically masculine norms of disaster – and especially bushfire – response in Australia (Reynolds and Tyler, in press).

States and Agencies

The creation and implementation of formal and informal rule frameworks can be viewed as a form of communication (Ayres and Braithwaite, 1992). Many authorities and agencies are charged with the responsibility of coordinating community action. These organisations create policy and/or rules to direct community action. This relationship between key organisations, their authority to formulate rules and communicate and encourage compliance with those rules, is critical to preparing and responding to disaster events such as wildfire. Problems arise when communications are inadequate; when they are not received or, if received, are not understood or followed; or when people face mixed messages from different agencies, organisations or communicators.

In Australia responsibility for wildfire prevention and management lies with the States and Territories rather than with the Commonwealth government. Despite the distinctive emergency management arrangements in each State, there also are commonalities between them (Bennett, 2012). Statutory authorities, for example, are largely responsible for rural fires. Moreover, volunteer brigades are constituted under a statutory authority and are organised by both group and regional structures.

In addition, Acts and related regulations detail landholders' responsibilities for fire prevention and suppression, which can be summed up as individuals should take 'reasonable care'. Setting agencies' responsibilities in legal terms provides a basis for understanding how particular state agencies function.

But it is important to go beyond the formality of legal arrangements and consider more sociologically based accounts. Pierides and Woodman (2012), for example, focus on the 2009 Victorian bushfires to develop their object-oriented sociological theory and argue that focussing on organisational structures and processes tends to overlook actual objects and their place in a disaster and so produces a sociologically weakened account of events. Others focus on emergency management arrangements and levels of readiness among residents and officials as well as the response and recovery from major bushfire events (see Wettenhall's 1975 critical account of the Hobart, Tasmania 1967 fires). A natural and social history of Steels Creek, Victoria, which was an area burnt in the February 2009 bushfires, describes accounts from residents affected by the fires and includes a robust critique of the so-called 'Stay or Go' policy (Hansen and Griffiths, 2012). The authors argue that encouraging people to stay and defend their properties was based in part on a skewed reading of data relating to deaths in previous large bushfires (see also Reynolds and Tyler, in press).

Of equal importance it is critical to understand the ways in which disaster events and activity in relation to such events, before and after, raise questions about power relations and the capacities of many social actors to engage in these processes in purposeful and active ways. The state has a moral and political obligation to address disaster episodes, particularly in liberal democracies, but this does not necessarily mean that it is a benign actor. States have preoccupations with the society as a whole and the ways it is structured and organised to meet competing demands. This dimension raises troubling and often contested questions as to who is responsible for what in relation to bushfire events, illustrated starkly in relation to debates about 'Stay or Go' over the decades (see McLennan and Handmer, 2012; Reynolds, 2017). Furthermore, these relations play out in complex ways between disaster agencies and the populations that make up communities impacted by disaster events. It also results in expressions of an equation between the impacts of disaster events, presenting building losses or fatalities as if they have an equivalence (see van den Honert *et al.*, 2014–15). Many dimensions of these relations become visible in relation to communication and disaster events, preparation and recovery.

Communication Dilemmas

Governments via state agencies have promoted public communication about disaster events and specifically in relation to communities and fire.

While debates about the process of public communication, the modes of such communication and the outcomes of communication campaigns are long-standing, one influential view is that such strategies provide public benefit (e.g. Dewey, 1927) and another critique of these views in terms of power relations (e.g. Williams, 1958). More recently, these analyses have been broadened to include mass media (e.g. Morley, 2005).

These debates have been qualified in relation to disaster events via 'social marketing' (Kotler and Zaltman, 1971). Campaigns under this rubric are informed by marketing and public relations rather than by more traditional theories. The intention is to draw on a range of social science analysis where the emphasis is on the application of communication strategies. Critical to this type of consideration is an analysis of communities as audiences. Additionally, communication strategies involve a tailoring of communication medium (see Shaw and Jones, 2005). Such concepts are increasingly utilised in public communications in relation to disaster events.

In addressing disaster events, agencies (within parameters set by the state) and social actors within localities in principle work together to develop procedures, prepare for disaster events and respond to them and their aftermath. These localities are defined by the social relations that constitute the communities, the ways agencies organise and operate, and the communicative relations that have been developed over time. Public communication is key to this process between agencies and those within localities and their constitutive communities.

For people to appreciate the risk of the 'hazards on their doorsteps' one claim is that they should be personally engaged with the messages coming from the emergency services organisations (King, 2000: 226). Another claim is that key messages should be consistent, easy to understand and relevant to the area where people live (Fairbrother *et al.*, 2010). Thus, it is not enough to just send generic material and expect that people have the knowledge and skill to apply that information to their own situations (Prior and Paton, 2008). Bushfire-related communication, whether awareness or education, should engage individuals directly; provide relevant, tailored information; and maintain preparedness. Our research investigates the interactions between communication and behaviour through a study of the multiple relationships between community; authorities; and agencies engaged with fire prevention, preparedness and recovery.

While there is an extensive body of international research to date on risk communication that addresses some of the dimensions of the communication process (e.g. Kasperson, 1987), there has been little integrated research focussing on the community and its intersection with the authorities and agencies engaged in wildfire safety and risk management, including how this affects the effectiveness of messages. Three aspects should be considered in relation to community awareness, preparedness and resilience. First, community is a contested concept that will be rigorously defined and substantiated in relation to wildfires as disasters. Second, the bases of mobilisation at a locality level in relation to wildfire risk involve a consideration of organisation, capacity and purpose. In this respect, social networks that are built up over time in localities provide the possibilities for awareness, preparedness and resilience in the context of wildfire risk. Third, authorities and agencies, such as emergency services and local, State / provincial and federal governments, often appear disconnected and poorly coordinated, with ill-defined or overlapping jurisdictional authority and roles. This focus on institutions, the way they organise, interact and affect community, extends to how formal and informal rules, as forms of communication, facilitate or impede appropriate forms of social organisation and operation in relation to wildfire risk.

The other side of these relationships is that of communities within localities. While there is a tendency for fire and emergency community strategies to be based on a view of community in relation to locality, there is often a complexity in relation to community cohesion, inclusion or exclusion, and coverage. At a minimum, it is important to map the bases of segmentation and cohesiveness in communities to inform policy development and implementation. Such mapping is likely to draw attention to the social changes experienced by communities in many localities, the long-term residents and recent arrivals, recent immigrant and sometimes refugee arrivals, those who speak English as a first language and those who do not, men and women, old and young, rich and poor. Such demographics are common and matter for policies and practices in relation to disaster events.

These demographics also matter when the composition of agencies, particularly in localities, is considered. Often this aspect of agencies is characterised by an ageing demographic, a white demographic and a male demographic. When developing connections with other members in the locality, such demographics matter, not only in relation to who does what in the event of a disaster event but in relation to who speaks to whom and how, and who hears what. Research also demonstrates that those within localities, irrespective of background and demographic, often rely on the immediate message from people who are known rather than the disembodied message from far away (see Elliott *et al.*, 2013).

Such social complexity suggests that those in communities in localities and emergency management staff should become involved in a 'strategic conversation' about emergencies and disasters over the long term (Blair *et al.*, 2010). One way of stimulating such a conversation may be in relation to the social networks that often characterise communities in localities or indeed by building cross-cutting and inclusive social networks within communities. While not easy such developments may also be stimulated and affirmed by learning and awareness strategies.

In the end, it is likely that successful and effective communication strategies and approaches will rest on mutual understanding and respect. Again these processes call into question power relations and capacities.

An Approach

Wildfire is an increasing threat in Australia, with population movement and mobility, shifts in climate patterns and the unevenness in preventive measures across the country. It raises specific questions for populations living in localities as well as for governments and agencies tasked with the question of how to ensure the ongoing safety of the communities that constitute these localities. Effective communication is central to the processes of wildfire preparedness and response. The focus here is on the complex social relationships that constitute the ways agencies and communities interact in relation to wildfire events, covering preparation, experience and the aftermath of such events.

The context is the increasing wildfire risks resulting from rapid climate, socio-economic and demographic change, especially in peri-urban and rural communities. In studying disaster preparedness and response, it is necessary to explore the relationship between agencies and the public in wildfire-prone areas. Understanding the diversity and inequality within the communities that make up the intended audience for these communications is a first step in the right direction. But we assert, more broadly, that studies on wildfire in Australia and research on disaster, more generally, need to be opened up to provide insights beyond the sometimes insulated or isolated field of disaster studies.

Invocations of community are increasingly being used in Australian public policy. Yet the term 'community' is often used in confusing and conflicting ways. We consider the origin of this approach to public policy and its connection with related notions of social capital and community capacity building. Three different usages of the term 'community' are explored and the social-capital approach to community-based policy is examined and explored, particularly from the perspective of the voluntarist nature of Australian bushfire agencies. Our research focusses on the intersection between community, state institutions and related organisations in relation to communication. As a broad concept, communication is the process of establishing meaning, encompassing all forms of social interaction from the personal to public announcements. Communication takes on significance at multiple levels within the community, from organisational and operational communications, such as wildfire warnings, to community education programs and the communication of messages and information via public campaigns.

The analytic focus is on the intersection between communities and fire authorities and agencies, with reference to power dynamics and the forms, media and processes of communication that occur within these relations. The first analytic reference is a distinction between locality and community. People live in communities often based in localities, and especially so in relation to disaster events. For a variety of reasons emergency agencies view communities as localities, while in such situations community members make place a starting point to understand the processes and patterns of disaster events. The implication is that analysis should begin with an understanding of community in and of localities.

The second step in the analysis is to understand the place and role of emergency agencies within this process. The state encourages, facilitates and enables emergency agencies to operate in relation to disaster events. Often the state is caught in tensions between a commitment to intervention, for reasons associated with safety, preparation, recovery and facilitation, in relation to self-empowerment, resource and political reality. Such matters mean that the relationship between the state and community in liberal democracies is neither straightforward nor readily and rarely resolved to the satisfaction of all. Hence, the presentation of the argument begins with a detailed account and explanation of the communities in and of wildfire-prone localities. With this understanding, the states' involvement in fire awareness, prevention and recovery, via emergency agencies, is considered. The analysis focusses on the views and perspectives of agency personnel in relation to the experiences and views of those within the localities.

The third stage in the analysis returns to communities within and of localities to understand the complication and complexity of the state-community relationship. Via a focus on modes and forms of communication these relationships are disentangled. Thus, the analysis identifies strengths, shortcomings and complexities in communication and examines the salience of formal and informal relationships and their dynamics within communities and community networks. Education and capacity-building strategies are assessed in terms of identifying and exploring the ways that organisations can optimise the relevance, quality and timeliness of information they provide. As well as the modes of dissemination they employ, and to enhance the willingness and capacity of people to hear, understand and act on safety messages in the immediate and long term. As climate change proceeds, these activities are likely to become pressing.

Notes

1 'Bushfire' is the more commonly used term for 'wildfire' in Australia. When referring specifically to the Australian context, the terms 'bushfire' and 'wildfire' are used interchangeably. When referring to the international context only, the term 'wildfire' is used.

2 After the Black Saturday fires in 2009, the 'Stay or Go' approach came under increasing scrutiny, but the fundamentals of the policy were ultimately supported by the subsequent Royal Commission (Handmer and O'Neil, 2016).

2 Concepts of Community

Peter Fairbrother, Bernard Mees,
Richard Phillips and Meagan Tyler

National, State and local governments in Australia are currently look-
ing to integrate notions of community, social capital and community
capacity building into a variety of policy areas, including bushfire preparedness and safety. This development is part of an international trend
towards formally acknowledging the benefits of 'strong communities'
and the importance of fostering links between communities and government institutions. As Marsh and Buckle (2001) note, however, the
use of the term 'community', although widely established in the context
of Australian wildfire and wildfire management, has often been used
in different and conflicting ways. Linked with the volunteerist nature
of these fire agencies, understanding what is meant by 'community' is
an essential first step in developing a clearer conceptualisation to analyse current arrangements and determine what a community-focussed
approach to bushfire management may mean and entail. This chapter provides an overview of the concepts of community, social capital
and 'community capacity building, including an outline of how the
use of these terms is varied and contested. It presents insights into the
limits of relying on notions of 'community' in policy. This step lays
the foundations for the following chapters, which rest upon these understandings of community, connection and communication.

Community

Historically, the term 'community' has been employed to represent various collections and constellations of interests. The term literally denotes
an expression of commonality (cf. Latin *communis* 'common, general,
universal, public', *communitas* 'community, society, fellowship, friendly
intercourse'), but the first use of the term in the Australian context referred to rural townships; to the establishment and value of community
health services; and to involvement in local organised activities, such as
community gardens. The term could (and still can) refer to sections of
the populace that are associated with one another by dint of ethnicity
or activities, such as the Chinese, Italian or Jewish community, or the
business, sporting or motoring community. Its usage in newspapers and

other forms of civic discourse has traditionally occurred most remarkably in terms of service and benefit 'to the community' at large (such as the Victorian community or even the Australian community), rather than particular communities (cf. Radford, 1939; Bayne and Lazarus, 1940).

The term community may connote the nation, a province, a region or even a small locality. In these cases it acts to unite diverse sections of the collective population under one banner of belonging. At the same time, it often combines the idea of benefit with an imputed sense of civic obligation. Thus the notion of 'community' has often traditionally been held up as an ideal by which Australians should recognise a duty to the rest of the populace. This ideal has come to be especially connected with the ethic of volunteerism which characterises the wildfire services in Australia and the standards that all members of a populace can be expected to hold (Murray and White, 1995).

The usage of the term 'community' has often reflected the way that the nineteenth-century German sociologist Ferdinand Tönnies (1887) defined community (German *Gemeinschaft*), in opposition to society (*Gesellschaft*). For Tönnies, *Gemeinschaft* described a sense of community that included traditional social relations formed around face-to-face interactions. Tönnies separated associations into real or organic (a feature of *Gemeinschaft* – 'community') and imaginary and mechanical types (a feature of *Gesellschaft* – 'society'). According to Tönnies, 'society' represented the informal, distant and short-lived aspects of modern associative life, 'community' a sense of closeness, longevity and the personal. Beginning in the 1960s, critics of the distance between government and the people that public policy is supposed to serve saw calls to establish a renewed community-based kind of democratic association (a 'neo-Gemeinschaft') that restored a sense of the personal, deep and immediate to both local and public life (*cf.* Greeley 1966; Rivera and Erlich 1981; Kenny 2011).

Yet considerable divergence appears in how the term 'community' is used internationally today. Blackshaw (2010: 5) notes that community is traditionally constituted by three dimensions: locale, social network and a shared sense of belonging. Complementing this perspective, Taylor (2003) argues that there is a similar breakdown of contemporary public understandings of community, which are also usually anchored to one of three elements: geography, interest or relation. In both accounts, the three elements broadly align: geography with locality, relation with a sense of belonging and interest with social network. Broader sociological studies of what precisely 'community' represents in the Australian context are lacking, but a similar threefold understanding of the concept is evident in much of the way in which the notion of community is understood in terms of wildfire preparedness (see Fairbrother *et al.*, 2013).

Community as Locality

Understandings of community as linked to place are common in both popular conceptions and policy initiatives. The geographical element of community typically takes a community to represent a collective of people hailing from a particular place (Eng and Parker, 1994). But simply inhabiting the same space does not necessarily or automatically foster a sense of community, and so locality and community should not be conflated – it is not always correct to ascribe community status to a group of people simply because they live in the same area (Glen, 1993). It is also important to understand that the senses of community which may be associated with a particular place are not inherently 'good'. Some senses of community can, in fact, be exclusionary, and conceptualising communities as geographically bounded can engender nationalistic, racist, reactionary or fractious discourses (Brent, 2004). Thinking of community only in terms of locality also, of course, overlooks other competing definitions of community which are not so firmly linked to place – for example, the senses of community felt by groups such as travellers and ethnic diasporas. It may, therefore, be more useful to remember that multiple and overlapping communities, or senses of community, can exist at any one time in one locality.

Nonetheless, as Marsh and Buckle (2001: 5) note, the concept of community 'is of obvious importance within the context of emergency management and community recovery', but that 'it is a much abused and misunderstood term'. Taking community as a geographically bounded concept – an indication of where people live (i.e. in communities) – there has been frequent recourse to the notion and characteristics of community in discussions about preparing for wildfire and other natural hazards (e.g. Jones, 1987; Beckingsale, 1994; McClure and Williams, 1996; Rohrmann, 1999; McGee and Russell, 2003; Cottrell, 2005; Cottrell *et al.*, 2008; Chia, 2010). This geographic framing ensures that potentially affected Australians, both individually and as members of 'communities as a whole' (Rohrmann, 1999), are prepared for the possibility of wildfire and related disaster events (Chase, 1993).

Thus, community, as a locality, often becomes the focus of activity in relation to wildfire preparedness (Raphael, 1986; Cottrell, 2005). Moreover Cox and Holmes (2000) have suggested that thinking about place is crucial also particularly when considering recovery from bushfire or wildfire. These fires occur within a bounded geographic space that may or may not impact particular populated localities but sometimes do so with devastating consequences (see, for example, the Black Saturday Fires that impacted Strathewan and Marysville in Victoria, Australia; Teague *et al.*, 2010). Additionally, fire brigades (voluntary and professional) are located and named after specific places, and most volunteer firefighters reside in close proximity to the local brigade headquarters in order to respond efficiently to any event – so their physical connection to a place is a feature of being part of a brigade. While locality may be a significant and relevant element of community with regard to wildfire preparedness, recovery or response, however, the geographical notion of community has limitations, particularly as locality does not necessarily explain or take into account other elements of personal association, such as a shared sense of belonging, or links and connections to others regardless of their geographical distance.

Community as a Shared Sense of Belonging

Many contemporary definitions of community also refer to relational elements and an overall sense of belonging. Brint (2001: 8) views communities in this sense as:

> aggregates of people who share common activities and/or beliefs and who are bound together principally by relations of affect, loyalty, common values, and/or personal concern.
>
> (Brint, 2001: 8)

Consequently, it is often thought that the contemporary experience of community is increasingly more concerned with the configuration and sorts of relationships which exist between people – that community, by its very nature, is enmeshed in notions of communication (Lyon, 1989; Delanty, 2003).

One of the most prominent understandings of community as a shared sense of belonging is Anderson's (1983) contention that community is an 'imagined' phenomenon; that is, the focus of community is more on the sense of 'belonging' rather than on geography. The symbolism associated with this idea of community has been emphasised by Cohen (1985), where attention is given to the imagery, rituals and habits which are often seen to be markers of community. From this perspective, community is an extension of personal identity. As Blackshaw (2010) claims, the outcome from an analytical perspective has been a split in the basic sociological concept. On the one hand community can be seen as a socially grounded and focussed analytical category (as far as sociologists are concerned), but on the other hand community can be used as a form of political appropriation. It is the use of the concept of community to capture a sense of belonging, illustrated by much recent public policy reference (Blackshaw, 2010: 7–10; see also Brint, 2001), which has proved perhaps the most difficult aspect of understanding the idea of community as it is encountered in public discourse today.

The term community is often used as a symbolic reference to indicate a common way of life, a mutual understanding or a way of capturing a common resolution to deal with shared issues. But this concept of community (often in reference to a collective sense of 'the community') has been used variously, and somewhat confusedly, in more recent scholarly and public discussion. Indeed, an extensive debate about community and its supposed importance has emerged recently in discussion over current directions in Australian public policy (e.g. Adams and Hess, 2001; Scillio, 2001–2002; McDonald and Marston, 2002; Reddel, 2002; Simpson *et al.*, 2003; Reddel and Woolcock, 2004; Wiseman, 2006; Brackertz and Meredyth, 2009; Putt, 2010). The use of the term 'community' has often proved both confusing and ill-defined, and raises a series of practical and methodological questions when it is viewed in relation to communication and wildfire. Marsh and Buckle (2001: 7) contend, for example, that emergency management planners need to 'be more astute and sophisticated in the ways in which they analyse communities'. They need to understand that individuals are often members of multiple and overlapping communities, and that a community defined by locality cannot be assumed to be unified. Marsh and Buckle (2001) argue that if these new understandings of community are not incorporated, attempts to implement community safety measures will be largely ineffective.

Community as Social Networks

Community can also be defined through 'interest' when features such as religious belief, sexual orientation, occupation or ethnic origin join interest-community members together (Smith, 2001). Community expressed in this way can clearly represent a non-geographical phenomenon and shares much in common with the sociological conceptualisation of communities as being characterised by social networks (Stacey, 1969; Hoggett, 1997). The social network approach to community emphasises the links, ties and communications between individuals, and to a lesser extent, the connections between individuals and social institutions. Thus a community can be understood as a complex web of social connections, both formal and informal, which can be mapped. Indeed, the mapping aspects of social network analysis are becoming increasingly common in studies of community and the social sciences more broadly (Magsino, 2009). Mapping these networks of social interaction is seen to be important in such studies because such connections are thought to be significant in coordinating everyday interaction and decision-making (Gilchrist, 2000). Moreover, the mapping of networks is likely to be of particular interest to policymakers, and in *The Well Connected Community*, Gilchrist (2009) outlines why and how focussing on networks and network building may help governments in their efforts to create 'strong communities'.

The development and uptake of information and communication technologies may also influence social networks (Clay, 2008). Indeed, Sassen

(2002: 366) argues that mobile phones, email and the internet are social forms of technology as they have obviated the distance inherent to earlier communication technologies, and that traits of digital networks are dispersed access, interconnectivity and simultaneity. Consequently, virtual communities can be described as 'thin' communities, contrasting with 'thick' or organic communities based around tradition (Turner, 2001: 29). Moreover, Turner goes on to characterise 'thin' communities as ones that are not established around strong ties and are usually communities of strangers. One of the implications of this development is that such 'thin' communities may no longer be place or locality dependent. This aspect is examined by Castells (2001; and cf. Delanty, 2003) who suggests that these new forms of 'personalised communities' are grounded in networks and focus on the individual. Castells (2001) also notes that while virtual communities can frame and support existing social relations, they rarely facilitate the establishment of new relationships. However, recent developments in relation to the technology and practice of social media (Facebook and the like) may qualify this initial assessment.

Social-network theorists tend to detail the social ties which exist within particular settings rather than adopting a more normative approach that suggests what communities should be (Papacharissi, 2010). There is an acknowledgement that these networks can produce both positive and negative social outcomes. Social networks can bind people together and be useful for the sharing of knowledge and helping others. The importance of social networks in post-disaster recovery situations has been emphasised in some literature (Cattell, 2001; Coates, 2007; Jirasinghe, 2007). It has been contended that:

> 'networks enhance people's ability to cope with difficulties and disasters by keeping hope alive and bolstering well- being, even in the face of ... sudden crises'
>
> (Gilchrist 2009: 4).

These networks may also provide useful material support in the wake of a disaster, with some evidence suggesting that community-based approaches to recovery are better targeted and more effective than state-led initiatives (Coates, 2007; Jirasinghe, 2007).

There is little doubt, therefore, that social-network approaches to community have much to offer policymakers and that existing research and policy on disaster recovery could potentially be extended to disaster preparedness. To suggest that interest in community and related terms is a contemporary development in policymaking, however, would be misleading. As Goodwin (2005: 95) remarks, 'community' development was already a theme in Australia, for example, in the 1960s and 1970s. Writing over 30 years ago, Bryson and Mowbray (1981), for example, criticised the sloppy and cynical use of 'community' in social policy.

More recently, Gilchrist (2009) argues that despite limitations and criticism there has been an international trend towards the increasing use of notions of community in policy discourse. In the Australian context, there has been a recent focus on 'community resilience' (COAG, 2011), 'strengthening community' (Government of Victoria, 2008; Pope and Zhang, 2010) and a shared responsibility between the community and the state (Fire Services Commission, 2013). Assigning community status to certain groups, however, is only a relatively recent tendency among policymakers and social commentators (Glen, 1993), and it is important to note that assigning the term 'community' to a group, simply to legitimate a political program or to support a plan of action, does not actually create communities (Ramphele and Thornton, 1988: 29).

Competing Concepts of Social Capital

The notion of social capital is often invoked in contemporary discussions of community and the two terms are often seen as closely related (Coleman, 1988; Kenny, 2011). Social capital has become a concept used in a wide range of academic disciplines, but like community, an exact and widely agreed-upon definition of social capital remains elusive. Social capital is usually understood to refer to the benefits acquired through the membership of communicative networks and other social structures (Portes, 1998). It is possible to identify the foundational theorists of the literature on social capital as Coleman (1988), Bourdieu (Bourdieu and Passeron, 1977; Bourdieu, 1985) and Putnam (1993, 2000).

Levels of social capital have been linked to a variety of issues, from economic growth to public health to political participation. There is also a growing interest in the relationship between social capital and the delivery of social and community services, such as healthcare provision (see, for example, Kawachi *et al.*, 1997; Gillies, 1998; Baum, 1999; Campbell *et al.*, 1999; Kawachi 2001). The idea of social capital usually includes a concern with levels of civic participation and the characteristics of local networks. And in this sense social capital can, as Campbell (2000: 186) notes, be a:

> useful starting point for conceptualizing those features of community that serve to enable and support the identity and empowerment processes that are most likely to facilitate health enhancing behaviour change.
>
> (Campbell, 2000: 186)

In addition, as Gilchrist (2003a: 151) observes:

> the discourse on social capital recognises the importance of these [networks] in the terms "bridging" or "linking" ties, which are distinguished from the more intimate bonds of kin and friendship.
>
> (Gilchrist, 2003a: 151)

In developing this idea, Harpham and colleagues (2002) argue that 'bridging' capital refers to social capital which joins different groups or communities, whereas 'bonding' capital describes social cohesion within a group (Narayan, 1999). Harpham and others (2002) also suggest that the 'bond/bridge' construct is able to account for the role of government and the state in the generation of social capital.

Research suggests that relationships and regular interaction with other people have positive effects on socially desirable outcomes, such as health. Individuals who experience stable and varied networks, for example, lead happier lives compared to those who are more isolated or whose networks are uniform (Argyle, 1987; Yen and Syme, 1999). Social networks and social capital were found to have a positive influence on improving the quality of life for some participants (Cattell 2001), by ameliorating the effects of poverty and deprivation on health. As suggested by Cattell (2001), social networks and social capital produce different health-related outcomes, which might be explained by arguing that class structures are also reflected within networks. For example, middle-class people generally have wider, looser and more resourceful social networks, whereas working-class people have fewer opportunities to broaden their networks (Pearlin, 1985; Willmott, 1987). In addition, it has been argued that personal networks are crucial factors concerning the sustainability and effectiveness of the community sector and community life. Informal connections, for example, create a system of links and relationships which promote and develop communication and cooperation (Gilchrist, 2003a). The concept of social capital, then, bears particular relevance to the area of bushfire and wildfire safety and the role of informal communication in wildfire preparedness and response.

The concept of social capital was first developed in relation to capacity building. Coleman (1988) explored the links between educational attainment and social inequality, and developed the concept of social capital to refer to resources that characterise family and community relations which contribute to the cognitive and social development of young people. Thus, social capital can be viewed as a connection between structure and individual agents. According to Coleman (1988: 98), social capital is:

> [D]efined by its function. It is not a single entity but a variety of different entities, with two elements in common: they all consist of some aspect of social structures, and they facilitate certain actions of actors... 'within the structure'... social capital is productive, making possible the achievement of certain ends that in its absence would not be possible... Unlike other forms of capital, social capital inheres in the structure of relations between actors and among actors.
> (Coleman, 1988: 98)

Coleman identifies two important forms of social capital: information channels and social norms. For Coleman, information channels involve trusting others to give accurate information. Given the importance of communication in disaster preparedness and response, and the influence of informal networks on information channels leading up to and during a wildfire event, understanding social capital in this way may be of use in future bushfire and wildfire research and policy.

The other important form of social capital that Coleman identifies is social norms, that is, the behaviours which are accepted within a particular social network. Coleman suggests that social capital is promoted through the closed or restrictive nature of certain networks by members of such networks dictating the actions of others within the network through the threat of expulsion. In this way social norms, and hence social capital, are established and reinforced within a network.

The composition of social groups also draws attention to the exercise of power and Pierre Bourdieu's work has contributed significantly to the development of social capital theory in this area (Bourdieu and Passeron, 1965; Bourdieu, 1985). Bourdieu argues that in order to understand the social world the various forms of capital need to be explored, whether cultural, linguistic or social (all of which are rooted in economic capital). According to Bourdieu:

> Social capital is the aggregate of the actual or potential resources which are linked to possession of a durable network of more or less institutionalized relationships of mutual acquaintance and recognition – or in other words, to membership in a group.
>
> (Bourdieu, 1985: 243)

Bourdieu, like Coleman, broadly defines social capital as the social ties or association to specific communities that generate resources, benefits and opportunities available to individuals. In other words, social capital is constituted by social processes, both within and between groups that result in the accumulation of resources.

The final of the three main contributors to social-capital theory is the American political scientist Robert Putnam. His work is widely known and he is often credited with bringing the concept of social capital to the attention of policymakers. Gilchrist (2009: 9) contends that Putnam's 'more liberal approach has a particular resonance with communitarian models of social and family responsibility and therefore has wide appeal to politicians and policy makers'. Building on Coleman's work, Putnam defines social capital as those characteristics of social organisation – such as trust, norms and networks – that can enhance the efficiency of society by facilitating organised actions.

Whiteley (1999) suggests that Putnam's definition of social capital has three main aspects: first, a citizen's trust in other members of society;

second, social norms supporting cooperation; and third, networks of civic engagement. Putnam's seminal study *Making Democracy Work* (1993) examines the differences in democracy and economic development in regions of Italy. Putnam quantifies the levels of association and relations of reciprocity within a region by measuring factors such as voting activity, membership of sports clubs and newspaper readership. He suggests that involvement in such activities (especially voluntary) is a feature of a productive and engaged civic community. The overall finding of Putnam's study is that areas showing strong civic engagement and high levels of participation in civic associations are more likely to supplement the effectiveness and stability of democratic government. High levels of social capital correlate with positive government and economic performance.

According to DeFilippis (2001), however, Putnam redefines social capital in a number of ways. The concept of social capital evolved from being a process of interaction in the writings of Coleman and Bourdieu to being a resource possessed by individuals or groups with Putnam (whether within areas, communities or countries). Social capital became fused with a particular interpretation of civil society and 'voluntary, non-governmental associations, based on trust, become the institutions through which social capital is generated' (DeFilippis, 2001: 785). Thus, social capital becomes a normative characteristic assumed to encourage democratic government and stimulate economic growth.

Community Capacity Building

Community capacity building is a term found in recent discourses in relation to community development that is closely related to social capital (Kenny, 2011). Community capacity building, however, generally has clearer normative and political overtones (Phillips, 2007; Craig, 2007). It is less used as a label in the way that 'community' and social capital are, but is more often put forward as a strategy for greater community participation and development. The community capacity building approach has produced debates over its usefulness in the Australian context (Adams and Hess, 2001; Reddel and Woolcock, 2004; Wiseman, 2006; Verity, 2007). And it has been suggested that more research is needed into 'latent and actual community capacities' to help further develop appropriate notions of shared responsibility between the state and local communities with regard to wildfire preparedness and response (Goodman and Gawen, 2008: 35).

The origins of the concept of community capacity building can be traced to the idea of community competence. Different approaches to community capacity building have emerged, but Hawe (1994) argues that the origins of the notion of community capacity building can be traced to community psychology. In 1966, a group of American psychologists severed their connection with the American Psychological Association, arguing that communities have the potential or capacity to address their own problems. In so doing, this breakaway group challenged the idea that practitioners and programs should focus on what was lacking in a community and, for example, came to view health professionals not as experts but as resources. These arguments were developed into the concept of community competence (Iscoe, 1974; Cottrell, 1976), a notion which involves the provision and utilisation of resources in a geographical or psychological community so that community members can make reasoned decisions about the issues confronting them.

There are broad similarities in the way many academics define community capacity. Chaskin (2001: 295) describes it as:

> the interaction of human capital, organisational resources, and social capital existing within a given community that can be leveraged to solve collective problems and improve or maintain the well-being of a given community.
>
> (Chaskin, 2001: 295)

In a review of debates about community capacity in relation to public health, Labonte and Laverack (2001a: 114) describe community capacity building in terms of:

> a more generic increase in community groups' abilities to define, assess, analyse and act on health (or any other) concerns of importance to their members.
>
> (Labonte and Laverack, 2001a: 114)

A similar approach clearly underpins bushfire and wildfire preparedness programs in Australia, such as the Community Fireguard program in Victoria, which claims it is based on 'theories of adult education, participation and empowerment' (Boura, 1998: 60; cf. Fairbrother *et al.*, 2010).

Community capacity building has been a particularly common approach in health programs in recent times, although different approaches to community capacity building are often evident. For example, Labonte and Laverack (2001a, 2001b) refer to a model of empowerment and discuss community capacity in terms of a 'parallel-track'. In this context, community capacity is viewed both as an aim and as a health-enhancing process alongside health promotion programs. In retaining an emphasis on community capacity building as an end in itself, Labonte and Laverack are incorporating the empowerment values attached to a broadly developmental approach to community capacity building that is also found in the work of Banks and Shenton (2001). Another such study, based in Australia, by Crisp and colleagues (2000), reviewed the existing literature about capacity building and health, and drew attention to some of the implications for funding bodies. The authors identify four distinct approaches to capacity building: bottom-up organisational, top-down organisational, partnerships and community organising (Crisp *et al.*, 2000).

A bottom-up organisational approach involves the development of skills that benefit the individual, the organisation and the wider community. The focus of this approach is on internal organisations or group development. Such approaches can be illustrated by the training of staff attached to a health-related organisation. Hall and Best (1997) propose that rather than sending staff on external training courses, a more effective way of building capacity is for an organisation to adopt an ethos of continuous learning and improvement. In this context, it is assumed that members of staff will be motivated to become more reflective about their professional practice (individually and collectively), with the aim of making health programs more sensitive to the needs of the community.

A top-down organisational approach recognises the importance of organisational capacity and the primary concern, in this context, is the infrastructure of an organisation. Within this approach, capacity is built by restructuring the organisation. According to Bainson (1994), for example, the Ghana Leprosy Service devolved the function of planning and implementation of programs from a single central agency to a regional and district level. It was found that the Ghana Leprosy Service consequently became more responsive and effective to address local needs and health issues. This approach recognises the important role of institutions and that their effectiveness and efficiency can be improved by strengthening links with and listening to the communities they seek to serve.

A partnership approach to capacity building occurs through promoting an environment where knowledge and information can be exchanged. Vicary and colleagues (1996), for example, reported that 56 agencies in rural Pennsylvania formed a coalition in order to address the health needs of women and their families. Representatives from each agency met on a regular basis, and an increase in the interactions with other agencies was reported by 83 per cent of the members of the coalition. In addition, a majority of the representatives (87 per cent) reported that their involvement with the coalition had resulted in new inter-agency collaborations (Vicary *et al.*, 1996). In a sense this practice is making the most of the resources that are already available.

A final approach noted by Crisp and colleagues (2000), and one that would seem particularly relevant to bushfire and wildfire preparedness, is community organising. This approach involves working with excluded members of a community to address particular issues. Capacity building, in this context, aims to transform individuals from passive recipients to active participants in a process of community change (Finn and Checkoway, 1998). Goodman and colleagues (1993), however, suggest that community-organising approaches to capacity building tend to be more effective in communities that have good existing resources, such as health or welfare professionals who become involved with health promotion. It is important to understand that community organising, therefore, is not enough in and of itself. The state also has a role to play in terms of distributing resources. So again, this approach is not a cure-all but can be an important aspect of social inclusion and communication within communities.

Community Capacity Building and Policy

The move to include notions of community capacity building in policy is often expressed as 'empowering communities', 'strengthening communities' or 'increasing citizen participation'. As Gilchrist (2003b) notes, it is recognised, however, that for such initiatives to have a meaningful effect communities must have a significant role in identifying problems and suggesting solutions to address these concerns. To support these and other similar initiatives, resources have been allocated to fund community capacity building, particularly, in the Australian context, by the Australian Institute of Family Studies (and its Stronger Families Learning Exchange) and various initiatives proposed by the Victorian Department of Planning and Community Development and its Office for the Community Sector (Government of Victoria, 2008).

Gilchrist (2003b), however, raises a number of issues concerning this community capacity building approach. First, although there has been an emphasis on training and supporting members of the community, the establishment of systems to not only facilitate individuals in leadership positions but also ensure that they are accountable to the wider community has often been neglected. Second, there is an assumption that the procedures and organisational culture within local authorities are positive environments in which to manage partnership arrangements. Nonetheless other research has suggested that community representatives have felt estranged and hindered by the formal settings and protocols that they encountered at partnership meetings (Craig and Taylor, 2002).

Citizen participation is another way in which community capacity building manifests in policy discourse and is an important idea that informs current British social policy. Citizen participation is understood as 'the engaging of individuals and groups in the renewal and strengthening of their own communities' (Bentley *et al.*, 2003: 9). For example, according to the United Kingdom's National Neighbourhood Renewal Strategy (Neighbourhood Renewal Unit, 2002) launched in 2001, the primary objective of participation is to ensure that local residents and community groups have a central role in improving their neighbourhoods.

In terms of assessing community capacity building-based policy, Stoker and Bottom (2003) argue that it is possible to distinguish between policies informed by an assumption that people are largely responsible for problems within their own community and those policies which view these problems as originating from the inequalities and power divisions within capitalist societies. In other words, problems in communities are explained either by the inadequacies of community members or by the structures in society. For those who construct the locus of the problem at an individual level, the solution is to instigate focussed development on 'problematic' individuals, partially to encourage compliance to the moral standards of the rest of society and to reverse their addiction to a dependency culture. Conversely, those with a structural perspective favour confrontation and community protest, and encourage the powerless to challenge those in power.

Nonetheless, Stoker and Bottom (2003: 6) argue that as the debate has developed the two positions outlined earlier have largely been avoided and instead a 'system level explanation and solution' has been offered. In this sense, community capacity building policies can be viewed as attempting to take a middle way so that blame is neither allocated to the individual nor to social structures. Instead, the emphasis is on systems of relationships and institutions that influence how communities function. Such policies are considered reformist in nature and any changes that do occur do so within the boundaries of a market economy with a commitment to liberal democracy. It is within this broader social context that concepts such as community capacity building must be located in order to perform a useful role in policymaking and research.

Mowbray (2005), writing in an Australian context, is also critical of community capacity building approaches. After reviewing the Victorian Government's 'Community Capacity Building Initiative Program', Mowbray argues that the policy objectives of communitarian initiatives need to be considered carefully. In addition, such programs rarely achieve notable social change and usually involve 'low-key and modest local activities and services that people pursue despite government' (Mowbray, 2005: 263). Mowbray suggests a number of key points if governments are serious about empowering localities, including setting realistic and achievable objectives, committing substantial resources on a long-term basis, involving local government and ensuring that programs are fair and transparent through 'arms-length' mechanisms, thus avoiding micromanagement approaches.

Another issue relating to the broader political and social context is an apparent lack of critical thinking regarding how terms and concepts are used in community capacity building discussions. For example, Cass and Brennan (2002) highlight that a climate where funding for community groups is cut and where community is portrayed as a neutral term has resulted in a context that is curiously 'non- reflexive'. Smyth (2009) notes that supporters of community capacity building often fail to engage with its shortcomings and failures. This means that this apparently consensual approach stifles and suppresses critical debate and thinking, and renders community engagement addressing concerns regarding social justice invisible. Furthermore, Ife (2003) argues that while community capacity building and related terms can appear technical, apolitical and value-free, community development actually poses difficult political questions, for example, by challenging self-interest and promoting collective action. Such an ethos, if successful, Ife (2003: 6) suggests, 'will threaten some very powerful interests' and may lead to a loss of support for such activities, much as occurred with many social work programs in the 1970s (Rivera and Erlich, 1981).

Conclusion

The debates about community are long-standing and complicated, reflecting attempts at precision in the context of a looseness in the use of the term in the public policy domain. Even so, the concept has gone through a number of iterations since first popularised in the 1920s. To help focus the use of the concept, three aspects of community are considered here: locality, a sense of belonging and social networks. As the analysis proceeds, these three aspects will be highlighted so that their use and definition are as precise as possible.

In considering community, an equally confusing term is that of social capital, referring to the ways that those in communicative networks and other social structures benefit from such membership. Indeed, these relations are often invoked as a mark of civic participation and citizenship in contemporary society, although such relation can be both inclusive and exclusive in practice. Nonetheless, this concept is associated with understandings about the quality of life in communities, the exchange of information and the expression of social norms as well as the social resources individuals within networks can draw upon in their social lives. These aspects are crystallised in the analyses of civic participation and engagement in localities and other social settings (e.g. Putnam, 1993). While subject to critique, the important point for this analysis is that the idea of social capital lays the foundation for a consideration of community capacity building, a central feature of the ways in which residents and others in localities may prepare for and respond to disaster events, such as bushfire and wildfire, a now and again occurrence, although of increasing frequency and intensity.

One implication of the analysis is that it is important that fire and emergency agencies are aware of the many uses of community, since much preparation and responses to disaster events are predicated on ideas about community, even if the precise debates about origin and focus are not known. The principal point is that these debates draw attention to specific and particular understandings of terms like community and social capital. In particular it is important that fire and emergency agencies understand that the concept of community goes beyond 'locality'; otherwise policy is likely to be predicated on a one-dimensional understanding of community as locality. In such circumstances the development of communication and related strategies can become miscued.

This first step in the analysis suggests that the touchstone for understanding the social dimensions of disaster events requires an appreciation of the way such terms are used in communication strategies and practices such as policy documents, announcements and related modes of communication. The use (and misuse) of these terms can shape action in both positive and negative ways. It is, for example, important that emergency management policy consider how audiences of messages make sense of messaging from agencies and if agencies' representations of community fit with the existing understandings of residents. Equally, it is also necessary to understand how the recipients of messages and related communication hear, understand and value such communication, in relation to their social experiences in the communities in which they are located. These aspects will be elaborated later.

Community, thus, has become an increasingly important concept in recent sociopolitical policy and debate. A sense of community is often seen as a fundamental part of human experience, and academic literature has struggled for more than a century to define what this sense of community is. Thus the concept of community remains a contested one. In more recent times the notion of community has become a focus in a variety of policy discourses, covering everything from public health to political participation to disaster preparedness. Too often in policy, however, 'community' and the related concepts of social capital and community capacity building are simply taken as inherently good and left undefined. In terms of emergency management in Australia (and wildfire safety is no exception) an implicit understanding of community as a unified and geographically bounded entity has become common. Yet in order for wildfire safety research and policy to move forward, it is important to acknowledge the competing definitions of community, social capital and community capacity building, to be clear about the way in which these terms are used, and to be aware of their analytical and practical limitations. Scholars and policymakers must move beyond limited and static understandings of community as geographically bounded and of social capital and community capacity building as cure-all solutions to broader structural problems. We must also acknowledge and address the power dynamics within communities and between communities and the state.

3   Cohesion and Complexity

The State, Community and Communities

Peter Fairbrother, Bernard Mees, Richard Phillips and Meagan Tyler

As discussed in the previous chapter, understandings of 'community' vary. Usually academic discussions on community highlight the contested nature of defining the concept. Commentators often then proceed with a description of community in terms of three aspects: place, interest and identity. However, the contested nature of community has been questioned. To illustrate, Taksa (2000) argues that there is a commonality in debates concerning the loss of community in that many argue that 'community's recovery' should be based on unity and harmony. In taking a more critical view about community, the argument is that this view obscures the differences and divisions that often mark communities and so perpetuates social inequalities.

The debates about community raise questions about the state: the local state (councils), the provincial state (State government) and the nation state (Commonwealth). Communities are social formations which have salience in relation to arguments about the modern state. And in recent times, steps have been taken to refocus the direct relationships between the state and subnational entities such as regions. Specifically, the state as a multilevel form of governance, with both a downward and upward refocussing of the relations that make up the state. Nonetheless, there are particular areas of activity, such as wildfire and disaster events, which have always prompted a range of direct policy interventions as states attempt to deal with the impacts of such events. But often these have the appearance of *ad hoc* and reactive actions. The question is what are the implications of such approaches for disaster engagement.

The argument developed here is that an understanding of wildfire preparedness and disaster recovery requires a consideration of community as complex social arrangements involving inequality and diversity as well as cohesiveness and unity. Evidence points to the ways in which populations live in fragmented communities, at least socially. These features may involve a range of characteristics, such as age, gender, ethnicity, occupation and place of residence. Indeed, such features of community life have implications for the ways in which agencies and others address questions about wildfire. More generally, it is not clear how the state connects with communities, where people live and work, and deal with disaster events. These are the themes explored here.

The State

The state has been the focus of debate and enquiry for decades. While these debates are extensive and complex (e.g. Brenner *et al.*, 2003), the liberal democratic state rests on sets of relations that define the way the state organises and operates. Organisationally, the state comprises a series of institutions which function in relation to production and consumption, care and welfare, and discipline and control. When considering the state it is necessary to account for a distinct political sphere, alongside the economic, social and cultural spheres. This approach indicates that it is necessary to take into account that there is a degree of autonomy in relation to spheres of action, and in particular, the political sphere. The implication is that the state in capitalist society has relative autonomy in relation to other sets of social relations (Jessop, 1990: 354; see also pp. 196–220). Hence, governments are in a position to exercise power and implement policy in contingent ways over time (see Kelly, 1999 for a critical assessment of the strategic-relational approach as exemplified by Jessop).

Complementing the strategic-relational approach is the ways that governmental functions are structured and focussed over time (Clarkson, 2001). It can be argued that during the neo-liberal period these functions have been transposed upwards to international institutions and downwards to subnational states, incorporating regional levels of governance. But, this is not an argument for the hollowing out of the state (e.g. Strange, 1996); rather it is an analysis that is based on a:

> reconceptualised [state] as a set of interconnected jurisdictions that stretch from the local through to the global.
>
> (Clarkson, 2001: 504)

In this perspective:

> [T]he sovereign or territorial state is less a single entity fighting for its autonomy than the central component of a larger set of structures operating on a number of tiers ... processes and institutional forms rising from the municipal and the regional through the federal to the continental and global.
>
> (Clarkson, 2001: 504)

Such an approach draws attention to the ways that particular 'state' levels organise and operate over space and time, often with varieties of legitimacy, democracy and effectiveness. These levels include the municipal, regional, State (provincial), federal (national) and international.

The Australian state comprises three formal levels: Council, State and Commonwealth. As with all states, the precise relations between these levels have changed and evolved over time. Hence, following the logic of the transposition of state functions over time, and in relation to specific objectives, it is likely that the relation between state and community will be uneven, often partial and incomplete.

The task thus is to consider the ways that the interactions between the state, on the one hand, and community, on the other hand, play out. Theoretically, there is a place for agency in relation to both policy formulation and implementation, by and in the state, as well as within the community. This latter point has been developed in a body of literature focussing on the idea of state-synergy (Evans, 1996). This idea involves reciprocal engagement between state and civil society, in relation to a division of responsibility and in relation to personal networks within and between these spheres (Evans, 1996). Of course, this does not necessarily imply that the capacities within each sphere are equal; rather it is necessary to consider the strengths and weaknesses of different interest groups that make up each sphere, and the ways these relations are expressed in practice (e.g. Kalinowski, 2008).

While the principal focus in such analysis is on the interactions between the state and the social actors and institutions that make up civil society, there has been limited enquiry into the relation between the state and communities (e.g. Evans, 1977). At a general level, the view that governments should intervene to regulate and organise social and economic life has been transformed over the last three decades. From the late 1970s onwards, based on ideas associated with the role and place of the state in a modern economy, there has been a paradigmatic shift towards multilevel governance, with the national (federal)/provincial (State) increasingly seen as facilitators rather than as interveners in civil society (e.g. Pierson, 2005, particularly Chapter 7). Although an often overstated distinction, the point of noting this shift from intervention (social democracy) to facilitation (neo-liberalism) is that the tensions associated with these ideas are likely to play out in complicated ways in relation to communities.

Disaster events impact regions and thus localised communities. There is a long-standing debate about constituent features and parameters. These debates have been distilled into questions relating to the multi-dimensionality of a region (Jessop *et al.*, 2008). Recent contributions, moreover, identify questions relating to territoriality, scalarity and network-connectedness (Macleod and Jones, 2007; see also Goodwin, 2012 and Morgan, 2014). The focus is first on the ways in which territorial and topological perspectives can be deployed to analyse internal relations within a 'region' (*cf.* Macleod and Jones, 2007: 1185 where they point to the importance of trans-territoriality and connectivity) and second on the relational processes of scalar structuration (MacLeod and Jones, 2007: 1186). And there are other dimensions to consider, not least the '*provisional* nature of political power' (MacLeod and Jones, 2007: 1187), and this aspect is alluded to in this analysis, via an exploration of the decision-making processes involving disaster agencies and civil society.

These debates provide a focus for the analysis. Territory refers to spatiality, while the relational dimension addresses their connectivity (Goodwin, 2012: 1182). Interaction between the territorial and relational dimensions produces regions whose spatial boundaries may be unclear (Massey, 2004: 3). Hence, the first task is to explain both 'the scalar and territorial dimensions of particular political practices' (Goodwin, 2012: 1189). While regional governance often appears institutionally bounded, it can be porous and impermanent (Morgan, 2007, 2014). It is this instability that allows diverse actors to contribute to strategic regional economic and social agenda (Mackinnon, 2011). As a result, the scalar politics that surround the establishment of regional institutions and policies may involve social and material interests that are both wide-ranging and fluid. The second task is to explore who is involved in these processes and who is not, and why.

In the case of disaster events, the state, via its agencies, often aims to shape and mould the way in which different interest groups are integrated into the structures of government or operate in relation to state initiatives and practice. This view is of the state as relatively interventionist, where the state seeks to create the conditions for managed communities in and of localities. One implication may mean that state institutions need to have a sufficient presence to ensure that the involvement of the citizenry within localities is accomplished in ways that enable their participation. Another is that those who make up communities in and of localities also have agency and, moreover, their interactions with emergency and disaster agencies are complicated.

Of note, the Australian state rests on two contradictory relationships in relation to disaster events: first, between the administrative and representative structures that comprise the state apparatus in liberal democracies and, second, between professional and voluntary relationships in connection with disaster events. Thus, it can be argued that the state plays a distinctive role in shaping policy and decision-making processes, promoting engagement by citizens within communities. The premise here is that effective policies and practices are likely to emerge where a co-productive partnership, that is, 'shared responsibility' (Teague *et al.*, 2010; McLennan and Handmer, 2012), is developed between the state *qua* agencies and the locality-based social groups within a disaster-prone area. These relationships work out in complex ways. But before examining these matters it is necessary to consider community(s).

Community

Communities are dynamic; a characteristic that is often missing in conceptualisations of community in disaster management literature (Mulligan 2013: 281). In this chapter, the starting point for considering the concept of community is from Calhoun (1980: 107) who argues that community is both 'a complex of social relationships' and an 'a complex of ideas and sentiments'. Ideas about community based on uniformity are common. Nonetheless, some scholars criticise the conceptualisation of community and philosophical underpinnings for its tendency to privilege unity, agreement and communion, and in so doing marginalise and hide differences (Secomb, 2000; Diprose, 2003). Others critique the idealised conceptualisation of community which favours face-to-face relations based on small, decentralised groups of people (Young, 1986, 2001). As Brent (2004: 217) notes 'face-to-face can mean eye-ball to eye-ball' and as other research has indicated, Australians are living in increasingly fragmented communities based on interest rather than locality (Hughes *et al.*, 2007).

These aspects are relevant to wildfire communications and are also reflected in agencies' practices. Following the Royal Commission into the February 2009 ('Black Saturday') Victorian bushfires there were recommendations for fire agencies to produce more tailored information (Teague *et al.*, 2010). In addition, fire agencies produce communication materials aimed at different communities of interest, such as farmers and horse owners, but also encourage small groups to organise themselves in programs such as the Community Fireguard Group (CFG) in Victoria. Yet such approaches involve greater costs and more sophisticated approaches in relation to subject and audience. In short, agencies need to know more about the residents in wildfire-prone areas. This raises questions about the nature of the information required and the capacities of fire agencies facing budget restraints to collate and analyse such data. In this context, government agencies often view communities as 'things' that can be measured and 'treated' in some way to achieve a certain goal such as increasing wildfire readiness. Such practices should be scrutinised.

Scholars interested in analysing power and politics have examined the rise of community programs aimed at a range of social issues. Rose (1999: 176) argues that:

> government through community [occurs when] in the institution of community, a sector is brought into existence whose vectors and forces can be mobilized, enrolled, deployed in novel programs and techniques and identity construction, of personal ethics and collective allegiances.
>
> (Rose, 1999: 176)

In this context, communities are subjected to a range of measurements with which 'community professionals' can explain and interpret a community. Rose argues that 'community' became subject to this form of governing partly through a reconceptualisation of the remaining 'space' left by the state and the markets. As Rose notes, this way of governing should not be viewed as naturally occurring, but rather was constructed through particular forms of economic, political and social policies, and ideologies.

One way to understand the idea of 'government through community' is to examine what groups of people do. For Calhoun (1980: 110) actions are the distinctive characteristic of a community as people may feel that they belong in a wide variety of social contexts, but these self-identifications do not always modify their action, let alone produce collective action. Moreover, this observation points to the two-way relationship that underpins agencies and communities. The question then becomes how do communities address wildfire risk and what is the place of agencies in this process.

Community and Wildfire Readiness

The view of 'community' as unified and cohesive consistently informs wildfire policy in Australia. This focus is illustrated in a past *Sydney*

Morning Herald editorial entitled 'Bushfire Disaster Reminds Us We Are One Community' where bushfires are claimed to:

> remind us that we are a community, with a need to help each other, and that our communities do rally when natural disaster threatens
> (Sydney Morning Herald, 2013).

This surge in collective cooperation during times of crisis has been termed 'communitas' by Turner (1985), although as other scholars have highlighted this collective activity is usually short-lived (Moore *et al.*, 2004). Other examples of appropriating 'community' in this way include official and academic publications.

The idea of 'community' is central to wildfire preparedness and disaster recovery (Jakes *et al.*, 2007). In Australia, the Victorian Bushfires Royal Commission stressed that responsibility for wildfire safety should be shared (but not equally) between the 'State, local government, individuals, household members and the broader community' (Teague *et al.*, 2010: 6). Webber and Jones (2013) describe how community development approaches have been used in the recovery from the Victorian 2009 wildfires. According to Elsworth and colleagues (2009), invoking 'community' in the emergency management literature was influenced partly by community safety approaches which assume that communities can be engaged and empowered to examine their risk of wildfire and devise solutions to manage this risk. Consequently fire agencies have been trying to work more effectively through education, awareness and engagement programs to promote network and capacity building within communities (Fairbrother *et al.*, 2013).

Several points can be made about the existing literature about community in relation to emergency management, natural hazards and wildfires in Australia. First, community is not confined to political or administrative boundaries (Buckle, 1999). Further, there have been various attempts to define community beyond 'a merely local place' (Goodsell *et al.*, 2011) as well as cautions about assuming community and place synonymously (Clark, 1973; Brent, 2004). Place does appear, however, to be a salient factor when thinking about wildfire management and processes of recovery (Cox and Holmes, 2000). Other observations about the role of place in the context of wildfires can be made. Cottrell (2005), for example, suggests that a broad understanding of 'community' is relevant and argues that geographical location is a relevant factor as it influences the types of hazards to which people are exposed. The conclusion offered is for an acknowledgement that each 'community' is different and that service providers should understand this feature. Research concerning the relation between social capital and disaster preparation also suggests a positive association with the sense of belonging to a place (Jakes *et al.*, 2007). Finally, volunteer brigades are located and named after specific places, and most volunteer firefighters reside in close proximity to the local brigade headquarters in order to respond to any emergency. So, their physical connection to a place is a feature of being part of a brigade.

Individuals may belong to different communities that may or may not be related to one another, and Buckle (1999: 23) suggests that mapping communities effectively could reveal the:

> complex relationships, networks, hierarchies and nested groups... Any affected community is likely to cross some defined administrative boundaries.
>
> (Buckle, 1999: 23)

Within locality-defined communities there may be groups competing for scarce resources (Marsh and Buckle, 2001). We argue that current analyses should be extended to reflect this diversity when devising engagement strategies for communities. One way of addressing this aspect is to consider the manners in which groups of people often interact 'within and between a number of sub-communities' (Sullivan, 2003: 20). Previous research concerning community and wildfire highlights the ways in which people associate with multiple subcommunities and indeed communities. These interactions are not confined to a specific geographic location. Unfortunately, we know little about how ideas of community and social divisions influence levels of wildfire preparedness.

Communities: Unity and Division

In terms of the perspectives of residents themselves, many participants we interviewed across the different types of localities reported that they generally felt there was a sense of community where they lived. When asked to elaborate about what this meant, participants would refer to examples of collective activity, including festivals and voluntary groups, or report a perception of a communal response to drought conditions. In areas recently effected by wildfires, participants spoke about people helping one another in different ways, such as by providing food, shelter or transport. But, as Calhoun (1980) asserts, this feeling does not account for how these communities are constituted and sustained by other political, economic and social influences. Calhoun's work points towards aspects of division within and between communities which are important for fire and other agencies to consider when working with people in wildfire-prone areas.

Many examples of contrast and difference were reported, such as newcomers and established residents; holiday home owners and local people; those who maintain their land (keep grass and vegetation trimmed) and those who do not; urban and rural people; and environmentalists and anti-environmentalists. These categories provide a way for people to talk about their communities by making distinctions that enable people to locate themselves within the locality and the communities that comprise the locality. The purpose was to explore how such perceived or real differences impact capacities to prepare for wildfire, rather than assess the validity of these claims that people made about others.

Unities and Tensions

Many have a strong sense of community, as illustrated by the residents in an old and established rural community based on an agricultural service town in New South Wales (NSW). This region in particular had been severely impacted by drought conditions for a number of years. Some participants suggested that people pulled together to cope with the adverse conditions. Others felt that people in the area were friendly and willing to help one another. Another example of community collaboration cited by a few participants was the annual Ute (Utility car) Muster Festival which was organised by volunteers, attracting around 18,000 visitors. One participant suggested that the region was typical of rural areas in that those with a sufficient population would have strong communities born out of the processes to sustain a livelihood.

A sense of community may be confirmed via references to collective responses in relation to a perceived crisis, as evidenced in a Tasmanian (Tas) locality. A number of respondents stated a belief that people would help each other in the event of an emergency (2 male and 1 female, Tas, rural and a focus group). However, other respondents stated that a sense of community can be limited. More specifically, some participants (2 male, Tas, rural) identified that for some there was a sense of community via organisations, such as sport-related clubs. A number of participants noted a sense of community through membership of charitable organisations and involvement in collective events. One observed that 'community spirit' is a characteristic of rural areas in general and went on to state that a sense of community was manifested around organised economic activity in terms of raising money for charity or for local people who needed support (female, Tas, rural).

Various signifiers of community diversity and division were expressed. There was a notable division recognised between those who prepare their properties and those who do not. Some participants characterised the relationship between council officials and community members as 'them' and 'us'. It was also noted that for new arrivals it can be difficult to feel part of a 'community':

> Amongst certain groups there is, and amongst other groups- well theirs is probably a division, but you probably have that anywhere. There are certain groups of people that do get on. The thing in [place name removed], to be blunt, is if you're a newcomer you're not accepted as a local.
>
> (male, Tas, rural)

Another local, for example, doubted if the community could be organised to prepare effectively for a bushfire. Participants in the focus group implied that they felt a loss of community, primarily caused by bureaucratic processes and legal concerns impacting local activities.

A more qualified assessment was evident in a seaside Victorian (Vic) town. Here there was some evidence of tensions within the locality where the relationship between neighbours appeared strained when one household did not maintain the vegetation on their property. A number of residents also drew attention to permanent and non-permanent residents (such as tourists). Some participants argued that tourists represent a major problem in the event of a bushfire, since the high numbers of tourists is assumed to mean that the routes out would be too congested to be viable.

Others expressed a more collaborative ethos in the same locality. Participants who belonged to CFGs reported that a range of residents cooperated to watch over one another's homes during threatening conditions:

> In [one resort] there's a number of Community Fireguard Groups [educational and awareness groups promoted by the Country Fire Authority (CFA)], and they range from being all local residents to a mix of residents and absentee land owners, to other groups that are all absentee land owners. It's interesting how they look after their immediate group of people, where there's a court or a close within the development of the settlement, or it's a broader street, or some neighbours over the back fence, and just keeping a watch on their neighbours on bad days.   .
>
> (male, Vic, tree/sea change)

Other participants reported more general positive aspects of belonging to the community and also particular strategies to feel part of the community. One semi-retired resident described the need to be active in the community in order to become accepted, while, in a joint interview, a couple described the importance of social contract, or understanding, between neighbours.

All residents and others interviewed in a rural Western Australia area stated that it generally was a close community that was friendly, with most usually supportive of each other. Community-mindedness was displayed, in particular, according to some participants, in response to recent bushfires in the area. They were also able to identify some of the key changes to their communities. These included an increase in retirees relocating to the area, an increase in the number of small holdings (a lot of subdivisions) and other residential developments. Some participants (agency personnel and some brigade volunteers) identified negative consequences of these changes. It was suggested that some newcomers did not have the knowledge or experience to adequately prepare for bushfire.

Nonetheless, others spoke more positively about how the newer residents had contributed to the local economy and community. A few suggested that there were distinct groups within the community, such as older established families or distinctions based on residential location: urban/rural fringe, town and rural. While participants did not report any examples of conflict between these groups, one participant, who had been in the area 4 years, suggested that she would not be considered a 'true local' even if she lived in the area for a further 20 years. In terms of community diversity, from observations and participant's responses, the area was not significantly diverse. It was characterised by one participant as being a 'WASP' – White, Anglo-Saxon, Protestant – community. However, a few participants did refer to small numbers of people from other ethnic backgrounds living in the area.

It is against this background that the themes are brought together in one high-risk area in Tasmania. At the time of the interviews, new residents were moving on to blocks located in gullies and on steep hillsides. As these blocks often have poor access, they pose many difficulties for bushfire management for homeowners and volunteer fire brigades. When these accessibility issues are combined with a lack of bushfire awareness, the build-up in fuel load (due to the recent winter being one of the wettest on record) and the close proximity of many of the more recent suburban estates to bushland reserves, the result is a very high level of risk.

The main town and the larger council area have many of the characteristics expected of rural-urban interface areas. A resident of a smaller community provided an example of the diversity in this population when she described who lived on their road. Residents included farmers, couples from England, France, Western Australia and Queensland, along with themselves (originally from NSW) and local Tasmanians (female, Tas, urban-rural interface).

In these circumstances, residents provided contrasting assessments of the locality. For one participant, the local fire brigade was seen as embodying the community because it is:

> [Q]uite a hub of the community, so we're very connected with a lot of people. I joined that in order to get a better understanding of bushfire, being a resident there, and also wanting to sort of put back into the community.
>
> (female, Tas, urban-rural interface)

For another person it is:

> The community organisations down there are very vibrant and very active. When a local community issue comes up, everyone is willing to put their hand up and say their piece and present options.
>
> (male, Tas, urban-rural interface)

Overall, many people felt that the community was actually comprised of many different communities, based on location, length of residence, and socio-economic status. But rapid population growth meant that the area was changing. With an influx of commuters and 'weekenders' many residents now spoke of taking advantage of the area's amenities rather than being involved in local community activities. Thus, according to some of our participants, the area was beginning to assume the characteristics of a dormitory suburb of Hobart (the nearest city) rather than a separate community (female, Tas, urban-rural interface).

It is in these contexts that the different fire agencies promote various learning programs that focus on 'the community'. One of these programs is the CFG in Victoria, which encourages residents in a neighbourhood to organise and operate together to promote an awareness of fire and prepare for the possibility of dealing with bushfire (Fairbrother *et al.*, 2010). Trained facilitators lead these groups. The activities are primarily framed as educative but there is some recognition that the success of the education is tied up with 'community building', although, perhaps more accurately, building local social networks. (For a full report on this related project, see Fairbrother *et al.*, 2010.)

One specific intention of the program was to encourage a 'sense of community' and promote self-reliance in relation to bushfire preparedness, usually in rural locations or settings at the rural-urban interface. Via facilitated group sessions, the program encouraged the development of household bushfire survival plans. Fireguard groups generally consisted of six to ten households (10–20 members) but occasionally became larger. The CFG groups were usually limited to one street or small locality. Each group is allocated a trained CFA facilitator, usually by the Community Education Coordinators. These facilitators then took groups through the four core sessions of the Fireguard program. Such sessions involved a number of meetings (usually four to seven), normally held in the home of one of the group members. The ideal outcome was that each household represented in the group would produce written, practised and effective, fire survival plans with backup plans for different contingencies. In most cases, group members supported each other in making their properties 'fire ready' and, in the event of a fire, protecting property or helping more vulnerable members of the group.

An inaugural CFG meeting was typically held in a resident's home with neighbours invited to attend. They were expected to meet regularly while they underwent the CFG core program over 4–7 weeks with a facilitator. As Fairbrother *et al.* (2010: 18) report, CFA staff described CFG as:

> the ultimate, at the top: highly motivated people, shared decision-making, self-reliant communities. That's the overall objective of what Community Fireguard is.
>
> (CFG participant, Central Vic)

Such hyperbole is part of the process of legitimating the locally based groups, but similar sentiments were often repeated by CFG participants themselves. Many specifically mentioned that the CFG program helped to foster feelings of connectedness or 'community spirit' (Fairbrother *et al.*, 2010). As indicated:

> I would have thought – I mean – they're called Community Fireguard groups, so if you can't get that community feeling and everyone wanting to meet up and go through it, then I would say you weren't successful.
>
> (CFG participant, Central Vic)

A sense of community was defined as a complement of awareness by another:

> [The] community aspect, I think, is of definite importance...I mean awareness, of course, is the prime – of fire behaviour and what you've got to do. But without the community side of it, it's going to fall apart.
>
> (CFG participant, Central Vic)

For another this sense of community could be enabled by the Fireguard groups themselves:

> Maybe that's part of the role of the fire groups that actually, you can engender this sort of community spirit and go through that to actually encourage people.
>
> (CFG participant, Western Vic)

Indeed, several participants expressed the belief that fostering a sense of connectedness or community was the primary positive outcome or strength of the CFG program, above the importance of acquiring knowledge about bushfire safety and preparedness. For example:

> Fire is part of that but it is also... it's a sort of community thing to foster, but rather than look at just fire, that is just one part of it. Because we could be involved in something equally as bad but not necessarily fire and what do we do about it? So you can actually use community networking and those sorts of things.
>
> (CFG participant, Western Vic)

For this person, the Fireguard groups became a means of networking. Others agreed:

> One of the massive strengths, from my perspective, is community connection.
>
> (CFG participant, Urban Vic)

This sense of connection was a persistent theme. The group became an end in itself, a means of coming together:

> The strengths are binding the community so, not that I'm sure we're going to necessarily go and defend each other's property, but just that strength in numbers in a way, you know that other people around you are thinking about it as well and are aware, so the fact that we formed the group, I think that it is a very valuable function in itself.
>
> (CFG participant, Northern Vic)

A feature of many comments was that these groups were crucial to building and promoting a sense of community. As stated:

> For sure, it's been the community building, like everyone sort of knew everyone but it's really strengthened that sense of we're all in it together.
>
> (CFG participant, Urban Vic)

On this level, the participants spoke of a sense of connectedness rather like Anderson's (1983) imagined communities. It was a feeling or belief, group members felt 'together' and 'connected', that there were other people around them, moving towards common or shared goals. Yet, as will be explained in the next section, there were also tensions in communities.

Community Uncertainties

These communities were also undergoing change, even in the well-established and relatively stable areas. The New South Wales area mentioned earlier had changed for some but not for others. For example, farming practices had changed as farms were becoming bigger through amalgamation. This has seen an increase in corporate farms and an increase in farm managers. Consequently, smaller family farms run by one or two people are slowly decreasing in number. One resident felt that the community had changed because of the recent ongoing drought conditions (male, NSW, rural). He argued that many people of the same age had left and probably would not return. It was also suggested by two others that the skill base of the area had probably declined with some people leaving to find employment in the mining sector. These residents observed that local businesses could not offer the same conditions of employment compared to some other sectors and States and so some skills had been lost to the area. The local economy had declined as the drought affected farmers' incomes and so a lot of people were short of money.

This obviously impacted the local retail trade with shops struggling, and a number had shut. Other changes included the closure of a rice mill as well as an abattoir while a number of government department offices had relocated to larger population centres.

While, most residents did not report issues of division or conflict within the community, more generally, a source of conflict was evident around attitudes and values regarding the environment. For example, in many areas some people:

> [S]ee the trees as a threat and others who see them as habitat for wildlife and part of the amenity of the area... Then there's other people who are just wanting to realise the commercial value of their properties and don't care about the bush at all.
>
> (female, NSW, urban-rural interface)

Others across these localities also commented on this division over environmental values:

> We get very cross with people who move in and then decide they're going to do everything they can to get rid of the bushland because it's a threat. It's wrong.
>
> (female, NSW, urban-rural interface)

Interestingly, a local government officer suggested that there was a growing tendency for residents to complain to the local council about a neighbour's poorly maintained block. It was argued that previously people had known the person with the untidy land and would speak to them directly, but now the council was used as a 'go between' to avoid upsetting the neighbour. This view that untended bushland represented a threat in the context of bushfires was expressed by one volunteer firefighter in Tasmania:

> The attitude of we want to live in a green environment needs to change. It's all very well for them to live in a green environment, but their [uncleared] property just provides a stepping stone for the fire to jump between two properties that are well cleared and so on.
>
> (male, Tas, urban-rural interface)

However, others in this same locality viewed the process of clearing vegetation as a threat. For example, two participants who had moved from the mainland felt that the whole issue of people burning off on their own blocks had to be better regulated because of the risk such burns pose and the air pollution generated (2 female, Tas, urban-rural interface).

The issue of community change was viewed negatively by some participants. For example, another spoke about the increasing number of people from lower socio-economic background living in the locality:

> No, it's changing the way [the locality] – the dynamics of ... is changing because of the influx of...Dole bludgers, people who are out of work. ...They're very lazy, as a group and sometimes the children in those families are at a loose end and they are looking for mischief.
>
> (female, Vic, rural)

Economic and social status was also linked to levels of bushfire readiness, as one focus group participant in Victoria noted:

> It's only the riff raff we get in town that don't look after their place.
>
> (female, Vic, rural)

Participants from other States gave empathetic accounts towards others who had particular educational needs or financial difficulties:

> I think there's a lot of people that are not getting their voice out because of the illiteracy, but because it just seems like in Tasmania there's this divide because of the illiteracy. Like, there's 70/30, so there's 30 per cent of people and they're just strutting around like, you know, we do in Melbourne, or the 70 per cent which are a lot of people on welfare, a lot of people with illnesses, disabled, and they're just pushed aside. So this is the thing about the communication with fires as well. You wouldn't know if they knew stuff. I mean, yeah, I think it's a worry. I've been very disappointed finding that out living here for six years. It's sort of out in the country it seems to be a lot worse than it is in towns, like with ... up north, and when we lived in Hobart you sort of didn't get that, but living out here in the country you really feel that divide.
>
> (female, Tas, urban-rural interface)

And:

> Some families don't even have a car. I was thinking of one family that I was supporting. She would buy an old bomb, like under $1500 because she could sort of scratch up some of that money. Then she would buy a dodgy car and that would go for so many weeks and then that would go so she'd buy another one. You know, borrow some money. She had a couple of cars outside but you could never drive them. That wasn't even the working poor and she had about four children. So yeah, some of the families don't even have transport. So if they wanted to leave, they couldn't.
>
> (male, WA, urban-rural interface)

These examples demonstrate how some people struggle to comply with official advice concerning bushfire preparation or are potentially not in a position to activate a fire plan.

Economic status plays out in other ways in relation to its impact on bushfire preparedness at a community level. For example, owners of second homes were often perceived as not adequately maintaining their properties in terms of keeping vegetation trimmed. As a local government officer noted in one rural locality in NSW they were more likely to issue abatement notices enforcing the clearing of vegetation to absent home owners. Similarly in Victoria:

> I think that all the local community, the people that live here all the time are basically ready, whether they've got it [fire plan] written down or not, they're basically ready and they've basically cleaned up. There's a lot of holiday homes that are never cleaned up. That's a risk to permanent residents.
>
> (male, Vic, tree/sea change)

While this perception was noted in other states, participants actually gave examples of home owners maintaining their properties:

> I can understand why Weekend Warriors [people only living in the locality at weekends] perhaps wouldn't be on top of it, because they're only down here for two days. With the ones next door to us, they seem to keep their places really well maintained. They're all very wealthy and their properties just look like something out of *House and Garden* [magazine]. But I can understand why perhaps sometimes people might be negative about it and why it is probably the case with a lot of Weekend Warriors.
>
> (male, WA, rural)

Another participant from the same Western Australia (WA) locality who was also a volunteer brigade member suggested that there was a risk of people not maintaining fire breaks because they were trying to sell their investment property and so were reluctant to spend further money on a house that was for sale. However, this participant added:

> I mean, I haven't personally seen much evidence of it. We're pretty good in our little area.
>
> (male, WA, rural)

Another way in which socio-economic status influenced preparedness was provided by a participant from a tree-change area in West Australia. Here it was suggested that educational attainment among volunteer firefighters was connected with higher expectations regarding brigade equipment:

> We get basic supplies from the local shire and training ... but, proba-
> bly because of the sea-change – tree-change component and the higher
> education level amongst our fire brigade, we're much more conscious
> about safety. The masks that the Shire provides us with, we don't con-
> sider good enough, so we fundraise to buy better ones.
>
> (female, WA, tree/sea change)

Thus, communities as localities often are becoming more diverse and when reflected in terms of socio-economic differences can also become a source of unease, if not in some cases tension as residents grappled with social change and sometimes uncertain futures.

In many localities, there was a recognised urban/rural division. Specifi-cally, this related to newer residents who had moved from an urban envi-ronment to a more rural location. These 'newcomers' were characterised as not understanding the country way of life and lacked certain skills and knowledge that would enable them to be accepted. This argument was particularly related to bushfire preparation and awareness; the implication being that people with an urban background would be more vulnerable and less able to cope if faced with a bushfire. However, such views were challenged by other perspectives. For example, a participant who moved from Sydney to Tasmania asserted that simply being from a rural area did not equip people with an appropriate knowledge about the environment:

> That's what it comes down to, and there are a lot of people in rural
> areas that don't really have much respect or regard for the natural
> environment. The fire brigade is one of those organisations gener-
> ally, in rural areas. Generally, I mean in one way I've got a lot of re-
> spect for them, because when there is a fire it's obviously important
> that people actually are prepared to go out there and deal with them,
> but politically, and their value system, the majority of people in fire
> brigades aren't interested in the environment. They don't actually
> care about it that much. So there's a fair bit of tension there.
>
> (male, Tas, tree/sea change)

There were a number of examples of people coming from an urban back-ground with no previous experience of bushfires and who reported high levels of bushfire readiness. Another newcomer, this time in West Aus-tralia, provided another view regarding what they expected:

> Newcomers like myself and my family – I think the perception is that
> the newcomers want to come in and in one respect they want things
> to change, and the people that have been [here] long don't want it
> to change. Then, the flipside to that coin is that new people want to

come to work because they like what it is, and they don't want anything to change, but yet some of the families who have been here for a long time, have seen a change over time and want it to continue to grow and develop. So really, the issue in the people is really too hard to generalise that one. But I'd say most people are pretty tolerant and just want to see the best for the town and the community.

(male, WA, rural)

The issue of new residents was also a feature in a NSW locality which attracted large numbers of retirees. Some gave accounts of being involved in various voluntary groups such as a golf club (entirely run by volunteers) as well as informal arrangements designed to offer support for neighbours with mobility issues. Overall, this locality was characterised as having high levels of voluntary activity. In the following account, a participant reflected on the changes that had occurred and gave a particular view linking these circumstances:

There used to be quite a good sense of community. It was a lot smaller. Most people knew each other. There's been quite an influx of people coming into the town. So there is newcomers, but there are more community activities … I feel that there is a bit of exclusion by the older or original people, if you like, towards the newcomers. There is a sense that they are going to be excluded, so they do start their new things. I think a lot of the older ones, and I include myself, feel a bit threatened by these new ideas.

(female, NSW, tree/sea change)

Conversely, from the same locality, a different view was expressed concerning newcomers:

There's an older population here and they tend to not really want to get involved. They've come down here because they want a nice peaceful, quiet life.

(female, NSW, tree/sea change)

Another broad difference reported was between those who regularly cut the grass and vegetation on their land and those who did not. Nonetheless, even the issue of clearance prompted conflicting views. For example, one person from a New South Wales peri-urban area noted that:

[I]f you're in a bushfire prone area you should have the right to cut down whatever tree you think could be a danger to your house. I mean there's going to be guidelines, that you follow the guidelines.

(female, NSW, urban-rural interface)

An alternative view from the same locality was that:

> I don't want to live here if you end up having 50 metre fire breaks,
> there's no point in living here then you won't have any bush left ...
> The reason I like living here is because of the vegetation around here.
>   (male, NSW, urban-rural interface)

These varied ways of viewing preparedness informed some of the complex ways in which communities as particular types of localities, in this case peri-urban communities, viewed bushfires.

Many participants expressed negative views of their local council (as the local state), speaking of 'them' and 'us' relationships. A commonly expressed view was that the council seemed to be a hindrance rather than helping local people. For example, participants from a focus group in Tasmania argued that bureaucratic processes and legal concerns prevented certain types of communal activities and consequently contributed to eroding a sense of community. Another issue raised involved the role of local government and regulations concerning preventing the removal of trees and other vegetation. According to a focus group participant in Tasmania:

> I would say that the biggest issue for me is the contradiction between
> what I know should happen and what is the reality of where I live.
> So for example, I live on a road that's terribly dangerous and the
> council will do nothing to remove those dangerous trees and part
> of the reason is because we have at least one close neighbour who
> believes in having untouched trees or on roadsides and he has more
> influence with the council that other neighbours who have tried for
> years to get that changed. I can't touch the trees. But we are not even
> allowed to cut trees down over the road. Yet there are dead wattle
> trees all along there and you would think it was our fault.
>   (female, Tas, tree/sea change)

And, an example from a Victorian resident expressed similar sentiments:

> It's widely known that council is completely dominated by greenies,
> completely and as a result the rules up until that overriding rule set
> in place by the State Government, the rule was that you couldn't re-
> move any vegetation from your property, your property, the property
> you own, you couldn't remove it without permission from the shire.
>   (female, Vic, urban-rural interface)

The sense of animosity was felt by those working for local government. A Tasmanian local council employee was asked how the local residents viewed the Council. The response was:

> They think we are arseholes. They put their plans in and we shat-
> ter their dreams. We take their money. They think we waste their
> money. You show me where there's a good relationship between a

community and their council. But in saying that, if we do something right, well then they'll say thank you.

(female, Tas, tree/sea change)

Another example of conflict between residents and agencies concerned water usage. In one account from New South Wales it was suggested that the poor management of the process of water usage had led to a possible reduction in the capacity of brigades (made up of farmers) to respond to fires through targeted action:

[Some] people at Brigade level [threatened not] to go into the parks because they've now pinched water. You've got to remember a lot of the farmers have got a resentment of what's happened. If you go back over the last 15 years, a lot of the water has been taken off farmers or efficiencies and has been given to the Environment [agency] but what the Environment has done which is really the main thing, they haven't used the water for the environment because the Environment at times haven't needed it. They've then sold the water, which has then provided them with money to then lobby the Government against the famers who they pinched the water from.

(male, NSW, rural)

These findings suggest that councils (as the local state) and other state agencies and authorities can inadvertently create or worsen divisions within communities.

These varied localities all displayed to different degrees lines of division, focussed on the environment, the peri-urban setting and class relations. While the tensions often associated with these divisions were relatively muted, they nevertheless pointed to the ways in which a view that communities are by definition cohesive and thus susceptible to uniform and standard messages is misconstrued, as will be elaborated in Chapters 6 and 7.

Conclusion

This chapter draws attention to the complexity of the idea of 'community' as locality. The vignettes displayed the range of understanding and variation across the localities studied, irrespective of State. Attention was drawn to the importance of network building in promoting and encouraging a sense of identification with particular localities. Others drew attention to the complex relations that can emerge where old established communities are presented with newcomers, or indeed in the case of seaside resorts, a sudden seasonal influx of people, often from distant urban settings. These complex social settings provide the context for the ways in which people may understand, prepare or indeed respond to disaster events such as bushfire.

The chapter reaffirms the view that 'community' is defined in a range of ways by residents and others, often for specific purposes. In some cases, it is defined with reference to length of residence, whereas in other cases the population was long-standing and relatively stable, and in yet others there had been a significant incomer feature to the locality. Of course, it is hard to draw conclusions from such factors, often with older, more long-term residents experienced with bushfire events, while in other cases, particularly in Tasmania, incomers were sometimes more likely to be bushfire aware. This sense of preparation was also often associated with prior experience. In this respect, the importance of experience should never be underestimated, although it also must be acknowledged that experience can also be associated with poor or inadequate practice.

Empirically, this account raises a number of questions about the ways in which the different localities deal with bushfire events, either in relation to preparation or response. First, there was considerable evidence of the ways in which many residents in the different types of localities covered by the study built a sense of 'community' not just for the purpose of wildfire events, by collective actions (festivals), local assistance and help, and the social life of the area (see Calhoun, 1980). But, in the same observations, residents drew attention to differences: those who do not maintain their land in safe ways those who do not live in the area all the time and those who have ideas about the environment that counter the views of those who make their living from the area. It is in this sense that analysis needs to take into account the underlying tensions that can define a locality.

The tendency to understand community in terms of commonalities has been criticised for overlooking differences and inequalities. The dilemma in relation to policy development and practice is to recognise such variation of understanding and experience. One of the obvious ways of enabling such a proactive development is via the embedded local state representatives and agencies, local councils, brigades and so forth. But as illustrated earlier these relations are complex and can be both integrated and divisive in outcome. Divisive, not because of ill-intent, but because of varied understandings, senses of identity and the associated complexities connected with the exercise of power, control and inclusiveness in different social settings.

By addressing both unities and divisions within localities and as well as noting the tensions that may develop between residents and agencies, a more nuanced view of the world with which disaster agencies engage is presented. The challenge for agencies and their volunteers is twofold. First, to avoid deepening social divisions. Second, to work within the current social context that may be characterised by conflict rather than developing strategies that depend on cohesive communities. These are the themes that will now be addressed, beginning with an account of the institutional ways the state attempts to shape awareness, the challenge of a disaster event and recovery within localities via the emergency and disaster agencies.

4 The State and Communities

Peter Fairbrother, Richard Phillips and Meagan Tyler

Disaster events impact localised communities. The state, via its agencies, seeks to shape and mould the way in which different interest groups are integrated into the structures of government or operate in relation to state initiatives and practices (Trebilock and Daniels, 2006; for contextual reference see Clarkson, 2001 and Peters, 1996). Such inclusion tends to rest on state initiatives to secure the conditions for managed communities in and of localities. In turn, the ways in which these objectives work out in practice draws our attention to the role and place of state institutions in these processes. Via wildfire agencies, and in relation to the residents of wildfire-prone areas, the state has sought to address the threat of wildfire as well as consequences of wildfire events. In this respect, the way the state organises and operates is determinate.

As indicated earlier, the liberal democratic state rests on sets of relations that define the way the state organises and operates. As noted, the state comprises sets of institutions that operate in relation to production and consumption, care and welfare, and discipline and control. Nonetheless, the changing nature and expectations of the state comprise an important background context for understanding the way in which wildfire agencies operate. The intent of state agencies is to promote behaviour that will ensure the safety of residents and others by mobilising them to prepare for, deal with and recover from disasters. This objective, however, is difficult to put into practice for two reasons. First, the ways that populations interact within and in relation to localities are complex and multifaceted. Consideration should be given to the composition of these populations, their experiences and understandings, the ways they come together (or not) and their relations with state agencies and statutory organisations. In addition, firefighting services outside the main metropolitan areas are largely composed of volunteers, drawn from the localities that they often defend. These aspects of community provide the bedrock for disaster awareness, frequently a complex and insecure mosaic of social relations. Second, the interconnection and relation between disaster and emergency agencies and the localities they address can be partial, infrequent, intense at times, and seemingly disconnected, and even remote. The outcome is that an understanding of these relations is elusive.

The chapter comprises four main sections, one for each Australian State covered by the research: New South Wales (NSW), Tasmania (Tas), Victoria (Vic) and Western Australia (WA). As wildfire response is organised on a State (rather than national) basis the different contexts of each State are important in terms of understanding the analysis in the subsequent chapters. The different institutional arrangements for each State in the study are outlined, and further insights are added from participant interviews. The information on each State offers a snapshot of each locality at the time that the research was conducted (in the years following the Black Saturday fires), outlining major themes raised by participants in relation to inter-agency cooperation, communication and the relationships between agencies and the localities they serve. This is particularly important as much of the information here was not freely or publicly available at the time of the research, and wildfire agency personnel themselves often commented on the complexity of inter-agency relationships (both formal and informal). As noted at several points in this book, the agencies themselves, as well as the relationships between them, were often in a state of flux. The information here does not represent how the various State-based services were running in 2018, but how they operated in the years following Black Saturday. To explore these relationships, the first step is to present the institutional arrangements involving the wildfire-related agencies, in the four Australian States covered by the research.

New South Wales

NSW is Australia's most populous State, with over 7 million people. Nearly two-thirds of the population live in the capital city, Sydney. The total area of the State is 10.4 per cent of Australia's total area. The State is susceptible to wildfires (in the bush and across grasslands). Over the last few years, fires have threatened the environs of Sydney. The main agency is NSW Rural Fire Service (RFS), a statutory body that is volunteer-based. The RFS comprises 74,000 volunteers and over 900 career employees. Fire and Rescue NSW comprises career and retained firefighters who are also responsible for wildfires. Additionally, NSW National Parks and Wildlife Service (NPWS) and the Forestry Corporation of NSW are land management agencies and listed as fire authorities.

State Institutions as Emergency Services

At the time our research was conducted, there were four main agencies in the State with bushfire suppression capabilities: RFS, Fire and Rescue NSW (FRNSW), Forest NSW and NSW NPWS. In 2012, the RFS had 920 salaried staff and 70,448 volunteer firefighters across 2,039 brigades. The RFS has one head office, four regional offices and 49 district offices. In 2010/11 the RFS received $257 million dollars in funding.

These contributions were from the following sources: Local Government (11.7 per cent), insurance industry (73.7 per cent) and NSW Treasury (14.6 per cent). FRNSW has a total of 7,312 staff and 338 fire stations. One significant bushfire suppression scheme managed by FRNSW is Community Fire Units (CFUs). Residents in at-risk areas are trained in initial fire suppression techniques and are provided with a trailer containing basic firefighting equipment. In 2010/11 FRNSW reported that 577 CFUs had been commissioned (Fairbrother *et al.*, 2014).

The processes of bushfire management in NSW were shared among 13 organisations and administrative bodies (Montoya, 2010) and are formalised in legislation. The State Disaster Plan (Displan) ensured a coordinated response by all agencies that have responsibilities and functions in emergencies. A significant piece of legislation in this regard was the passing of the *Rural Fires Act 1997*. This saw the replacement of the NSW Bushfire Service with NSW RFS. While a detailed review of legislative changes is beyond the scope of this chapter, a key amendment occurred following the 2009 Victorian bushfires. The *Rural Fires Amendment Act 2009* included provision for the RFS to assume responsibility, from local government, for bushfire hazard management. Montoya (2010) notes that between 1994 and 2010, 14 bushfire inquiries or reviews were conducted in NSW, along with other inquiries after significant fire events (e.g. ACT bushfires, 2003; Victoria bushfires, 2009) in other States, and have influenced and informed bushfire management in NSW.

Much of NSW is vulnerable to bushfire events. The RFS attended 1,897 bushfire and 2,316 grass fire events in 2010/11, and in the same period FRNSW attended 6,933 bush and grass fires. Forest NSW reported that in 2010/11 only 703 hectares of state forest were burnt from wildfires and no Section 44 (significant incident) wildfires were declared. From 1 July 2015 until early February 2016 RFS members attended over 13,000 incidents, including forest fires, assisting with storm damage and involving several interstate deployments. In October 2013, a series of bushfires occurred across the State. At its peak, on 18 October, over 100 fires were burning across the State. Previous significant bushfires in NSW were in January 1994 from Batemans Bay to the Queensland border and in 2001/02. These were important events as they informed subsequent bushfire management legislation and prevention strategies. Overall, there appears to be an increasing trend in the scope, number and impact of wildfire in the State (Duttan *et al.*, 2016)

The RFS is said to comprise the largest volunteer fire service in the world. The NSW RFS is the lead combat agency for bushfires in NSW but it works closely with other agencies in their response to a range of emergencies including structure fires, motor vehicle accidents and storms that occur within rural fire districts. A number of committees have been formed around the emergency services and have relevance to bushfires: The Bushfire Coordinating Committee (Statewide), Bushfire Management Committees, Fire and Rescue Bushland Urban Interface Section and Fire Services Joint Standing Committee (liaising between Fire & Rescue and the RFS). There is also an inter-agency operations working group between Fire and Rescue, National Parks, State Forest and RFS. The RFS is deemed to be a combat agency while Fire and Rescue, police and ambulance form support agencies in bushfire incidents. Incident Management Teams are usually multi-agency.

State Bushfire Services

How bushfire-related agencies are organised to respond to incidents is variable and context specific. Bushfires are classified according to their potential severity. 'Level 1' bushfires are low-level events involving one fire agency. 'Level 2' bushfires require a coordinated response from agencies. Significant and potentially extreme bushfires are classified 'Level 3'. Under these circumstances bushfire(s) should be managed according to Section 44 of the *Rural Fires Act 1997*, whereby the RFS Commissioner assumes responsibility and appoints incident controllers to act. At Level 1, the organisation of agencies can be characterised as being fragmented. As an agency official explained, 'everybody does their own thing until a significant fire' (male, NSW, state RFS). For more serious events, more resources are deployed and often involve other organisations and agencies, for example, the police and utility companies.

The arrangement for bushfire management planning appears to be collaborative and multi-agency. For example, another official (female, NSW, State FRNSW) reported that there were over 60 bushfire management committees and that FRNSW has an executive role on some of these. A description of the role of one such committee included preparing five yearly risk management plans which identified assets and mitigation strategies. Based on this data annual work plans were developed.

While some aspects of bushfire management are centralised, localised initiatives were welcome:

> So the local areas though will often develop - and we do encourage this - they'll often come up with initiatives that work in their local area. We're quite comfortable with that. Everything doesn't have to go through a state level control. Local people can - as long as it's consistent with the general, broad message we have it's fine for people to develop local things and then we try and share them.
>
> (male, NSW, state RFS)

However, the extent to which the RFS at a State head office level was aware of all localised brigade activities is unclear as this would depend on effective reporting procedures.

Reaching Out

Analysis of the communication products collected showed that in terms of material development and production, the RFS is the lead agency, although materials were also produced by the NSW Department of Primary Industries (e.g. products for farmers). Like other fire agencies in Australia, the RFS has adopted the Prepare, Act, Survive framework which is incorporated across a range of communication products. There were plans for householders and the *Bushfire Survival Plan – Protect your family, protect your life* includes information about Neighbourhood Safer Places, creating a 'Plan to Defend' and a 'Plan to Leave'. The RFS has produced other printed materials that addressed a range of issues, such as 'Prepare your Property', with basic information on mowing grass regularly and removing excess ground fuels, and a checklist to assist householders: 'Liquefied Petroleum Gas Cylinder Safety Checklist'; 'Bushfire Alerts'; and 'Total Fire Bans Factsheet'.

For homebuilders, there were products relating to environmental plans and development plans. More specialised information was available and related to building in a fire-prone area, residential subdivision and landscaping. Two requirements of relevance were the Asset Protection Zone and the construction of firebreaks. There was information 'for a well-planned garden' to create an Asset Protection Zone. Information was also available detailing the Assist Infirm Disabled and Elderly Residents (AIDER) scheme. This is a one-off free hazard reduction service, supporting vulnerable residents to live more safely in their home around bushfire prone land.

The FireWise fact sheets were also documented. These fact sheets are available through the RFS website and in fire stations. A sheet covers a specific topic, for example Bushfire Survival Plans (Issue 01), Leaving Early (03), Fire Danger Ratings (07), and Fire Safety for Your Pets (08). It should be noted that the whole sequence of FireWise fact sheets is unavailable on-line, and when asked, it was explained that some of the missing fact sheets could be made available, should they be required.

Other forms of media also were used to communicate bushfire information. Television commercials about bushfire preparation, for example, can be viewed via the RFS website and YouTube. Social media is used through the RFS Facebook page and Twitter. In 2012, an iPhone application was released, titled 'Fires near Me', that sends an alert about bushfire activity in NSW. There is also an application 'NSW RFS Firefighters pocketbook', a reference guide for volunteers and staff.

The RFS website contains a wide range of materials and other resources. The 'Household Assessment Tool', for example, was designed to help householders make an informed decision about whether to 'Leave Early or Stay and Defend'. Bushfire-related information from the RFS aimed at younger people is also available. *Firesafe*, for example, is a Science and Technology program for teachers to deliver in schools. Another program, the Kids FireWise Program, includes a home escape plan. These materials are also delivered by the RFS to schools in bushfire-prone areas.

These materials are supplemented by other forms of communication. Street meetings (where residents in a particular street are invited to meet and discuss bushfire preparedness issues), for example, have been organised by locality personnel, as community members or groups, such as Progress Associations. For some, these are deemed more effective than RFS-led meetings.

These communities as localities are diverse, located in widely varied terrain across the state, with uneven experiences of wildfire events, ranging from the deadly to the relatively minor, but events which seem to be increasing in the frequency and impact. The agencies have taken steps to meet these challenges, with an emphasis on the obligations expected from community members in the preparation for and the response to such events. How these steps work out in practice will be discussed later, in subsequent chapters.

The point to make here is that bushfire management is carried out through complex arrangements via multiple committees and hierarchical functional provisions, from head office to regions and to brigades in localities. This complex of professional and volunteer staff means that the engagement with communities in and of localities is likely to be ambiguous at best and often quite opaque at worst. The agency assumption is that communication should largely be from the top down, or more accurately from the professional staff, as mediated by volunteer staff, to a diverse and differentiated population. It is thus not surprising that the idea of shared responsibility plays out in unclear and, as will be demonstrated, in taut ways.

Tasmania

Tasmania is an island State to the south-east of the Australian mainland. At the time our research was conducted, the population was approximately 515,000 people and, unusually for Australia, 58 per cent of this population live outside the capital, Hobart. The land area is 68,102 km², 0.9 of the Australian land mass. Just under 3 million hectares, or over 42 per cent of the state is managed by Tasmanian Parks and Wildlife and Parks and Reserves. The Tasmania Fire Service (TFS) remains the primary agency responsible for fire suppression and control for the state (including a number of surrounding islands). The TFS employs around 250 career firefighters and can draw on approximately 4,800 volunteer firefighters. This agency is complemented by Forestry Tasmania (FT) and the Parks and Wildlife Service (PWS).

State Institutions as Emergency Services

Three agencies provide the lead in relation to fire services in Tasmania: the TFS, PWS and FT. In general, the PWS is responsible for managing National Parks and other conservation reserves; FT is responsible for managing the state forests; and TFS attends a diverse range of emergencies, including bushfires, structural and vehicle fires, hazardous material incidents, urban search and rescue, and high-angle rescue as well as other types of incidents. Of note, these three agencies are all part of the Interagency Fire Management Protocol, at the time, the only one in Australia. These three agencies coordinate their management of activities to deal with large fires under the auspices of the Multi-Agency Coordinating (MAC) group. They seek to provide a coherent and where desirable an integrated approach for all bushfires, irrespective of level (large, complex and multi-tenure) and irrespective of land tenure.

The TFS incorporates over 230 fire brigades across Tasmania and its islands. It comprises both career fire and volunteer firefighters, who provide coverage for both urban and rural districts. The origins can be traced back to 1827, when the then Colonial Government imported fire suppression equipment (State Fire Commission and Gill, 2009). Insurance companies and local businesses established fire brigades from 1835. The subsequent years saw the reorganisation and development of the fire service and led to the creation of 22 urban fire brigade boards, the Rural Fires Board and the State Fire Authority. The *Fire Service Act* 1979 unified the service into one organisation; the State Fire Commission and its operational arm the TFS incorporate over 230 fire brigades across Tasmania. These brigades are comprised of around 250 career firefighters and approximately 4,800 volunteer firefighters. In recent years, the governance and organisation of the fire services have changed. The TFS now acts as the operational arm of the State Fire Commission which reports to the Minister for Police and Emergency Management. It has a close cooperative relationship with the other emergency services in the state, the Tasmania Police, State Emergency Service (SES) and Ambulance Tasmania.

Forestry Tasmania is a government organisation responsible for 1.5 million hectares of state forest land, 39 per cent of Tasmania's forests (http://www.forestrytas.com.au). It is a Government Business Enterprise and hence operates as a semi-autonomous body, albeit operating within the auspices of a number of key statutes, including the Forestry Management Act 2013. Nonetheless, the role of FT has been controversial in relation to the way in which it seeks to meet its mandate, with the FT, the labour unions, the Tasmanian Government and the logging industry attracting public criticism in relation to forest management (Krien, 2010). Nonetheless, FT is a key firefighting agency and many of the staff are trained firefighters, as well as 'incident controllers'. It also organises and carries out fuel reduction burns and related activities in relation to bushfire management.

The PWS is a division of the Department of Primary Industries, Parks, Water and Environment. It is responsible for 2.4 million hectares, 40 per cent of the land in Tasmania. It manages reserved lands, including National Parks, reserves and conservation areas. This responsibility covers 800 reserves and 19 National Parks. The agency prepares fire management plans for some individual reserves and strategic fire plans for each PWS region. These plans present strategies to protect neighbouring settlements and towns, as well as visitors and within reserves. In terms of fire-related activity, one estimate is that PWS dealt with 55 incidents a year and that in 2010–11, 40 planned burns covering 20,000 hectares were undertaken (male, Tas, state PWS).

In Tasmania, the Minister of Police and Emergency Management approves a major plan for the state, the Tasmanian Emergency Management Plan. The thrust of the plan is to ensure an appropriate framework for disaster and emergency responses in the event of emergencies, focussing on layered command and control arrangements. A significant review of the plan followed what has been termed the 'worst bushfires in almost 50 years' in 2013 (Department of Police and Emergency Management, 2015: iii) when more than 60 bushfires burnt across 40,000 hectares, causing the loss of homes, businesses and public infrastructure.

There are also significant planning initiatives relating to the protection of public assets and infrastructure. A community protection planning project has been implemented. It is a State Government initiative to develop Community Protection Plans (CPPs) to mitigate the impact of bushfire on Tasmanian communities and to enhance resilience. The CPP project is supported by the Department of Primary Industries, Parks, Water and Environment and three types of plans are developed, namely the Local Bushfire Plans, Local Bushfire Response Plans and Local Bushfire Mitigation Plans. Significantly, as part of CPP, the Local Bushfire Plans are developed to support personal Bushfire Survival Plans and focus especially on nearby safer places. There are two aspects to Local Bushfire Plans: first, identifying vulnerable people within communities and the places where they might meet during a bushfire event and, second, the local planning process, engaging the community to identify 'community assets', such as key businesses or infrastructure that should be protected by a brigade during a bushfire.

State Bushfire Services

As noted, the key agencies for managing bushfires are TFS, FT and PWS. A number of participants reported that these three organisations have a close working relationship. It was also reported that the fire service liaises with other state agencies, such as the police, Health and Human Services and Housing Tasmania.

Inter-agency cooperation started in 1992 between PWS and FT, and in 1995, the TFS also signed up an Interagency Fire Management Protocol (male, Tas, state PWS). There was evidence of a close working partnership between TFS and FT in the context of fire suppression:

> We work together under a unified Incident Management Team and a lot of our preparedness and training is also done in the same co-operative spirit.
>
> (male, Tas, state PWS)

In summary, it would appear that the key bushfire suppression agencies in Tasmania have close working relationships with each other in practice.

FT has its own fire suppression capacity to protect assets and when using fire in forest management. There is, however, a fire management arrangement and resource sharing agreement between FT, TFS and PWS, described as follows:

> the nearest and best able respondent will respond to a fire report irrespective of land tenure and commence initial fire suppression work.
>
> (male, Tas, state FT)

Nonetheless, one telling division was between career firefighters and volunteers (a common theme across different Australian States). In some localities, amalgamations have taken place with shifts from the previous urban and country brigades to one brigade. There was also some evidence of animosity between the career firefighters and volunteers. As one interviewee stated:

> It still needs to get better…there are some occasions where a career brigade will want to come out into a volunteer or retained brigade area, for whatever reason, I don't know other than to say they've got more cause…all I'm saying that in my observations it's much better but there are still some pockets out there that are not helping the situation.
>
> (male, Tas, state other)

Notwithstanding, the participant said that the main objective was to engage the community with a unified message. He continued to emphasise the importance of a consistent message.

Agency Activities and Their Audiences

In the event of a wildfire, the TFS provides information, principally through its website (www.fire.tas.gov.au) and the media. Further, a system of three levels of messaging, namely the Bushfire Warning Alert Levels, is used to assist the public to make choices regarding their own safety. The explanation of the Bushfire Warning Alert Levels is also available in print and on the TFS website. There is an embedded advertisement explaining 'What it's Like in a Bushfire', advising the public of the conditions to be experienced in a bushfire. In addition, the website also contains embedded playlists for ongoing television bushfire awareness commercials.

Bushfire-related messages were communicated to the public through a variety of other methods, including television advertising, radio, brochures and booklets. The TFS encourages the public to prepare Bushfire Survival Plans and provides planning templates for early evacuation or staying to defend, Emergency Contact Cards and also a Fire Season Calendar. In 2012, the TFS distributed 55,000 copies of a DVD to homes in bushfire-prone areas. It guided householders through the steps to prepare a home against bushfires. It also provides information and advice about whether to leave early, well before a bushfire arrives, or to stay and defend a well-prepared property. Additionally, an information sheet titled 'Advice to householders when a bushfire threatens' is sent out. It contains a key message, saying 'Today, fire crews may be protecting other homes nearby, and may not be able to attend your home when the bushfire arrives'. This information sheet directs readers to the ABC Radio network for news of bushfire events.

There was an increasing use of social media, such as Facebook, YouTube and Twitter, to communicate bushfire-related messages to the public. But, at the time of the research in 2012, social media was only used by TFS to release information and that traffic received from the public via Facebook or Twitter was not monitored by TFS. The PWS also used Facebook (but not Twitter) in 2012, although one participant suggested that the use of social media was a recent development and had not been heavily promoted among the public.

Individual and group face-to-face contact was used by TFS staff to identify and work with community leaders and local volunteer brigades. After making these links, attempts often were made to engage people in the locality, for example, through forums and street walks, where fire service staff would incorporate group property inspections. While Community Fireguard Groups had been established in Tasmania in the past, most had been disbanded because of limited resources. More recently, CPPs had been initiated to provide a means to communicate bushfire safety messages. CPPs involved attempts to consult and discuss evacuation strategies during a significant bushfire event. This process was done through established community groups in localities and local brigades (male, Tas, state TFS).

The use of such participatory methods was seen by some as a community development approach to promote bushfire preparedness, initially through building networks in localities (male, Tas, state TFS), although it was qualified by another:

> So I don't think that we would describe anything we do as true community development necessarily in that it [is] being driven and evolving from within the community. We're still going into communities and we have a particular agenda.
>
> (female, Tas, state TFS)

These staff went on to suggest that the current approach was characterised by consultation and partnership working and they considered that communities in localities had the capacity to find their own solutions (female, Tas, state TFS)

The other two agencies also encouraged fire safety awareness and preparation. First, the PWS also uses face-to-face contact to communicate bushfire safety messages through the Discovery Ranger Program (male, Tas, state PWS). This involves rangers conducting activities with the public to communicate fire safety messages in National Parks and reserves during the summer (December–February). Second, FT communicates messages about fires through its website and publications that are in its offices rather than being widely distributed. The other way messages are communicated is by direct correspondence with people who contact FT:

> I reckon 90 per cent of our public information effort goes into either the pre-emptive provision of information on the re-gen [regeneration] burning program or responses to emails, to abuse, to petitions, to people who come and blockade the office.
>
> (male, Tas, state FT)

There were some examples of the joint branding of some materials: For example the *Guidelines for Development in Bushfire Prone Areas of Tasmania* is co-produced by TFS, Department of Primary Industries, Parks, Water and Environment (DPIWE), the building industry and local government. In terms of local government involvement, the *Property Bushfire Risk Management Plan Development Kit*, a bushfire risk assessment kit for residents, is an example produced by The Tasman Council and was freely available on the Council's website.

The focus of these agencies, at the time, was on increasing public safety, from promoting household-level preparedness to the development of CPPs at the higher level, including nearby safer places. The DVD on bushfire preparedness was widely circulated to households in risk areas. There was also an increased activity in the planning for public assets by the responsible agencies. Overall, as indicated these were top-down processes, resting on an interventionist rather than a participatory set of strategies.

Victoria

Victoria is a small and densely populated State, with over 5.5 million people. It is the fastest growing State or Territory, with around 75 per cent living in Melbourne (capital city) and environs. Victoria is recognised as one of the most naturally fire-prone environments in the world due to its vegetation and summer climate (Buergelt and Smith, 2015; see also CFA, 2018). Much of the State is covered by designated 'bushfire prone' areas, although highly populated metropolitan areas are excluded. In Victoria, the Country Fire Authority (CFA) provides firefighting and other emergency services to country areas and regional townships within the state, as well as large portions of the outer suburban (peri-urban) areas and growth corridors of Melbourne not covered by the Metropolitan Fire Brigade (MFB). In 2015–16, the CFA employed over 1,000 professional career firefighters and was able to draw on around 35,000 volunteer firefighters from local communities. In addition, there were around 21,000 support volunteers (CFA, 2016). The Department of Environment and Primary Industries is the lead fire agency on crown land, which covers roughly 20 per cent of Victoria.

State Institutions as Emergency Services

Four agencies form the core of the Victorian emergency services: the CFA, SES, MFB and the Victoria Police. In Victoria, the Office of the Emergency Services Commissioner provides leadership in emergency management with specific responsibility for ensuring the delivery of efficient, equitable and integrated fire and emergency services. The Office oversees the state's emergency management arrangements, which are described in the Emergency Management Manual Victoria. The position of the Emergency Services Commissioner was established by the Emergency Management Act 1986 to provide independent advice to the Minister for Police and Emergency Services, the Premier, or another Minister as required, on any issue in relation to emergency management. The Emergency Services Commissioner supports the role of the Coordinator in Chief of Emergency Management (the Minister for Police and Emergency Services) in overseeing emergency planning, response and recovery. The Fire Services Commissioner is linked to the Department of Justice and is an independent statutory officer, appointed by the Governor in Council reporting to the Minister for Police and Emergency Services. The Fire Services Commissioner provides leadership, support and expertise to work consultatively with the Victorian fire services to achieve continuous improvement and reform.

At the time of the research, the two organisations primarily responsible for bushfires in non-urban areas were the CFA and the Department of Sustainability and Environment (DSE). The DSE later became the Department of the Environment and Primary Industries (DEPI) and, since a change of government in Victoria in late 2014, it became the Department of Environment, Land, Water and Planning (DELWP). These rapid changes are indicative of tensions regarding the role of the state in managing the environment as a resource. Despite the name changes, the roles of the old DSE and the CFA have remained relatively constant. The Department for the Environment, under all these guises, is responsible for the State's parks and forests. The CFA and the relevant department also undertake strategic bushfire prevention such as construction of fire breaks and fuel reduction burning to assist in reducing fire intensity, slowing the fire's spread and providing firefighters with safer conditions to fight the fire.

Following the Victorian Bushfires in 2009, the CFA was one of the designated lead agencies responsible for delivering major components of the Government's Implementation Plan in response to the 67 recommendations made by the Victorian Bushfires Royal Commission (Teague *et al.*, 2010a, 2010b). In general, the emergency services agencies also work with the DSE, Department of Primary Industries, Victoria Police, Ambulance Victoria and local councils.

As part of the emergency management arrangements in Victoria, the control agency of the particular emergency is responsible for the dissemination of information. For example, during a bushfire event, the CFA is the control agency, and other agencies, such as the SES and Victoria Police, provide a supporting role. The organisational structures around bushfire communication have evolved around different State Departments and agencies. There have been significant changes since the 2003 Victorian Bushfire Inquiry.

The Fire Ready Victoria (FRV) Strategy (2004–7) was developed in response to recommendations from the 2002–3 Bushfire Inquiry, which identified the need for a joint agency to oversee the community education and information campaigns. Since 2004, the CFA, DSE Fire, Department of Health Services (DHS) and MFB have worked together under the 'Fire Ready Victoria Strategy' to provide joint education, information and awareness programs amongst residents of high bushfire risk areas, increasing understanding of how to mitigate bushfire risk and the adoption of preparedness measures.

In September 2005, the Department of Justice established a 'Fire Communications Taskforce' (For further detail, see: Teague *et al.*, 2009: section 4.9.). The Department of Justice's Strategic Communications Branch was tasked with bringing the relevant agencies together to ensure that there was consistency with messages, forming the Fire Communications Taskforce in 2005. The idea was to set up 'a whole of government approach to community education and communication about fires' (Teague *et al.*, 2009: section 4.9). This Taskforce oversaw a number of initiatives and projects. These included the State Government and CFA campaigns known as 'Fire Ready Victoria' 2004–7 and 'Living with Fire' 2008–12.

A number of agencies had representation on and input to the Taskforce. It was coordinated by the Department of Justice through the Strategic Communications Branch, to which the Office of the Emergency Services Commissioner and the Fire Services Commissioner was attached. The Taskforce met fortnightly during the summer and listed agencies and departments had legislative obligations in terms of bushfires. This task force managed the 2010–11 summer fire campaign. This campaign covered four phases: Fire Readiness and Planned Burning, Fire Operational, Fire Recovery and Planned Burning (State of Victoria, 2011: 20–22). Such arrangements remained under review and were changed as agencies and the State government refined approaches to bushfire and like disasters, especially in relation to the Royal Commission findings and recommendations. Increasingly the emphasis has been on the integration and coordination of disaster and hazard mitigation.

In September 2010, a new role of Fire Services Commissioner was established in Victoria and enshrined in legislation in December 2010. The Fire Services Commissioner had legislative responsibility for the overall control of response activities in relation to a major fire that is burning or that may occur, or that has occurred in any area of the State. Moreover, in a formal recognition of 'community' the Commissioner led the 2011–14 fire services action plan. Via 24 work programs, this plan focussed on 'the themes of community fire safety, planning, state capacity and capability, operational interoperability, organisational improvement and governance and accountability' (CFA, 2012: 7). The position of Fire Services Commissioner was replaced by the Emergency Management Commissioner with the passage of the Emergency Management Act 2013.

Of note, there is a public recognition by the Fire Services Commissioner that the intent of emergency management should be to focus on the 'community as the centre of all activities and primacy of life as the single most important priority' (O'Byrne, 2015: 12). In 2011, the Victorian Government Fire and Emergency Communication Committee superseded the Fire Communications Taskforce (Victorian Government, 2012: 44). This committee sought to coordinate the whole of government fire communications. It was chaired by the Director, Strategic Communications Branch, Department of Premier and Cabinet (DPC) and reported to the Fire Services Commissioner (FSC – Victorian Government, 2012: 44).

On 1 July 2014, parts of the Emergency Management Act 1986 and Fire Services Commissioner Act 2010 and enactment of the Emergency Management Act 2013 were repealed, establishing the following positions and bodies:

- Emergency Management Victoria (EMV) as the leading emergency management in Victoria
- Designating the Emergency Management Commissioner with the responsibility to coordinate and control responsibilities over all major emergencies
- Giving the State Crisis and Resilience Council, Victoria's peak emergency management advisory body, the responsibility for developing and coordinating emergency management policy and strategy (Emergency Management Victoria, 2015)

The overall outcome of these developments is that the approach to bushfire preparedness and awareness is based on a whole of government approach to communication and education. These arrangements are likely to be further refined and extended over time.

State BushFire Services

As indicated, a number of organisations have a say in the process of bushfire preparedness with the corollary that responsibility for bushfire management was shared between different agencies, rather than being the exclusive domain of the fire services. Following the 2009 bushfire disaster, the Victorian State reviewed and revised its practice, informed by the 2009 Victorian Bushfires Royal Commission findings. This resulted in a focus on communications as well as a reconsideration of emergency management in the State (State of Victoria, 2012; Fire Services Commission, 2013). As part of these reviews there was a clear recognition of the importance of community embeddedness and engagement.

The shift in focus towards an integrated and comprehensive awareness and education program was established under the auspices of the Fire Communications Taskforce. These steps were explained by one agency staff person as

So the Fire Communications Task Force, chaired by the Director of Strategic Communications, Stratcoms, was set up, and basically would bring together all of the agencies across government's communications people that were putting out messages to sort of say, let's have a handle on what messages you're putting out there.

(female, Vic, state)

This approach in effect amounted to a 'systems' approach to risk mitigation. The focus was and remains on communication and education for bushfire preparedness. The same respondent went on to draw a parallel with road safety:

> You're going to have layers, or systems approach. So the way we complement risk communication of course is through effective other measures that aren't seen. So the driving system's a really good example. You get in a car. To keep you safe on the roads, you've got seatbelts, you've got airbags, you've got traffic lights, you've got speed cameras ... So in terms of bushfire, there's a lot of other parts of that system that can save people's lives to make it easy on them when they make that decision. So providing information is one thing, but [it should] fit in with their individual circumstances.
>
> (female, Vic, state)

The coordination of action and policy development involving a wide range of agencies and departments remains a challenge.

Agencies at Work

At the time of the interviews, the CFA, DSE, DHS and MFB had been working together since 2004 under the FRV Strategy to provide joint education and information programs and awareness amongst residents in high bushfire risk areas. The aim was to increase understanding of how to mitigate bushfire risk and the adoption of preparedness measures. Some participants explained that in fulfilling this aim, there was a clear division of labour between different agencies. For example:

> DSE focused on planned burning messages, CFA focused on getting the community prepared for the fire and understanding risk et cetera.
>
> (female, Vic, state)

As noted earlier, in Victoria the control agency of a particular emergency that occurs is responsible for the dissemination of information. The outcome of these arrangements is that the CFA acts as the control agency for bushfire events. While other agencies become supporting bodies.

Communication products were described as coming from a number of sources, including the Premier's Office, the Fire Services Commissioner, the CFA, Department of Health and Human Services (formerly DHS), as well as local governments. These measures involved examples such as letters from the Premier's Office outlining communication and FireReady programs in Victoria, from the Fire Services Commissioner, reminding recipients to ready for the fire season. We also documented an extensive range of brochures produced by and for the CFA as part of the research project. An indicative example is the CFA pamphlet titled 'Living in the Bush', originally published in 2004 and updated following the February 2009 bushfires. This brochure recommends actions to be undertaken in localities during periods of high fire danger and other natural disasters, and it is reflective of current practice in application of personal and community safety and survival at the time of writing. The Department of Health and Human Services also produced relevant information, including a pamphlet titled, 'Preparing your mind to deal with bushfire season', a fact sheet giving guidelines and tips on how to mentally and emotionally prepare for the bushfire season. DSE was found to provide traveller safety information when planning a journey to, or through, bushfire-prone areas. Finally, the then Victorian Bushfire Information Line (VBIL) was a CFA-managed customer call centre which provided bushfire information (mainly around preparation) to individual callers.

This range of communication approaches and products targets residents in localities, visitors and tourists, schools and so forth. It was clear that attempts were made to prepare localities via such practices as Community Fireguard, a locality-level initiative to prepare for and develop awareness of fire events. Via FRV meetings, which comprised meetings held at public venues, or Street Corner meetings, residents are informed of the CFG program in their respective areas.

One of the issues that became subject to extensive public debate was the 'Prepare to Stay and Defend or Leave Early' policy, more widely known by its colloquially shortened label 'Stay or Go' (Handmer and Haynes, 2008). It should be noted that in the 2014–15 bushfire season the main message sent in public education campaigns from the Fire Services Commissioner, however, was 'Leave and Live', a significant change. Still, this simplistic expression of recommended behaviour continues to rest on a complex decision-making matrix by community members in and of localities.

At the time of our research, the policy was still officially 'Stay or Go' (AFAC, 2006, 2013). Nonetheless, the 'stay and defend' aspect of the policy had become de-emphasised, according to a number of participants, following the experiences of Black Saturday bushfires and the subsequent Royal Commission. As one agency person stated:

> Well there's a philosophical shift which was an outcome of the Royal Commission of the way in which government reviewed what we had been saying as government to people. But the fundamental shift last season, it will be re-emphasised this season is that leaving early is the only safe option.
>
> (male, Vic, state)

Notwithstanding the message that leaving early was the only safe option, it has been recognised that staying and defending remains a valid option to be considered (Reynolds, 2017).

The organisational structures around the Office for the Emergency Commissioner and the Fire Services Commissioner were often complex and multifaceted, particularly in relation to the different reporting lines to the Minister for Emergency. As with the other States, and particularly WA, there was an evolving set of relationships between agencies and in relation to the localities they address. With successive disasters, bushfire and others, these arrangements were reviewed and adapted to the changing circumstances of disaster preparation, response and recovery. Over the last few years there has been a developing multi-agency awareness of the complexity of the different needs of the individuals in relation to bushfire awareness and education. The difficulty for the agencies is to bring clarity to these relationships.

Western Australia

WA covers over 2,500,000 sq km, nearly a third of the Australian mainland mass, comprising remote areas as well as urban settlements and sites for mining and natural resource extraction and agriculture. In WA wildfires can occur all year round. Demographically, WA has recently experienced rapid growth, with Greater Perth accounting for 78 per cent of its population in 2013, up from 71 per cent in 1973. The Department of Fire and Emergency Services (DFES) and the Department of Parks and Wildlife (DPaW) have joint responsibility for bushfire management in WA. DFES is an umbrella organisation supporting the Bushfire Service, Emergency Services Cadets, Fire and Rescue Service, SES, Volunteer Fire and Emergency Service, Volunteer Fire and Rescue Service, and the Volunteer Marine Rescue Services. Overall, the DFES employs 1,100 career firefighters and can draw on over 29,000 volunteers, of which 22,000 are bushfire service volunteers.

State Institutions as Emergency Services

At the time of the research, the three principal institutions involved in bushfire management in WA were Fire Emergency Services Authority (FESA) – now DFES – the DPaW (until 2013, part of the Department of Environment and Conservation); and local government, represented by the Western Australia Local Government Association (WALGA).

FESA was formed in 1999 under the *Fire and Emergency Services Authority of Western Australia Act 1998,* with the stated aim of improving the management of emergency services in WA. It comprised: Career Fire and Rescue, Volunteer Fire and Rescue, Bushfire Service, the SES and the Volunteer Marine and Rescue Service and other services.

This agency was an emergency management organisation (covering bushfire, cyclone, flood, storm, tsunami and earthquake). Under the *Bushfires Amendment Bill* 2009, FESA had legislative power to assume control of all bushfires. In 2011, the FESA authority was located within the portfolio of the Minister for Police, Emergency Services, Road Safety and was classified as the hazard management agency in WA for fire (both rural and urban). Following two reports in 2011 and 2012 (Keelty, 2011; Smith *et al.*, 2012), the DFES was established in 2013, triggering widespread changes for FESA staff and volunteers.

In July 2013, FESA was reorganised into the DFES (see DFES, 2013). The formation of the department was based on a recommendation from the Keelty Special Enquiry into the Perth Hills Bushfire (Keelty, 2011). This new department follows an 'all hazards' approach to emergency management, working in partnership with the community and other government agencies to prevent, prepare for, respond to and recover from natural disasters and emergencies (DFES, 2013). It delivered several safety programs to localities focussing on the management and recovery from emergencies. The department includes the State Emergency Management Committee (SEMC) (oversight of emergency management) and the Office of Bushfire Management (oversight of prescribed burning programs). In 2015, the department comprised 29,000 volunteers and 1,100 career firefighters.

The Department for Environment and Conservation (DEC) was responsible for managing land (pollution control, property licensing and visitor services) owned by the WA State government, such as National Parks and reserves. It ceased operating on 30 June 2013, and was divided into two departments, one of which is the DPaW and the other the Department of Conservation and Land Management. The DPaW is responsible for bushfire alerts on parks and other lands managed by the Department (http://www.dpaw.wa.gov.au/). It manages parks and wildlife areas, providing considerable information on tourism and associated activities in these areas. The DPaW has two specific bushfire responsibilities, prescribed burning and fire management and bushfire suppression. Of note, the prescribed burning and fire management often was done in conjunction with various traditional owner groups. In some cases, this engagement has led to partnerships between the department and indigenous groups and communities.

The SEMC remains the peak emergency management body in WA. It has existed in various forms since the 1970s. Following a review of emergency services, the State Counter Disaster Advisory Committee was established. Later, it was known as the State Emergency Management Advisory Committee and then the SEMC. When the *Emergency Management Act 2005* was proclaimed on 24 December 2005, the SEMC was established by legislation. The Minister for Emergency Services can appoint a chair, deputy chair, an executive officer of the SEMC, a representative of local government and up to seven other members from government agencies concerned with the state's emergency management arrangements.

The WALGA remains the peak body for local government in WA and represents local government on state-level committees and subcommittees. This association has a concern with bushfire preparation and awareness as they impact local council areas. To illustrate the Association emphasised the importance of 'local knowledge' in relation to bushfire preparation, awareness and recovery on the publication of the Ferguson report on the Waroona bushfires of 2016 (Ferguson, 2016; see also http://walga.asn.au/News,-Events-and-Publications/Media/Local-Knowledge,-Funding-Key-to-Fire-Improvements.aspx). Complementing this activity, from 2005 onwards, Local Governments had the capacity to set up Local Emergency Management Committees (LEMCs), comprising representatives from organisations and agencies that dealt with emergency management.

In response to the Keelty report (2011), the Inter-agency Bushfire Management Committee (IBMC) was established, with FESA and DEC as the lead agencies, providing an operations subgroup that met weekly prior to the bushfire season. The IBMC included representatives from FESA – DEC/DPaW, local government, the Bureau of Meteorology and the Department of Planning and Infrastructure. According to the State Emergency Plan for Bushfire (December 2010) the work of the IBMC was supported by five subcommittees: Bushfire Research, Fire Operations, Fuel Load, Training and Aerial Fire Suppression. Example of the work conducted by IBMC includes standardising both bushfire policy across FESA – DEC/DPaW and training for bushfire firefighters and incident controllers. On 2 December 2015, the DFES and DPaW signed a partnership agreement to deal with bushfires (DFES – DPaW, 2015). There have been further changes since then.

State Bushfire Services

At the time of the research, agencies organised Incident Management Teams that became the principal agents in response to bushfire incidents. Incidents were classified as Level 1, 2 or 3, with 3 being the most complex and longer lasting. These teams were deployed during the fire season and were staffed by 50–60 people, accredited to specific roles. In 2011, there were five teams in total, with one team covering the whole state. A second team might be activated during a very large bushfire, but generally one team would be rostered as available. This team would be operationalised if an incident went beyond the capacity of the initial, localised response, for example in the event of a longer lasting and complex bushfire. In 2011, in anticipation of the organisational changes that took place in 2013, both FESA and DEC staff were included in these preformed teams. This practice became operational for Level 2 incidents, a development that was in response to the Victorian Bushfire Royal Commission's criticism of agencies operating in isolation with negative consequences. In addition, this development was viewed as a positive opportunity to build and maintain working relationships.

Collaboration on Communication

In this State, there has long been a collaborative approach to modes of communication information and the procedures associated with dissemination. As with other States, prescribed burns were reported on the ABC, commercial radio, internet sites and the *West Australian* newspaper. During a bushfire event, the DEC adopted FESA communication message templates to ensure standardisation of the message. Social media was also used, for example, Twitter alerts about smoke, but only in very limited ways at the time of the interviews. The DEC also produced and distributed information for tourist outlets, such as information centres. At a local government level, there was some adaption of materials to suit particular local circumstance, although most used nationally produced materials.

FESA had an extensive list of communication products carrying the 'Prepare, Act, Survive' slogan including printed, and online, information about Fire Danger Ratings, Warning Levels and Total Fire Bans as well as a Prepare Act Survive DVD. Targeted material, for example, aimed at people with evaporative air conditioners was provided; there was evidence that recent bushfires had caused some homes to be lost by embers igniting uncovered evaporative air conditioning units. These practices continued under the DFES, although increasingly with reference to 'all hazards'.

Targeting rural areas, FESA and local government authorities produced information relating to harvest and vehicle movement bans during severe bushfire conditions. A variation of this approach was the 'Stay Ahead of Crop Fires', aimed at the farming community. A FESA program to assist pastoralists in the Kimberley and Pilbara areas encouraged landholders to develop fire management plans on their stations; comprehensive guidance on how to set up controlled burns was provided.

For landowners, communication materials explained the importance of enforcing Building Protection Zones (BPZ). This involves maintaining a '20 metre circle of safety' around the home, which is calculated to reduce the effects of radiant heat and lowers the risk of direct flame contact. BPZ guidelines also advocate reducing fuel loads (vegetation) around the home to increase its chances of surviving a bushfire. Firebreak notices, often distributed with council rates notices, were a commonplace form of communication mentioned by participants at a locality level.

As well as print and online materials, audiovisual resources were available. For example, *The Day the Flames Came* is a DVD documenting the 1961 Dwellingup bushfires. Produced by FESA, Bushfire Cooperative Research Centre and Department of Environment and Conservation, the film focusses on the actions of three men who fought to save their families. There was also targeted materials aimed at young people. For example, the 'Juvenile and Family Fire Awareness Program' details the free confidential education and support program for children between the ages of 6 and 16 who have been involved in arson. The program was delivered by a firefighter, with specialist training, in the family home. It included audiovisual materials and advice about developing a home fire safety plan. For the school curriculum, the Bushfire fact sheets (numbering 1–3) were designed for upper primary and lower secondary school students and linked to the health and physical education, and science curriculums.

Of note, WA has a relatively long history of encouraging Bushfire Ready Groups (BRAG). These groups comprise local residents who work and prepare together for bushfire events. They are based on residents working together in a facilitated way, drawing on practices relating to network building and shared understandings. This program was established by DFES in collaboration with local government, building on earlier programmes aimed at encouraging such groups. In 2017, there were 68 such groups, as had been the case for a number of years. These groups aim to:

> build the community resilience by providing an opportunity for neighbours to network, share ideas and information and develop and implement strategies a to reduce their bushfire risk.
>
> (DFES nd)

They are promoted and facilitated as 'a community driven program'. It is predicated on the assumption that self-reliance may be necessary in the event of a bushfire. Thus:

> In a dangerous bushfire, a fire truck may not be available to protect every home. This means residents and homeowners need to be responsible for their own safety.
>
> (DFES nd)

The program is coordinated by a trained volunteer facilitator and is supported in localities by local Fire Services personnel. Material for these sessions included information sheets, such as 'Playing Your Part in BRAG - Residents working together to prepare for Bushfire', as well as a significant amount of learning material through the Bushfire Ready publication programs. Thus, in facilitated ways residents learn and prepare.

One feature of the agency development in WA was that there had been a history of tension between the then two main fire agencies, FESA and DEC. Following the major fires in the state in 2011 and subsequently, these agencies underwent considerable organisational renewal and reorganisation. Over time, there was an increased emphasis on inter-agency organisation and collaboration. Nonetheless, as indicated by the analysis of these agencies within communities, there was evidence of cooperative and collaborative activity across the agencies. These steps were part of a top-down process, with governments actively involved.

Final Comments

Each State has established sets of disaster-focussed institutions which intersect with the communities that face the possibility of wildfire from time to time. While there are broad similarities in each State in relation to organisational structures and the composition of these bodies, each also has its own differences. Moreover, as illustrated by the WA example, disaster events are often the occasion for subsequent reorganisation and a refocussing of the activity of these organisations, which can leave them in a state of fluctuation for a period of time. In the last two decades, there has been an increased emphasis on the social dimensions of both wildfire awareness and preparations as well as the ways that communities seek to learn from such disaster events. In this respect, it is the case that for such events, the state is not just a facilitator but often actively intervenes to secure a greater degree of preparedness and awareness of the dangers of disaster events.

Governments have sought to establish firefighting organisations and related bodies as specialist agencies capable of meeting the challenge of disaster events in effective and economic ways. Increasingly, there is an intermingling between administrative and representative arrangements to prepare and implement risk management plans, refine and focus the mechanisms for dealing with disaster events and rebuild after such events. Steps have been taken to give communities a voice in these procedures, although often there is a degree of happenstance in promoting such distributive arrangements.

Complementing and indeed qualifying these moves by successive governments, an ambiguous relation between professional and voluntary activity remains. Attempts have been made by governments to develop the narratives and practices that will result in positive working relationships: for example between firefighting bodies and the population that comprises a community as a locality. Most recently such aspirations are indicated in Victoria by the 'shared responsibility' approach to disaster preparation and events.

Overall, the state actively seeks to shape policy and develop accountable decision-making processes to ensure the engagement of citizens within communities in and of localities. Increasingly the assumption is that effective policies and practices require the facilitation of co-productive partnerships, as indicated by a 'shared responsibility' (Teague *et al.*, 2010; McLennan and Handmer, 2012) relationship between the state *qua* agencies and locality-based social groups situated within disaster-prone areas. As will become evident, these relationships work out in complex and uneven ways.

5 Communities
Relationships and Responsibilities

Peter Fairbrother, Richard Phillips and Meagan Tyler

In Australia, as in most wealthy nations, the state seeks to address the possibility of disaster and deals with the consequences. Policy is developed and, via state agencies, communities are encouraged to address wildfire events. Recently, there has been a recognition by fire agencies of the importance of 'shared responsibility' in relation to these events (Teague *et al.*, 2010). The idea of shared responsibility in relation to wildfire emerged out of the debates that inform risk theory (McLennan and Handmer, 2012). There are three core dimensions to the notion: obligation, multiple parties and multifaceted risk management. These ideas represent a qualification of the dominant narrative about self-reliance in the face of disaster events (see McLennan and Handmer, 2012: 2). While the emphasis in policy discourse had long been on 'Prepare, Stay and Defend, or Leave Early' (PSDLE) in practice the relations between fire and emergency agencies and households and others in localities are more complicated. Here, we build on the outlines provided in the previous chapter to illuminate how participants understood the function of agencies and the relationship with communities on the ground. Rather unsurprisingly, at times, their experiences differed from the formal representation of how policies, procedures and functions were supposed to operate. These accounts are especially valuable as this level of information about the actual practice can be difficult to acquire, and official documents and websites do not tell us about the realities of how processes function.

The thrust of much debate about disaster events and the preparation and recovery from them focusses on policy narratives and implications, the disconnect between policy and practice, and measures such as communication modes and methods as ways to address these problems. Some of the insights from the policy domain, such as McLellan and Handmer (2012), and the broader literature on risk management, lead to understandings about the ways that narratives are developed and have impact. Other insights can be gained from the repertoires of action literature, focussing on 'the ways that people act together in pursuit of shared interests' that is repertoires of collective action (Tilly, 1995: 15). Nonetheless, much of this analysis focusses on the contested relations of political engagement and conflict (Traugott, 1995). The construction of such relations often in episodic ways may help understand these more mundane relations at a locality level. A third set of analyses focus on the modes and mechanisms of communication, drawing attention to the changes wrought by social media in recent times (e.g. Dufty, 2015). Even so, a comprehensive analysis of these social relations requires an understanding of the dynamics of communities as localities and their connections with disaster and emergency agencies.

The task is to understand the ways communities in and of localities can build their capacities to address the prospect of disaster events. One way to open up these considerations is to focus on the dominant approaches that have been articulated and promoted in relation to disaster events. The recent elaboration of a 'shared responsibility' narrative points to the multiplicity of actors, their constructions of meaning and the supposed varied obligations at play in relation to disaster awareness. These relations raise questions about the appropriate modes and levels of state intervention in relation to disaster awareness, the ways and degree to which individuals can take responsibility in relation to such events and the working out of these relations in practice.

As noted, community capacity building refers to participation, engagement and resilience, a set of concepts that have been debated in relation to wildfire in the Australian context (Adams and Hess, 2001; Reddel and Woolcock, 2004; Wiseman, 2006; Verity, 2007). But, research to date has tended to underplay the distinction between latent and actual community capacities and such neglect has implications for both the elaboration of ideas about shared responsibility between the state and local communities as well as the ways in which this notion can be implemented. The purpose of this chapter is to explore the dimensions of such capacity building in relation to disaster events, involving the wildfire agencies.

As with the previous chapter, this one comprises four main sections, one for each Australian State covered by the research: New South Wales (NSW), Tasmania (Tas), Victoria (Vic) and Western Australia (WA). There has been only very limited, publicly available work bringing together such material on the range of state-based fire agencies in Australia. The aim here is to extend existing knowledge and to give a picture of how processes relating to wildfire agencies and communities operate in practice. It will then be possible to disaggregate and develop an understanding of the processes of population engagement with wildfire preparation. Such an approach combines both the recognition that the political economy of localities must be explained and understood as well as the importance of considering substantive social and political relationships define a community as a locality. Moreover, it is necessary to note the way in which many wildfire-prone areas in Australia also constitute regions, with their often partial and flawed forms of sub-national regional governance (e.g. Pape *et al.*, 2015).

New South Wales

As noted in the previous chapter, there has been a process of working out the precise capacities of agencies and in the process establishing the basis for inter-agency cooperation in relation to wildfire events. In part, these complications point to the long-standing relations between professional and volunteer staff. The critical dimension to consider in relation to these matters is to examine the relationships between agencies (professional and volunteer) and those who populate the localities subject to the possibility of wildfire events, the communities.

Agency Responsibilities

In NSW a number of agencies play key roles in relation to wildfire management: the Rural Fire Service (RFS), Fire and Rescue NSW (FRNSW), Forest NSW and NSW National Parks and Wildlife Service (NPWS). In various ways these agencies work together and complement each other in relation to wildfire preparation, events and follow up. The key questions are who does what and how do different agencies, local government and community members interact? One distinction that was drawn in the previous chapter is that FRNSW was responsible for the internal built environment and urban fire risks, whereas the RFS was responsible for rural areas. Nonetheless, there was, and there remains, a working arrangement between the two fire agencies through agreements and joint committees. Further, the RFS has primary responsibility for bushfire-related messaging.

One pattern of engagement involved a hierarchical downward set of relations, from the RFS at a state level to the locality. In this model, the RFS head office produces communication materials, which at the time of the resarch were implemented through the 44 RFS designated districts. District-level staff supported brigade volunteers, and, in turn, the brigades tried to target at-risk localities through forms of community engagement. These activities included community education and hazard reduction work. There is also an ongoing onus on a volunteer brigade to inform district staff as to what they plan to do.

The joint work between the agencies could take explicitly formalised forms. The FRNSW worked with RFS around hazard reduction burns. In addition, the FRNSW were also represented in four bushfire management committee areas, along with NPWS as the other land manager involved on the committee. Generally, land management agencies had a responsibility to mitigate the threat of bushfire and prevent bushfires from escaping from their property onto other land. FRNSW also had a role in assisting such agencies in mitigating the threat of bushfire. Of note, and unlike other States, the FRNSW was also responsible for the management of Community Fire Units (CFUs). This practice complemented the way the RFS had a responsibility for the establishment and support of CFUs in other non-FRNSW localities.

The FRNSW also managed CFUs. These CFUs 'provide a group of neighbours with the necessary skills and equipment to protect their own properties before, during and after a bushfire' (Gilbert, 2007: 10) The CFU initiative was extended following a pilot program, with CFUs now also managed by RFS. It should be noted that both agencies were responsible for their own CFUs. Anecdotal evidence (personal communication, August, 2016) indicates that some CFUs were organised around a group of people rather than a group and an equipment trailer. In addition, it was difficult for the RFS to consistently monitor the ongoing effectiveness of CFUs (e.g. even knowing if the equipment in the trailer was used).

The focus on community engagement captures the two sides of responsibility, from agencies to the community and the obligations expected from communities in and of localities. This sense of responsibility and obligation was explained by one participant as follows:

> to mitigate bushfire threat it has to be a joint community, fighting agency, even broader community commitment strategy. It can't be just reliant on one or the other. That's the key to it, you know. There is reliance on the fire agencies to make sure we do a lot of the mitigation work. We do the community engagement program so they're relying on the community to actually prepare their homes, to prepare a bushfire survival plan.
>
> (male, NSW, state FRNSW)

It was also suggested that public expectations could also act as a barrier to engaging in preparedness measures:

> If we can ensure that people are well prepared whether they are staying with their property or whether they are going to leave their property. If they're well prepared their property stands a much better chance of surviving a fire and they have a much better chance of surviving a fire. It is a message that we have used. I will be honest that in New South Wales we have had some difficulties around that message as well because people do say 'well I pay taxes and it's my right to call 000 and expect a fire truck'.
>
> (male, NSW, state RFS)

The implication of this observation is that calling '000' would result in the fire brigade attending their property during a bushfire event (Bushnell *et al.*, 2007). This sentiment ran counter to the idea of self-reliance, often emphasised by agencies.

Agencies Targeting Their Audiences

As noted earlier, the RFS produced a range of materials aimed at specific groups within particular localities. First, school workbooks were available, where primary and secondary programs were regularly reviewed and updated to comply with the syllabus prepared by the NSW Department of Education and Training. Education programs and resources produced by RFS also catered for students completing tertiary and community education courses. Second, some materials were designed to meet the needs of rural communities, such as advice about preventing hay shed fires. Third, information aimed at the elderly and people with a disability is produced in a fact sheet explaining the Assist Infirm Disabled and Elderly Residents (AIDER) program. Another significant program is called 'Hotspots', which was described as working with rural landholders to manage fuel on their property in an ecologically sustainable way. Lastly, translated versions of a range of fact sheets into different languages can be found on the RFS website (see NSW Rural Fire Service nd).

Communications professionals interviewed differed in their approaches to and evaluation of these materials. Interestingly, none of the State-level participants commented on the diverse range of materials already available; instead a number spoke about gaps in addressing diversity. Some participants articulated the need for targeting information. Two State agency personnel argued that women in rural areas required specific information (male and female, NSW, state RFS). In addition, migrants with little or no experience of bushfires were also seen as a particularly at-risk group. Another State agency official also recognised the issue of diversity and offered an explanation as to why producing appropriate information was challenging:

> Look there is a huge need for diversity but it's not just cultural diversity; it's business diversity as well. South Australia (another State) is just developing a really good package of materials for large businesses. We haven't got the resources to do anything for large businesses, tourism, or anything like that, [let] alone going into cultural diversity. I would like to do a lot more work with the organisations that represent those culture... and start dealing with those and getting into them, which is very time consuming. But we just don't have the resources.
>
> (female, NSW, state RFS)

A different perspective on audience segmentation and diversity was given by another official, who argued that there was a limit to how targeted the messages could be:

> The community is smart and they're - we're not going to know the limitations of an individual family or an individual person. We can't structure our messages to that singular audience. So people need to take responsibility themselves in terms of their own vulnerability and be that physical, mental, socio-economic location based, whatever it's going to be and to be taking action themselves. I think what the fire services need to do is to put a huge amount of energy into getting the best information, that really good situational awareness and posting that as quickly as we can so that people can actually [be] making those informed decisions. I think that's probably the gap at the moment.
>
> (male, NSW, state RFS)

In addition to the communication 'gaps' identified earlier, there was no evidence of material relating to holiday makers. However, this may be because it is developed at a regional level rather than centrally.

Challenges

Agencies faced a set of challenges in fulfilling their remit. First, agencies often found it difficult to maintain locality interest in bushfire preparation outside the fire season. It was argued by several participants that during times of colder and wetter weather interest in bushfire preparedness lessened. Preparedness complacency was also linked to the frequency of bushfires, where it was suggested that long periods between bushfires led to lower levels of interest:

> Looking back over the last two or three years, after a big event like Victoria we knew that there would be heightened interest but then last bushfire season in New South Wales we saw practically no bushfire activity. So it was a really difficult year for us trying to get that message out that 'hey, fires can still happen'.
>
> (male, NSW, state RFS)

Second, agencies faced a set of challenges about information on fires. There could be difficulty in obtaining information concerning a bushfire event as it was often a fast-moving incident (male, NSW, state RFS). Moreover, there was a question about accurate information, especially in relation to social media sites such as Twitter:

> The next challenge is pulling information in through social media. There's a lot of info out there which could be used but the processes

around verifying that information - turning information into intelligence that's probably the next big challenge.

(male, NSW, state RFS)

This concern is recognised. Bird and colleagues (2012) analysed the use of Queensland Police Service Facebook page and surveyed people who were members of community Facebook pages about their experiences of using social media during floods in Queensland and Victoria. These survey respondents (432 in all) indicated high levels of trust in the information posted on Facebook. Of note, information is often assessed in terms of source, so that government Facebook pages are rated higher for accuracy and trustworthiness when compared to community groups' Facebook pages. However, for timeliness and usefulness of the information, community groups' Facebook pages were rated higher compared to government Facebook pages.

The use of social media in disaster and emergency situations is a relatively recent development and a growing area of research. The study cited earlier related to flood incidents, and so questions remain as to whether or not similar results would occur during a bushfire; these can be notoriously unpredictable and dynamic events, and can impact telecommunications and electricity supply. However, social media might be a useful communication tool at specific periods rather than during an actual fire, such as before impact or after the event, in aiding recovery efforts.

Assessment

This case points to the efforts undertaken by agencies to address the perceived situations of communities in and of localities. First, the agencies have developed a range of measures to promote awareness of the dangers and challenges involved in wildfire events. In complex ways these processes involved professional staff and lead personnel in the volunteer sector. Second, relatively comprehensive and seemingly sophisticated communication procedures have been formulated or were in the process of development as varied modes and technologies of communication are put in place. These procedures were complemented by a range of engagement processes across the State, involving a range of training, educational and awareness activities.

There has long been ambiguity in the relationships between the FRNSW and RFS. Some participants identified the expansion of urban development into rural areas as one influence on this tension. However, it was also stressed that at a senior management level the working relationship between these two fire agencies was a positive one. It was suggested that the RFS also worked well with various media outlets and had established links with journalists through providing accredited training for those reporting bushfire incidents (male, NSW, state RFS).

A few participants expressed concerns about, or were critical of, the NSW RFS. Two officials suggested that the value of community engagement was perhaps not appreciated throughout the service. This view is encapsulated as follows:

> We do measure how many community engagement activities happen each year. But even that's an extremely flawed model because, things like our open days or a school visit they will capture as community engagement when they're not really that - they're a public relations activity. So there's a very low awareness in the organisation of the difference between public relations and community engagement. We have members of our executive saying frequently that when you're on the back of a truck and you wave to the community, you're engaging.
>
> (female, NSW, state RFS)

Criticisms were also expressed about the state mitigation teams, seen as a focussed response to the Victorian Bushfire Royal Commission (2010) (female, NSW, state RFS). This participant implied that in her experience there had not been any consultation within the RFS about how the extra resources allocated to respond to the recommendations from the Commission were to be spent. Another participant who spoke on behalf on the volunteer brigade members was also critical of the state mitigation teams who were salaried staff. It was also suggested that resources should have been used to address inadequate equipment or outdated premises at a local level rather than being used for other technological-based investment.

More generalised concerns related to other internal practices. It was suggested that there was a lack of good communication between salaried staff and brigade volunteers and that some administrative procedures were too onerous. Simply stated, there was a lack of trust between RFS senior management and volunteers. References to the relationship between the fire service and the public, particularly around expectations, were also recorded (male, NSW, state other).

Generally participants felt that public expectations of the RFS had increased, particularly with regard to the increased variety of modes of dissemination and specificity of information. As an example of demanding accurate information, it was reported that during a recent bushfire incident an individual had asked the RFS to provide them with GPS longitude and latitude coordinates of the fire. This story was retold by several participants and was also heard by the researchers during a fire agency conference. It was suggested by one participant (male, NSW, state RFS) that residents have an expectation of being 'looked after' by agencies and other state bodies, a sentiment that the researchers heard echoed across interviews in other States. This again highlights the tension between the agencies delivering what they were required to do, with a sense that communities should take responsibility for themselves. In addition, it was also argued by some participants that agencies generally underestimated the capacities of communities to engage positively with bushfire-related information and that an ideal-type community would be one taking action for itself using the information provided by an agency.

Tasmania

Cross-agency collaborations have long been a feature of the Tasmanian approach to wildfire events. By and large these collaborations have been supported by the State and have worked. These relationships were further developed in the aftermath of major events such as the 2013 bushfires. In this way the agencies have gone through a comprehensive and reflective learning curve in relation to wildfire preparation and management. This multilevel approach to emergency and disaster management has played out in complex ways with the communities challenged by the prospect as well as the experience of disaster events.

Responsibilities

The formal division of responsibility for fire events between lead agencies was fairly clear at the time of the data collection. The Parks and Wildlife Service (PWS) was responsible for responding to and managing fires occurring in Tasmania's national parks and reserves, while Forestry Tasmania (FT) was responsible for responding to and managing fires occurring on Forestry property, and the Tasmania Fire Service (TFS) was generally responsible for fires on privately held land.

Of note, the TFS has responsibility for public engagement, which involves developing and distributing appropriate information and material to the public at risk to ensure they were prepared for and able to respond appropriately to bushfires. Nonetheless, there was an ambiguity about the protection of public assets seen by some agency personnel as the responsibility of property owners:

> So we need to talk to the owners of those other assets and critical infrastructure and have them being to take responsibility for mitigating bushfire's impacts as well. To some extent that's been ignored up to now... But... if they want those assets to be available for communities after fires then they need to take steps to protect them now.
>
> (male, Tas, state TFS)

Safety was to be achieved in several ways, as noted by the same officer:

> if they're not prepared to prepare their homes, they need to prepare to leave in plenty of time. It's about engaging with local government

also because it's important to look at assets other than simply people's homes. There are people's businesses and there are other community assets that need to be protected, like telecommunications towers and power substations and water treatment works, public facilities that the communities rely on.

(male, Tas, state RFS)

It was explained that developers and property agents should ensure that bushfire safety was outlined – in terms of preparation and procedure – to the individual purchaser. Furthermore, the purpose was not to prevent subdivision (where a piece of land is split into smaller plots) and sale of land. As one participant (male, Tas, state TFS) said:

we also want people to develop responsibly. We find one of the biggest problems is the developers will subdivide or whatever, but that information's not passed on to the individuals that purchase those blocks, that they need to continue on with those protective measures - needs to be continued.

Thus there was a view that there was a need for land development to be undertaken with consideration for bushfire safety.

But the public have to make decisions about their response to fires. One staff member said:

It means continuing to encourage people to make decisions about how they're going to prepare for and/or respond to fires. So they don't need to prepare their homes, but they at least need to accept responsibility for the loss.

(male, Tas, state TFS)

Also of note was that little was said about the policies relating to advice for individual responses to fire events.

Agencies in the Localities

The agencies targeted particular audiences within localities, including families with young children and migrants. Some information was aimed at parents of school children and school principals. This included advice when a facility was not deemed safe to protect staff and students if impacted by a bushfire, when the school's relocation and evacuation plans would be activated. For families, the TFS also provides information on 'The Juvenile Fire Lighter Intervention Program (JFLIP)', which was a free, confidential, state-wide service to help families deal with child fire lighting behaviour. Animal owners were also targeted with materials emphasising the need to decide whether to evacuate animals.

The TFS also issued a pamphlet titled 'Bushfire information for parents'. The TFS has taken the position that it is safer to keep young people in schools where they would receive adequate and appropriate direction/ advice from teachers and staff rather than be located at home where guardianship arrangements may be quite variable and may or may not be adequate in the circumstances prevailing at the time. Therefore, school children were also catered for where the TFS worked closely with the Department of Education (DEC) and others to ensure that government and non-government schools in bushfire-prone areas were bushfire-ready and that children, staff and visitors at schools would be safe if bushfires threatened. There was also a separate information sheet for school principals.

In the context of community diversity, there was some reference to particular groups such as recent immigrants. In the latter case, work with organisations supporting migrants was focussed on home fire safety rather than bushfire safety (male, Tas, state TFS). Other agencies noted that different groups of people visited reserves and parks, such as bushwalkers, four-wheel drive drivers and families involved in camping (male, Tas, state PWS). A more recent development was a move to work with aged care facilities to promote bushfire safety and awareness (female, Tas, state TFS).

Work on bushfire safety aimed at women was also highlighted by some participants as women were seen by some as a particularly vulnerable group. In some localities, women were seen as more likely to be at home during the day while men were more likely to be absent, often at work. Trial bushfire preparedness programs were being undertaken that were specifically aimed at women, based on the view that some women did not frame their intended actions within a correct bushfire response framework:

> Most things we've run, there've been less women attend than men and the women have tended to say, 'but we're just going to go early with the kids'. But they don't associate that with preparation.
>
> (female, Tas, state TFS)

These steps were taken in recognition of the consequences of different gender roles in relation to bushfire (2 male and 1 female, Tas, TFS).

One claim that was repeated by a couple of participants was that some communities are better prepared compared to others (2 male, Tas, state TFS). Characteristics of a bushfire resilient community included previous bushfire experience, awareness of fire behaviour and being materially equipped. Communities less able to manage a bushfire were seen as those that included more people who had recently moved to the area and were unused to living 'in the bush', who had no knowledge of fire behaviour and limited social networks.

But, overall, diversity was not seen as a significant issue in the interviews. Many participants in Tasmania noted that there were low levels of what they classified as 'diversity'. For example, one interviewee (female, Tas, state TFS) argued that Tasmania was not culturally diverse and that, where diversity did exist, it was usually in urban areas with a low bushfire risk. Rather, the focus was on 'the Tasmanian community' which, in the context of bushfire communication, was defined as those living in bushfire-prone areas.

Challenges

The relationships between agencies and members of communities were uneven and often partial. A first main challenge evident in Tasmania was for agencies to recognise the importance of community engagement. The focus of many local fire brigades was on fire suppression and incident management, with limited attention to community engagement:

> At the moment 98 per cent of our brigades have a focus on fire fighting. It's only a handful that also do community development work... So an early challenge for us is to encourage other brigades to take that approach too.
>
> (male, Tas, state TFS)

And another, also in the TFS:

> I think the main challenge is perhaps that the organisation hasn't really embraced community development as a process. So they tend to be more focused on response.
>
> (female, Tas, state TFS)

This challenge arose out of an emphasis on the technology of fire suppression, as noted by the first respondent:

> However, emergency services, more broadly, still have that emphasis on community service, but it's a very responsive, reactive, something happens, we go and fix it...I think it's very hard for fire services to see fire trucks and stations as anything other than 'must have' and community based programs as anything more than 'nice to have'. I think that's a cultural shift that everybody's struggling with around the country.
>
> (male, Tas, state TFS)

However, the amount of time that volunteers could commit to a local fire brigade underwrote the importance of technological solutions to wildfire. As yet another state official noted:

> Quite a few of my brigades are made up of farmers who just don't
> have the time. They're happy to jump on the truck, but they don't
> have that time to get out there and engage.
>
> (male, Tas, state TFS)

Nonetheless, there was evidence of a changed perception emerging. It
was suggested that members of some volunteer brigades had begun to
see a community-focussed approach in a more positive way:

> They are more willing to take and wanting to be resourced and
> trained to be able to do this within their communities. Whereas
> when I first met them, they were 'no, we're just operational, we don't
> do that sort of stuff.' But now they're saying, 'we would like to enlist
> someone to do this [community development] role'.
>
> (female, Tas, state TFS)

At the time of the research this recognition was relatively recent and
underdeveloped.

The second challenge, and related, was the recruitment of volunteers, which at the time was becoming a problem. As stated by a senior
volunteer:

> At the moment the average age of volunteers is around 54 years. I'm
> past midway in the 60s, heading towards the 70s and there are peo-
> ple much older than me that are still in there. The younger set, some
> certainly want to get involved and I'm very appreciative of that but
> there's not enough of them.
>
> (male, Tas, state other)

In some respects, this evaluation also reflects the age profile of rural
industries and the associated populations in many areas.

The third challenge paradoxically arose where there was an awareness
of the importance of community engagement. It had become apparent
that achieving behavioural change was not straightforward. As one participant stated, 'It's one thing to inform people, it's a different thing to
get them to act' (male, Tas, state TFS). Others also noted that achieving
behavioural change can be extremely difficult (1 female and 2 male, Tas,
state TFS). A related concern expressed by some was how to make the
brigade membership more representative of the community, through for
example, increasing the numbers of women and people from different
ethnic backgrounds.

The fourth challenge, centred on communication, was increasingly
seen as a critical issue for the agencies. One difficulty facing agencies
was to ensure that messages were consistent, no matter when they were
issued. As noted:

each and every one of us going out and giving out what we perceive is the same message but doing it with different aspects of priority and the community getting mixed messages.

(male, Tas, state other)

These communication strategies were potentially problematic in terms of ensuring the consistency of messages. As a corollary, there were often different responses to messages, even when presented in a seemingly clear way. It was unclear how key messages were communicated to appropriate audience segments. In relation to public information, for example, the planning of organised burns raised quandaries. On the one hand, fluctuating weather and environmental conditions may mean that a planned burn could be delayed or postponed. On the other hand, it was not clear what an effective mode of communication would comprise in such circumstances. And, of course, audiences vary in terms of language, time availability, age and gender.

Finally, the complexity of media arrangements and processes had begun to emerge as a concern. Agency staff spoke of both the possibilities and deficiencies of social media (male, Tas, state TFS). Moreover, how messages were prioritised was not clear. During a disaster event, for example, it was likely that a range of social media came into play, carrying messages often of varying quality and accuracy. At other times the more conventional media outlets did not view bushfire information as a priority. So:

You send a media statement out and you're at the mercy of whoever at the media and whether they think it's relevant and interesting. With bushfire stuff they'll only cover it if it's likely to impact on communities; if it's remote they're not interested.

(female, Tas, state PWS)

The corollary of communicating via the media was the development of agency information sites, accessible all year around, and part of the promotion of disaster awareness. The TFS internet site, for example, was accessed sporadically throughout the year, although during an incident, there would be high demand for access to TFS website. This, in turn, could lead to resourcing questions:

It makes it quite expensive for the organisation to say ok, for one week a year we've got to spend hundreds of thousands of dollars to put this hardware in for a short amount of time. It's got to compete with other budget initiatives that the organisation has.

(male, Tas, state TFS)

In addition, the infrastructure to manage infrequent, but high surges in demand had obvious resource allocation issues.

Other infrastructure problems involved radio communication systems. It was reported that under certain conditions, frequencies in the North and South of Tasmania could be interrupted by users. In addition, it was reported that different agencies use different frequencies:

> They [FT] work on different frequencies than us. They're still in switching distance but they work on different frequencies, so I'm not really hearing what they're saying and they're not hearing what I'm saying. Unless we switch to each other's frequencies and communicate directly, there's no overseeing in what's happening.
>
> (male, Tas, state other)

This person, a senior volunteer, went on to say:

> If I've got a police car at that fire, I've got to physically go and hunt them down. I can't talk to them on radio. If I've got an ambulance there, now I can, but back in the days of 2007–08, I can't speak to them.
>
> (male, Tas, state other)

Such disconnections could have severe consequences during disaster events and limit planning and preparation at other times.

Assessment

While agencies have a history of working together in constructive ways in Tasmania, there remain challenges. Working across agencies could be a problem in enforcing bushfire safety measures. As one officer stated:

> To get around all the areas - or some areas there's a crossover with ownership to Crown and wildlife reserves and quite a lot of different groups involved. It's very hard to serve abatement notices when you've got these individual groups controlling the different land areas. So it's very hard to come up with one set of rules for quite a diverse range of land management groups.
>
> (male, Tas, state TFS)

Such difficulties were evident in relation to planning and the role of the fire services. When new land developments were planned in bushfire-prone areas, for example, some participants reported that there was no enforcement, even though municipal councils often approach the TFS for an opinion. As one person explained:

> I suppose the problem... is because we're dealing with so many bodies it's very hard to get a consistency across the board... I suppose

all we can do is recommend it. At this stage, it's not legislated as such, although we can be a lot stronger now because of the new Australian standards for building in bushfire prone [areas]. So we do actually have a standard that we can apply to these places now.

(male, Tas, state TFS)

Overall, there is a lack of clarity about responsibilities, between fire agencies, and between these agencies and other areas of public responsibility.

Of note, bushfire ready communication products come from a unitary source, namely from the TFS. There was no evidence to suggest that local brigades were using other source materials. Citing financial limitations and lack or resources, local brigades relied on TFS materials. Notwithstanding the multilevel approach, the importance of individuals taking responsibility for their own safety was emphasised. Individual responsibility and action were also spoken of as multifaceted; this was articulated as either being prepared to undertake action to reduce their own fuel loads or being prepared to accept the responsibility for the loss of property.

The cross-agency collaboration between TFS, PWS and FT was formalised, with considerable support from the state. Steps had been taken to review and refine these relationships, especially in the aftermath of major events such as the 2013 bushfires. Overtime a multilevel approach to emergency and disaster management has been developed, involving the three major agencies, and especially the TFS.

Victoria

The State of Victoria is an especially fire-prone region. It also has a history of a well-established and relatively large volunteer firefighting force. In this context, the procedures and practices of the agencies have been subject to much review and extensive political debate over the decades. As part of these reviews there has been a clear and contested recognition of the ways in which community embeddedness and engagement may be recognised.

Responsibilities

The responsibilities of government and other agencies to manage bushfire risks and support preparation at a locality level have been subject to debate and enquiry for decades. This focus is particularly evident at times of major bushfire and the enquiry often associated with them. More recently, the focus on these matters has been with reference to shared responsibility (Teague *et al.*, 2010; McLennan and Handmer, 2012).

These debates raise difficult questions because they are often part of a broader consideration about the nature of the responsibilities of government and emergency agencies towards the public. For some, the concept is ambiguous giving rise to practical questions about the division of responsibility, which they argued needs to be more clearly defined and perhaps even quantified. One participant stated:

> So how much are we sharing this? Is it an 80/20 split or a 50/50 split or a 70/30 or what is it? So that's something that needs to be articulated more carefully in future. But clearly it is a shared responsibility. The message is you won't get a fire truck. So we are encouraging them [the public] to do things because the state can't actually provide - while we have a broad duty to do fuel reduction burning, provide fire services, whatever.
>
> (male, Vic, state)

From the perspective of the state agencies, there was a strong sense that the public should have a significant role in preparing and building capacity for coping with bushfires. The same participant used the Country Fire Authority (CFA) as an example of shared responsibility, commenting:

> In a sense the CFA is a living breathing example of that notion of shared responsibility... People forget that CFA is actually a community based organisation. It's made up of members of local communities who volunteer their time to go off and fight fires.
>
> (male, Vic, state)

But, as recognised there were limits to the capabilities of agencies in disaster settings:

> I think the government has a responsibility to manage public land and we have a responsibility to communicate with the people and prepare, and we have responsibility to deliver as best service as we can and commit and provide as much service as we can.
>
> (male, Vic, state)

Another issue was an anxiety expressed by those working in the agencies that residents in the localities may not fulfil their responsibilities in accordance to the advice given by the fire services and other related organisations:

> But the agencies have legislative responsibility as well for ensuring that things happen from the agencies' end as well. Ultimately, the agencies, when push comes to shove, can't make people behave in a way that's contrary to how they're going to behave in this country.
>
> (female, Vic, state)

So, there are formal demands and requirements on agencies, but there are limits to what agencies can expect, or as noted earlier, require.

Targeting Communications

In general, the focus of communication and education has broadened over the last two decades. Increasingly steps have been taken to distinguish between different audiences and in ways that have been assumed to be more appropriate for these varied groups. One method has been to send letters and planning templates out through the electoral role, although this process means that residents who are not eligible to vote are overlooked. Some communication products were directed towards children in the form of games and colouring sheets. Many of the public events, such as the Department of Justice Roadshow or Fire Ready Victoria (FRV), were publicised in local newspapers. In addition, attention has been given to the different modes of communication, social media, face-to-face engagement, mail-outs and so forth. Unfortunately, there often appears to be an *ad hoc* aspect to these steps rather than as part of a well-integrated and resourced communication strategy.

Over the last decade there has been an incremental identification of target audiences. Emergency services organisations have begun to consider the socio-demographics of localities in focussed ways, drawing on research. As expressed by one interviewee:

> Okay, as part of our research agenda, we've had from time to time projects that have set out to identify where those gaps are. So our stuff looks closely at gender differences, either as a matter of course in the terms of doing our research or it quite specifically sets out to do that. In terms of multicultural communities, we have an interest in that.
>
> (male, Vic, state)

Here there is recognition that gender differences and multicultural experiences matter, and the state bushfire services are taking them into account. These measures were part of an emerging realisation of the specificities of localities. As stated:

> one of the gaps that was found, very much so in the rural areas, was the - engaging women, our rural women. So they've just launched a rural women's program up in the north-west because what happens in the small country towns - all the blokes go down to the shed and get on the trucks and the women just stay at home or get to face the fire alone or work out their own thing.
>
> (female, Vic, state)

The steps taken to engage women in bushfire awareness processes have been relatively limited in practice (Tyler and Fairbrother, 2013). Often, these measures saw women as the problem; they focussed on the ways in which bushfire activity and organisation was a masculine endeavour.

These matters were further highlighted in relation to the needs of other groups, such as Culturally and Linguistically Diverse (CALD) communities and those with disabilities. Attempts were made to address these groups via specific programs and tailored materials. As one interviewee stated:

> We've got a lot of publications in different languages but we're also engaging different groups now as well to get the best channel into, say for example, the deaf community. Vision Australia - working very closely with them. Scope - so trying to tone down a lot of our information so that it's in easy English and much more accessible to people with disabilities.
>
> (female, Vic, state)

Hence, over the last decade state bodies increasingly took steps to disaggregate the target audiences in ways that addressed the socio-demographic specificities of different social groupings, underwriting the sense of belonging.

Another agency member also highlighted the different initiatives in place for engaging members of CALD communities, saying:

> We [CFA] have programs that target all those groups. So we have a culturally, linguistically diverse program which largely focuses on making sure all materials are translated into 22 different languages across the state. We also have community spokespeople, translators that can be called to come in and run a Fire Ready Victoria meeting in any other language. We've got 35 of those trained presenters across the state. We're targeting Centrelink [social security] offices because in the migrant sense, the first place that most migrants go to is Centrelink.
>
> (female, Vic, state)

Further insight was given into how one agency targeted populations considered to be vulnerable and how this would consequently change the way in which communities were accessed:

> We have a program where we work with health and community care workers who go into public housing. They're all trained by Fire Ready Victoria staff to give information to people living in public housing, particularly again at risk areas. We also work with - in terms of a passive sense as opposed to an active sense - on providing services to make sure that homes of residential care people, whether they're defendable or not. So we do assessments of those properties.
>
> (female, Vic, state)

Increasingly, the various social groupings were defined in terms of perceived risk. Such a focus was relatively recent. According to many, these
developments were very much a feature of the period just before and
subsequent to the bushfire events of 2009.

An important step was taken in 2007, when a bottom-up approach
was trialled to engage the members of a locality in relation to bushfire preparedness and awareness. This community development initiative, titled 'Strategic Conversation', was promoted by the then DSE and
succeeded by 'Community Engagement' (e.g. City of Greater Bendigo,
2016). Strategic Conversation was explained as a community building
paradigm with the emphasis placed upon understanding the impact of
the communication campaigns by the use of qualitative measurement,
focussed on relationships (Department of Sustainability and Environment, 2012). It was used as a process of referral, the claim being that
network building did not work through structures or hierarchies but
rather relied on a process of recommendation and referral. The content
and process of Strategic Conversation was largely driven by the community with support from the 'Knowledge and Learning' team in the
Department (Blair *et al.*, 2010).

The purpose of the Strategic Conversation approach was to facilitate an appreciation of the social context of bushfire preparedness. In
explaining the purpose, another State official pointed to a certain ar-
rogance of the 'top-down' assumptions made in many communication
programs, saying:

> Whereas we don't even know what a particular community's need is.
> We are - if we take that approach-totally arrogant and ineffective. We
> can spend millions and millions on programs to push out messages
> and tick all the boxes for evaluation...We still need them [communi-
> cation campaigns] and that's important. But just allow a little bit of
> space for something different to sit alongside and complement it.
>
> (male, Vic, state)

This emphasis complemented the concern that agencies had with the
effectiveness of messages, assessed by market testing methods. Of this
procedure, another official from a government department said:

> So we [the department] got them to do key message research with
> groups from high risk areas and general Victorian population so
> that we could get a lot more direction on what the key messages
> should be and which were resonating with the community.
>
> (female, Vic, state)

Thus, the challenge facing the state in relation to targets and audience
was both in relation to the audience itself as well as in relation to the

delivery of the message. Step by step a more sophisticated communication strategy has been promoted in Victoria. Still, while the effectiveness of communication strategies and implementation at the locality level was recognised as important, it was generally acknowledged that there still was no systematic engagement and assessment of these processes.

Challenges

Given the practicalities of bushfire events, there was a pragmatic acknowledgment that shared responsibility was a formal recognition of something that must take place if people were to survive. Agencies were not in a position to help every individual resident, or even every household, when a bushfire threatened. As a Victorian official remarked:

> there is absolutely no way that CFA can manage - or any fire service in any capacity with any resources - can manage a bushfire if people don't also look after themselves. We cannot save everyone and we never will... but in the end it's a survival question. If you want to survive, you have to take responsibility for yourself to some degree, because you will be on your own, most likely. It's not a, we're choosing to leave you. It's a fact of life that you - most likely - will face a bushfire on your own. It's just the truth.
>
> (male, Vic, state)

But the practical exigencies of a disaster event were not the only complications for agencies in their approaches towards bushfire-prone localities.

The character of locality also mattered. To illustrate, agency personnel expressed significant concern in relation to peri-urban areas on the ways citizens in these localities view emergency services, including the availability of those services:

> People are still very much in - and there's some really interesting demographic dimensions to this. People who live in an urban environment in particular have a service delivery mentality so you ring the fire brigade and it turns up.
>
> (male, Vic, state)

So, often coming from metropolitan areas, serviced by professional fire service agencies, there was a view that all one had to do was access emergency contact services and assistance would be there. This sense of availability also was encouraged by some of the messaging that took place:

> when push comes to shove, they still expect that the fire agencies will be there. I noticed it the other day. ... I went up through Warrandyte and up to Hurstbridge ... There's a big sign just out of Warrandyte

that says, CFA and SES protecting our community. So we've got this, 'yes, we're heroes protecting you - and you will be self-reliant and can't rely on us and we won't have a fire-truck' - so there's that kind of mixed messaging, I think, still very strongly out there.

(female, Vic, state)

In effect, this depiction of availability was a misrepresentation in the sense that a service is not only on 24 hours a day call out but that the staff are also available on this basis. The contrast with the voluntary service was that availability was 'voluntary' in the sense that there was a juggling with other demands and requirements of peoples' lives. Of course, this observation is not to suggest unwillingness. It indicates that there may have been competing demands on people's time, such as returning from a paddock to a vehicle to reach a fire station, which may take 30 plus minutes rather than 1 minute.

Complications also arose when the interests of messaging for bushfire awareness clashed with the interests of other organisations. As another Victorian official explained:

I was invited to a meeting ... at Tourism Victoria, talking about the impact of all this [warning messaging] on tourism, particularly for the rural sector. How concerned they are about people are losing big dollars because they won't go in the bush anymore and when they do it says there's a code red and high alert and they don't come back or they don't go at all.... So we're under a bit of pressure from Tourism Victoria to mellow our wording.

(female, Vic, state)

Hence, it was not always straightforward to issue a statement stating that there was 'a code red and high alert'. Such alerts, for example, could impact tourism in the bush areas. So there were pressures and limitations on the style of messaging from a variety of internal and external quarters.

Assessment

In general, the focus of communication and education has broadened over the last two decades. Increasingly steps have been taken to distinguish between different audiences and in ways that were assumed to be more appropriate for these varied groups. One method has been to send letters and planning templates out through the electoral role, although in doing so, residents who were not eligible to vote were overlooked. Some communication products were directed towards children in the form of games and colouring sheets. Many of the public events, such as the Department of Justice Roadshow or FRV, were publicised in local newspapers. In addition, attention was given to the different modes of communication, social media, face-to-face engagement, mail-outs and so forth. Unfortunately, there often appears to be an *ad hoc* aspect to these steps rather than as part of a well-integrated and resourced communication strategy.

The bushfire communication options developed by agencies came in a variety of formats, from television campaigns and mail out of pamphlets to household planning templates following the 'Prepare, Act, Survive' slogan, mostly formed in top-down ways. In contrast, there were also local agencies advocating for programs at the grassroots level, such as the locally delivered FRV programs. Some of these FRV programs were also tailored for the audiences partly based on the knowledge of the local brigades. The tailoring of the programs was done in contrast to what was perceived as the top-down corporate initiatives. And, yet these messages stretched the capacities of agencies in a variety of ways and clashed with the interests of other agencies and groups within localities. The outcome was a mosaic of activities and sometimes tensions as these relations were worked through in the bushfire-prone localities.

Complementing the organisation and approaches of the agencies is the challenge of tailoring and localising these relationships in effective ways. While there had been some experimentation with embedded programs, such as the 'Strategic Conversation' initiative, they were often time and labour intensive, and hence faced resourcing problems. In such circumstances, a top-down approach from the agencies to the localities seemed to prevail, not necessarily because it was believed to be the most effective, but because it was easier – in terms of time and other resources – to deliver. Often the outcome was a set of stretched relations within localities and between agencies and localities.

Western Australia

In WA bushfires can occur all year round. There were significant fire events in the lead-up to the data collection for our project: for example, Dwellingup February (2007); Boorabbin National Park (December 2007); Toodyay bushfire (December 2009); Lake Clifton (January 2011); Red Hill and Roleystone/Kelmscott (February 2011); Margaret River (November 2011) and a series of fires at the end of 2014, throughout 2015 and subsequently. Succeeding reviews and inquiries into these events have made recommendations to improve the management and prevention of bushfires. These developments and the more extensive history of the State mean that bushfire policy and management in WA is an ongoing and dynamic process as the state and agencies seek to learn from the findings and adopt recommendations.

Responsibilities

The last decade in WA saw debate and public concern about the in-stitutional boundaries in relation to responsibility. Successive reports (Keelty, 2011; Smith *et al.*, 2012; Ferguson, 2016) have commented on these tensions and solutions to them. Staff within the agencies also referred to the problems of responsibility. Some accepted the formal arrangements and noted, for example, that the Fire and Emergency Services Authority (FESA) was responsible for gazetted areas, while lo-cal government looked after unmanaged reserves and allocated Crown lands (male, WA, state local government). Others highlighted the point that local government managed volunteer fire brigades and ensured compliance with fire control notices (male, WA, state local govern-ment). These different aspects were drawn together in anticipation of the changes to the Department of Fire and Emergency Services (DFES), with observations that 'recent' legislative changes mean that the DFES is now the overarching hazard management agency for WA. In prac-tice, this was assumed to mean that DFES can assume control of a bushfire incident regardless of where it started (male, WA, state local government).

The idea of shared responsibility in this State was outlined by a number of participants. For some, this was framed as a logical stepped process:

> We talk about shared responsibility. We try to get people to - well, as I said, one of the first things is to understand what the risks are, and about what are the sort of things that they can do and what's the benefit in them doing these things? If we can do that, and we can empower them and understand that there's something in it, get some motivation going to have them acting rather than just knowing, then we're well on the way to having that shared responsibility.
>
> (male, WA, state FESA)

Shared responsibility was about raising the awareness of people living in high-risk areas and reminding them that they had to take action and responsibility to manage the threat of bushfire (female, WA, state FESA). A further dimension was that fire should be seen as an issue for everyone in WA as it was a natural feature of the environment (male, WA state DEC). In other words, government agencies were not solely responsible for dealing with bushfire events, or preparing for and recovering from such events.

The increasing emphasis on community responsibility was informed by the Victorian Bushfire Royal Commission in the 2009 bushfires. It was suggested that if agencies expected communities to make appro-priate decisions during an event, then the public would require the cor-rect information to make informed decisions (female, WA, state FESA).

This aspect of responsibility refers to the possibility of shared responsibility between agencies and a developed role for individuals and communities in and of localities. These narratives also provided a powerful account of the individual responsibility felt by agency personnel, especially during significant bushfires:

> People have to prepare and have realistic expectations and that fire prone, fire vulnerable community of Australia that we live in, in a drying climate, this has to be shared. That's that shared responsibility that we need - people like me, with that other experience, need to step up but it's fragile, you know? If a lot of people get matted [criticised], people will just go away.
>
> (female, WA, state DEC)

The personal and emotional cost of being involved in a significant bushfire event was also evident in Keelty's review of the Margaret River bushfires in WA (Keelty, 2012). It was noted that the DEC staff, when giving evidence, had clearly felt a burden of responsibility for what had gone wrong. Importantly, the Keelty review also points out that some of the staff involved lived in those areas impacted by the bushfire. This highlights the point that lines between the agencies and the residents of particular areas often overlap and interweave.

Targets and Audience

FESA, and subsequently DFES, was the main provider of information and related materials on bushfire preparation and awareness at the time of our research. Further, it was the main facilitator of network building and planned activity in bushfire-prone areas, in anticipation of fire events.

While subject to significant resource constraints, the agencies had taken steps to address specific social groups, with some of FESA/DFES's main publications, for example, translated for non-English speakers. In addition, some of the materials were adapted for use with remote indigenous communities. Nevertheless, such focus was limited, illustrated by the attention given to questions around gender and fire awareness and preparation. Nonetheless, it was reported that a 'women's program' about bushfires was in place mostly in agricultural areas and was managed at a district level (3 female, WA, state FESA). There was also some commentary from agency staff to the effect that DEC messaging did not reflect the needs of language groups other than English (3 male, WA, state DEC).

Another set of concerns relates to information management, such as communicating timely and clear information during a bushfire event.

Clearly, it takes time to receive, process and approve information from staff dealing directly with a bushfire. This scenario was vividly described by one participant:

> That's why I think when a fire is ripping through at 3000 metres an hour and the fire is behaving - the fire is doing more damage than you can get the intelligence back, it is very difficult to make sure you're communicating the right message. Because if you put out the wrong message, (1) you can cause unnecessary panic or (2) you get people to switch off. They won't have confidence in you.
>
> (male, WA, state DEC)

And:

> I think there's a very, very real danger that fire agencies have raised the level of expectation that people receive information beyond the capacity to deliver.
>
> (male, WA, state DEC)

State agency staff were concerned that managing expectations had become more problematic. Although the number of bushfire incidents had not changed, there has been an increased demand for information. In the 2009/10 bushfire season, for example, 744 pieces of information about fire were issued compared to 177 for the previous season (female, WA, state FESA). While this may indicate increased activity by the agencies, it was claimed that this increase in part was due to an expectation that such material should be available. As stated:

> In the space of 10 minutes during the fires we would have five calls from the same media outlet, just all different arms...We had calls from Japan, London, Mongolia, all these international media agencies about our fires here, as well as the increased local demand with all the channels and they all want their own angle.
>
> (female, WA, state FESA)

A corollary of this focus by the agencies was that staff had begun to question the adequacy of messaging and the different ways of engaging with localities. Hence, some questioned whether people understood the structured advice that was given, suggesting that perhaps too much information is provided (male, WA, state DEC). When asked, this informant said this understanding was based on views from friends, family and other members of staff. Others noted that many misunderstood messages; 'People don't hear what they hear, they hear what they think they hear' (male, WA, state DEC).

When asked to provide an example, the agency staff suggested that it was a 'gut feeling'.

Challenges

The challenges faced by Agencies in WA are stark. Ensuring 'cooperation consistency' between fire agencies was an important issue to address, and is one reason why the Interagency Bushfire Management Committee (IBMC) was established. While acknowledged, this problem had yet to be resolved:

> We still have issues. In the recent fires that we had, there [were] issues about; when the pressure was on, there [were] still people wanting to put up different pieces of information that weren't consistent.
>
> (male, WA, state FESA)

Nonetheless, this matter had received ongoing attention from planners in the State, and with the establishment of DFES, and the further reorganisation following the Ferguson Report (2016), the IBMC was reformed and relocated.

Another challenge was to persuade volunteer brigade members to adapt to a community engagement approaches. This was explained in terms of 'culture':

> It's a cultural thing that we all talk about and it's definitely changing but the volunteers can be a bit response focused and they join up to do the sexy stuff.
>
> (female, WA, state FESA)

More generally, the role and activity of the volunteers is of ongoing concern. While some volunteers were keen to adopt new ways of working with communities, others were less inclined. In addition, in WA, as in other States, the relationships between professional and volunteer staff are often a subject of debate (Varischetti and Prendergast, 2016).

For Agency staff, scepticism about institutional arrangements and the promotion of community engagement was often framed in a historical context, where the organisational restructuring that resulted in DFES and other arrangements was located in ongoing tensions:

> There's a huge amount of resentment from career fire-fighters. I'll give you an example. If I send out a letter to a Station Officer and put FESA Station Officer, they'll return to sender because they're not a FESA Station Officer, they're a Fire and Rescue Station Officer.
>
> (female, WA, state FESA)

These responses were seen as jeopardising moves towards the elaboration of community engagement approaches:

> Until it's led from the top that there's to be this community engagement approach and risk-based approach to our business, so we form that shared responsibility with the community, I think we'll be struggling.
>
> (female, WA, state FESA)

Concerns about staffing levels were also raised by this person:

> So even after the Victorian Royal Commission, we put up a fairly substantial bid to improve our capacity of more than three staff and $120,000 and we got more trucks and helicopters.
>
> (female, WA, state FESA)

These ambitions and the ensuing difficulties again raised questions about resourcing.

One problem that faced the agencies, echoing comments from colleagues in Victoria, was that residents receive, in some senses, mixed messaging about the role of the state agencies. That, on the one hand, they were painted as 'heroes' saving the community, but that they also needed to convey a message of shared responsibility and that residents cannot always expect direct help from those same 'heroic' agencies. As one participant explained,

> I think there's a bit of a Catch-22 for our agency where we have to be seen to be doing the right thing by the community but if we make ourselves out to be heroes too much then people are just going to assume that they're going to get rescued.
>
> (female, WA, state FESA)

Thus, raising awareness about what residents should do when faced with the risk of bushfire was a challenge. Not only were there issues of message across localities, for example, that some people live in rural areas, others peri-urban or regional and the risk is not evenly spread and of audience segmentation and diversity. There were also issues relating to the cultural construction of what agencies did and were seen to do, by residents in the localities they served. This added an additional layer of complexity regarding appropriate messaging.

Assessment

A key to the arrangements and practices of the agencies in WA was the relationship between them, and in particular FESA/DFES and

DEC/DPaW. Historically there had been tensions between FESA and DEC (http://news.smh.com.au/breaking-news-national/wa-bushfire-report-surprises-premier-20110815-1itwr.html). These tensions were highlighted as problematic to effective bushfire management in recent enquiries into significant bushfire events. As a result a memorandum titled 'Heads of Agreement' was signed between DEC and FESA in November 2011 (DEC – FESA, 2011). This, together with the Keelty reports, set out clear statements of intent and a set of underlying principles informing effective bushfire management (see also Western Australia State Government, 2012).

Paradoxically, these tensions occurred in the context of effective and cooperative working relationships at a local level. In 2012/13 many noted that the DEC, for example, worked closely with FESA in responses to bushfires and prescribed burning. But there were confusions about accountability and responsibility and there had been attempts to develop clear lines of responsibility for bushfire management. The legislative changes following the Keelty report also created some disquiet since there was a view that the creation of the all-hazard management had been passed with little consultation and that one of the implications was around perceived expertise being usurped (2 male, WA, state, 1 DEC and 1 local government). Nonetheless, others viewed these changes more positively. Part of the problem seemed to be in relation to locality responsibility, with FESA seen as having a more urban focus than DEC (female, WA, state DEC). In this context, the changes that set DFES up as the lead hazard agency may be beneficial in the longer term. But, as argued elsewhere, while legislative changes may contribute towards more effective collaboration, other factors including historical tensions and bushfire frequency can also impact the relationships between agencies (Brummel *et al.*, 2012).

The steps towards collaboration were part of a top-down process, with governments actively involved; they acted on the comprehensive reviews following the fires and addressed some of the problems that had become evident. Nonetheless, as indicated complications continued to emerge when attempting to promote community engagement and involvement. Still, one challenge facing the renewed fire agency arrangements was how to achieve mutually supportive relationships between residents in fire-prone localities and agencies. Of note, there had been debate and discussion about the meaning and relevance of 'shared responsibility', with agencies seeking to define the concept. While consideration had been given to ways of developing such approaches, they remained at a relatively early stage of development. These matters draw attention to the composition and involvement of the populations that made up these bushfire-prone communities.

Final Comments

The Australian state has a long history in addressing the circumstances and outcomes of disaster events, and particularly wildfire. Although the rhetoric occasionally is different, the overall approach has been one that is top down. In part this comes about because of the complex relations that define communities as localities. It is a complex mosaic of relations – age, gender, ethnicity, linguistic communities, class – and agencies often struggle to both target and relate to these different dimensions of community.

The prevailing approaches by agencies seek to enable communities as localities to build their capacities to address disaster events. This objective took the form of a range of communication practices involving agencies and the residents, and others, located in wildfire-prone localities. It also involved working with those in localities, at schools, public venues and other activity, such as hazard reduction work, to create the conditions whereby those in these areas are prepared and can anticipate such disaster events. In each State, a number of agencies either complemented each other and in a range of ways would work together to provide seemingly integrated approaches.

In a number of instances, a feature of agency activity was the promotion of neighbourhood activity, creating the conditions not only to address the prospect of wildfire but also to work together to develop the basis of cooperation and collective engagement. The CFUs in the case of NSW and the Community Fireguard approaches evident elsewhere are examples of such measures. Nonetheless, there was an unevenness in these approaches between them in terms of the scope of activity covered as well as across the different types of localities that made up the wildfire-prone areas within a State. In the former instance, the CFUs focussed on 'skills and equipment', whereas in other States, the focus tended to be in terms of education and awareness strategies. And, across States the agencies sought to engage people with varied experiences and involvements in localities as residents or visitors.

Of note, over time, these approaches have been refined and developed, especially in the aftermath of major wildfire events. It is evident that that there has been a relatively long history in cross-agency collaboration in Tasmania and less so elsewhere, especially in NSW and WA. Nonetheless, in all States, subject to histories and resources, steps have been taken to facilitate collaboration between agencies. Of note, on the ground, there is considerable evidence of such collaboration and engagement in relation to the communities that make up these localities.

Increasingly, agencies have opened up discussion about shared responsibility between these agencies and the citizens within wildfire-prone localities. Based on a view that all have varied obligations in relation to such events, and the awareness and preparation associated with them, there was a scepticism amongst agency staff about the degree to which such ambitions could be achieved. It would appear that questions remain as to how community capacities can be enabled in ways that allow participation and engagement by citizens in these areas to take place. As noted the socio-demographics of these communities matter. These localities comprise diverse populations with varied experiences; different forms of engagement within these areas come from a range of backgrounds, indicated by language, social practices and cultural understandings.

Agencies with limited resources face considerable challenges in developing effective communication methods and materials that meet the needs of Australia's varying and complex communities. As will become evident the approach adopted in much Australian wildfire preparedness communication often appears *ad hoc* and piecemeal – applying and adapting whatever is at hand from the broader media panoply – rather than involving a deliberative and comprehensively planned approach to community preparedness.

This chapter has set the scene for a series of detailed considerations of communities and disaster events. These include a consideration of agency involvement in communities as localities, the diversity within communities and communities as audiences, the messaging about disaster events, the gendering of communities and households in relation to preparedness and the challenges for wildfire policy.

6 Engaging Communities

What Happens Behind the Scenes?

Keith Toh, Bernard Mees, Yoko Akama,
Vanessa Cooper and Richard Phillips

Governments and their agencies play varying roles in relation to natural disasters. Strategies and policies are developed internationally, nationally and locally (see for example, UNISDR, 2007; Forest Fire Management Group, 2012; and FSC, 2013 respectively). Governments act in response to natural disasters for different reasons. In their research on three natural disasters in the United States, Trebilcock and Daniels (2006) refer to a range of perspectives/values with which to understand why and how governments intervene. A corrective justice perspective, for example, is when a government provides legal redress in the case of negligence. Others have focussed on disasters and critical infrastructure and the role governments have in its maintenance. Here it is argued that the growing interdependence and complexity of different systems, such as utilities, telecommunications and food transport, have increased their vulnerability to disruption from events including natural disasters (Boin and McConnell, 2007; Edwards, 2009).

Evidence shows that governments and their agencies attempt to alleviate the impacts of natural disasters and encourage the public to prepare more effectively. It is also clear that there are different, and at times competing, reasons informing these interventions. Agencies have a broad aim of creating resilience at both an individual and locality level, together with an understanding about the risks associated with wildfires. It suggests that such programs need to include a diverse range of activities prior to, and during, the fire season.

An, integrated approach is called for using general media campaigns as well as localised information and events. It also suggests that audiences are diverse, and consequently programs need to be varied in content and format to meet the specific needs of a range of different groups, such as cultural and linguistically diverse communities, schoolchildren and those who are more vulnerable to wildfire risk.

Thus, the policy framework also should recognise that despite agencies and governments providing information and programs, some people will choose not to, or be unable to, engage with the information or initiatives. Key strategies and initiatives are outlined, including such examples as providing safety information in areas deemed to be at high risk of wildfire and delivering initiatives at a local level, via a range of delivery modes. The chapter outlines the kinds of communications outputs and practices that were commonly identified during our research. This provides the background to the following two chapters, which analyse, in more depth, issues of power and diversity within wildfire communications in the Australian context.

Understanding 'Community' and Communication

Achieving preparedness for wildfires is a complex process. It involves the production and dissemination of information by fire and safety agencies and the success of such communication depends upon its reception by the public. Wildfire safety or preparedness advice has become a significant responsibility for the relevant agencies and entails various management and communication perspectives. A central feature of preparedness for wildfire events is the relationship between fire emergency agencies and the residents of threatened localities across the country. Agencies spend considerable time and resources on developing communication products and facilitating the ability of residents to take steps to anticipate and prepare for wildfire.

Wildfire communication products are developed for the specific purpose of sharing existing knowledge to remind residents of dangers and to encourage preparedness plans to be put into effect. Communication materials produced by fire agencies in Australia include but are not limited to information pamphlets and DVDs, refrigerator magnets, bumper stickers, school activity books and children's games. Modes of preparedness information include television, public signage, leaflet drops, newspaper advertisements and features, internet sites and mobile phone applications. Sophisticated communication packages have been developed as well as more focussed approaches, such as community-based network groups and public roadshows.

The term 'communication' has the same historical root as 'community' – that is it literally indicates something that people have in common. Contemporary communication theory, however, is informed by a diverse range of disciplinary contributions, from philosophy, linguistics, literary studies, political science, psychology, economics, organisational theory and even computer engineering (Craig, 1999). Moreover, the most basic mode of communication is language, an essentially generative communicative form that develops from thought through interaction.

In Saussure's (1916) generative model of language, communication is a two-way process – communication is a system of reciprocal actions, thinking and responses. Much of modern communication theory, although informed by linguistics, is more obviously concerned with how to improve the effectiveness of communication, not merely how to analyse it. The communication theory of figures such as McLuhan (1967),

Postman (1985) and Castells (2009), however, mainly represents a critique of modern media culture rather than an obviously useful analytical framework suitable for wildfire communication.

In the 1950s, communication studies also first came under the influence of information processing and cybernetic theory. In keeping with the technologist view of communication pioneered by Wiener (1948), communication became increasingly seen in terms of technological metaphors such as 'transmission' and 'feedback' (Shannon and Weaver, 1949; Schramm, 1954). Many contemporary communications theorists promote a transmission model of communication which sees communication as a form of human-to-human information transmission, taking the model of a radio transmission as the underlying system of mass communication (Craig, 1999).

Other important contributions to understanding communication include Ikujiro Nonaka's (1991) notion of knowledge creation. Nonaka argued that some firms were better at managing their internal knowledge – principally by making tacit knowledge explicit, by codifying it, recording it and passing it on from employee to employee, hence making it more valuable. The resulting field of knowledge management seeks to establish efficiencies in communicating knowledge and represents another of the key practical areas which can impinge on the effective management of wildfire communications.

Perhaps the most notable framework for understanding public communication to have emerged since the 1960s, however, is Habermas's (1981) theory of communicative action. Habermas seeks to explain how communication works in a modern democratic state from the perspective of an individual's 'lifeworld' and how individuals in a democratic society may relate to the broader communicative reality represented by politics, government and the mass media. His separation of communications into public and private, system and individual, or macro and micro levels seems a particularly useful perspective from which to analyse the effectiveness of wildfire communication in Australia; the focus in much preparedness planning is on notions of community, with an advocacy of community participation that underpins much contemporary government policy in the area.

This model also dovetails well with theories of social capital and understanding how communication occurs at the community level. Putnam's (2000) separation of social capital into bridging and bonding aspects suggests that close and personal communication is a key determinant of establishing social capital. The argument is that in developing the highly context-specific conditions of trust, reciprocity and knowledge exchange which are experienced by people in close social networks. It is communication at the face-to-face level that seems most natural, most genuine and most trustworthy from a social capital perspective on communication. Bridging capital and communication originating at the agency or government level would be expected to be less immediately acceptable to inhabitants of wildfire-prone communities from a Habermasian perspective on public communication. Habermas's main focus is on how citizens can engage with the 'system' of politics, government and economics which exists in developed capitalist states without being 'colonised' by it. From a wildfire agency perspective, however, the main problem would seem to be inverted, that is, determining what is the best and most genuine way in which government agencies can communicate effectively with members of communities that are most likely to be affected by wildfire events.

Agency Practice

In Australia, communication products for wildfire preparedness have been developed separately by public agencies in individual states with considerable collaboration and cross-pollination of ideas occurring between various state bodies. Agencies also develop and produce their own communication products and tailor delivery methods to local needs. This can be useful to local residents but it can also be difficult to track, especially if materials are distributed without centralised control or authority. Our collection and analysis of wildfire communication products from a variety of agencies across all Australian states (Toh and Tyler, 2013), however, have allowed a more considered analysis to be undertaken of the current approach to preparedness communication from the institutional level represented by the various State and Territory fire services.

A 'Bushfire Communications Grid'

The research team established a 'Bushfire Communications Grid' to assess the current standing of knowledge management practices in Australia. The Grid is an Australia-wide collection of bushfire safety communication products, the first attempt to amass such a collection across Australia. As more of these products were produced, more knowledge from their design and production was accumulated from late 2010 up until a close-off date of December 2012. This content represents an extensive accumulation of knowledge that has been produced at considerable cost by individual agencies. The development of the Grid, however, also allowed several shortcomings in the varied and variable development of communication products by the agencies to be revealed.

In order to assess knowledge management and communication processes within, across and from Australian bushfire agencies, a range of communication products were assembled. In essence, the bushfire products can be considered artefacts that represent the outcome of the agencies' respective processes to convert tacit knowledge into explicit knowledge resources that can be shared with the general public as part of wider communication strategies for bushfire preparedness. Initially, the collection of products took place during the fieldwork in Victoria undertaken during 2010–11. During interview and field visits, local agencies provided samples of the material that was distributed to residents. Residents were also interviewed concerning the bushfire preparedness material they had received from the local agencies and gave accounts of the sources of their knowledge.

A variety of agencies were also approached during the data collection process, both those explicitly and tangentially engaged in bushfire preparedness communication. These agencies included the Country Fire Authority (CFA) in Victoria, the Rural Fire Service (RFS) in New South Wales, the former Fire and Emergency Services Authority (FESA – now Department of Fire and Emergency Services - DFES) in Western Australia, among others, as well as State governments, local governments and government-run health services. When approached, fire agencies provided examples readily, many offering to send their communication products through the post. One agency referred the researchers to its website as the source of all their communication material, which could be downloaded. While the vast majority of agency personnel expressed positive responses to the project and willingly provided materials, there was some concern in terms of the time required to collect products because of the large volume. This may, in itself, indicate the need for a better or more formal knowledge management system within the agencies themselves.

The communication products in the Grid were indexed and classified using the following categories (meta-headings):

Campaign: identifies products that are used in significant communication programs. The most common were the products branded 'Prepare. Act. Survive.', which since 2009 have been used in the wider media campaign with the same slogan.

Scheme: is used where products are deployed in sub-campaigns, under a parent or overarching campaign. This classification applies where communication products were packaged and distributed at a local level, such as a local schools initiative, or 'Farm Firewise'.

Originating Agency: identifies the agencies associated with the products in terms of visible branding. Often this would be the lead fire agency in conjunction with the local state government. Other notable originating agencies were the Victorian Department of Human Services and NSW Health.

Target Audience: is used to identify instances where material was developed for specific demographic groups, e.g. women in the SA Fiery Women program, or older and disabled residents in the NSW AIDER and QLD Senior and Safer programs.

Form (Mode/Media): is used to identify the form or mode of delivery, which included printed text, radio, television, DVD, CD, telephone, agency websites, social media (e.g. Facebook and CFA Connect), community meetings, bumper stickers, game boards and even local puppet shows.

The analysis presented in this chapter, of how agencies communicate with the public, has also drawn upon a number of other data sources including interviews with agency participants, residents in bushfire-prone localities and research notes drawn out from contacts with agencies in obtaining the communication products. In addition to the formal material that was distributed by agencies, there were also instances of informal modes and other publications, including summarised material (photocopied handouts) produced and distributed by a local resident. These were also captured in the Grid.

The Grid is also important as very little research is available on wildfire communication in Australia that takes an agency perspective. Yet increasingly, the analysis of communications within and across public agencies internationally is undertaken from the perspective of knowledge management. This approach shows how the adoption of internal communication strategies can be used to improve the quality of products and services, and to reduce costs and the use of time in producing and managing communication in organisations. The management of knowledge in the context of wildfire involves turning tacit or individual knowledge into knowledge that can be widely shared and appropriately applied to the development and deployment of wildfire communication products (for definitions and discussion, see Hackett, 2000; Alavi and Leidner, 2001; Schwartz, 2006; and Bartholomew, 2008).

Bushfire Communication Practices as Transmission

The starting point taken by many bushfire agencies when developing communication products has usually reflected a simple transmission model. Communication products are designed and manufactured at considerable cost and this basic communication function has traditionally been the domain of individual State jurisdictions. The result, historically, has been a diverse range of messages, formats and learning experiences for residents. Expertise is marshalled among fire agency specialists and disseminated to the public. This is a typical and traditional approach to public communication where expert knowledge is created and then communicated through various community safety campaigns and programs.

At the time the research was conducted, several initiatives had recently emerged which recognised that the process of knowledge creation and marshalling of bushfire communication products has often been too informal and not well governed. Most notably, the Victorian State Government revised its bushfire safety policy and adopted the national framework 'Prepare. Act. Survive.' following the interim recommendations of the Victoria Bushfires Royal Commission (Teague *et al.*, 2009). The adoption of what has now become a national framework resulted in revised bushfire safety publications and educational materials.

Even prior to the Black Saturday bushfires, however, policy and programs were undergoing a process of change. From 2004 onwards, the CFA, the Department of Sustainability and the Environment (DSE), and the Metropolitan Fire Brigade (MFB), led by the Fire Ready Executive Group, were brought together through the Fire Ready Victoria Strategy to provide joint education and information programs, and contribute their own education and information activities. Recognising the importance of the need for cross-agency communication, the Victorian Fire Communication Taskforce was initiated and, coordinated by the Strategic Communications Branch of the Department of Justice. One of the fire agency community safety personnel explained the purpose of the Fire Communications Taskforce as:

> bring[ing] together all of the agencies across government's communications people that were putting out messages to sort of say, let's have a handle on what messages you're putting out there.
>
> (female, Vic, state)

This development underlines the perception of a perceived lack of inter-agency conformity and the resultant danger of mixed messages being sent out to the broader society.

The process of policy learning across the states primarily occurs through subcommittees of the Australasian Fire and Emergency Services Authorities Council (AFAC). Here agency representatives from around the country meet and discuss best practice and formulate agreed positions. In February 2006, AFAC, in collaboration with the Australian State and Territory fire services, for example, released a position paper that was designed to 'provide guidance to householders in relation to both their individual safety, and the protection of their homes in the event of a bushfire' (AFAC, 2013). Underpinning the bushfire preparedness messages is advice, for example, that on a Code Red day the safest place to be is away from high risk and that members of the public should only consider staying in their properties on extreme or severe days if at least two persons are fully prepared and can actively defend the property (AFAC, 2006). Different wordings may be adopted by different individual agencies, but key messages are now provided through media and public engagement campaigns under the 'Prepare. Act. Survive' slogan which has been adopted across Australia.

Some examples of more informal comparison and collaboration, across States and Territories, were revealed during fire agency and State-level interviews undertaken in 2011. For instance, one participant explained how some of their agency's communication products were developed:

> So I did a bit of an environmental scan with all the other fire agencies around their publications and then we chose ours to be modelled around Tasmania's. Then we looked at – okay well this is Tasmania. What are the gaps we know about, what's the research telling us, what's come out of the Royal Commission that people were asking for?
>
> (female, WA, state FESA)

To enable a more coordinated approach across other agencies, however, another participant described the need for a lead agency to work more effectively with other key public-sector organisations:

> We have multiple agencies wanting to engage communities about fire at different times, so we've got the integrative fire management planning process. We've got municipal planning, fire operations planning which is DSE's burns program, we've got Township Protection Plans, we've got – I think that's about all. But they – they're often not coordinated... Working with Red Cross as well, so Red Cross have their ready plan which is their plans for emergencies so they've got a planning process to work with communities to get ready for any disaster. So we've been working with Red Cross this year to make sure that all fire planning's consistent with ready plan, not selling two different kinds of planning approaches.
>
> (female, Vic, state)

Despite the establishment of AFAC (and its associated internal committees and processes), a need to avoid fragmentation and install a single management process and structure is still evident. Fire safety remains a state responsibility, and the many difficulties in achieving interstate agreement in such matters historically should not be overlooked. The recent move to federalise occupational, health and safety law, though, under the Safe Work Australia Act 2008 (Cwth) suggests that better coordination and cooperation across State boundaries can be achieved given the right kind of policy leadership. A system of cooperative federalism has been a particularly noted development of Australian public governance since the 1960s when the first moves to federalise corporations law occurred (Mees and Ramsay, 2008; Fenna, 2012). Occupational, health and safety federalisation reflects an extension of the federalisation of responsibility for corporations and industrial regulations powers, however, not emergency management.

It should also be acknowledged that strategic communications and the communication of information and education messages designed to enable long-term changes in community behaviour may be reflected in different approaches to inter-agency collaboration. While the cases of AFAC and Fire Ready Victoria show that multi-agency communication programs can be formed, considerable informal policy learning occurring between the States is also evident.

Feedback and Change

The main limitation to a transmission approach to communication stems from the often false assumption that communication is essentially a one-way process. A lack of understanding of public reception and perception of information, and a lack of conceptualising the importance of feedback are typical flaws in a transmission-based approach. The transmission model of communication has therefore been criticised primarily on the basis of not fully accounting for the complexities of communication.

It is already clear, however, that some agencies are aware that a simple transmission approach to communication has considerable limitations. Most agencies are aware that an ability for public input into the communication process is necessary. This requirement is for what is generally called a 'feedback loop' in the transmission literature. Yet the adoption of formal feedback processes was not obvious from a review of the artefacts recorded in the Grid. Instead a rather more *ad hoc* arrangement often seems to apply. The development process in one State was described by an agency interviewee as:

> When we're looking at developing a publication, obviously we use the research that has come out. We put together a bit of a draft and then that goes for internal consultation. So it goes to our media and public affairs area that obviously look at the language to make sure it's congruent with emergency warning language and the right language that the organisation uses, as well as style. Then it will go to Operations or Bushfire Environmental Protection branch or Fire Investigation who are the subject matter experts in it and will make sure that we're representing the call to action appropriately. Then we'll commission a designer to do that process... We'll do consultation and we'll run it through our Bushfire Ready groups who are localised community groups. We'll seek input from them and then we'd obviously go through the design phase and then have to go into how we're going to distribute it and what's our marketing campaign around that.
>
> (female, WA, state FESA)

The development process begins with knowledge creation and includes a form of informal feedback. A commitment to 'double-loop learning' in the manner advocated by Argyris and Schön (1974) was not clear from the interviews, however. Instead of a 'modification of an organisation's underlying norms, policies and objectives' (Argyris and Schön, 1974: 3), community consultation appeared merely to have been added to an already existing system of publication development.

The collection of communication products during fieldwork also included the discovery of some outdated material, a situation that may arise when local brigades store bundles of printed material rather than distribute or discard it. Even though new versions of the text may have been issued, it was seen by some volunteers as a waste to throw out the old, outdated material. The problems associated with the continued circulation of outdated material were compounded by the development of products without a unique identification for traceability – many were issued, for example, without a date stamp. It was therefore recognised that there was a lack of version identification and hence a fundamental problem with consistency of message.

A further issue that became especially apparent during the development of the Grid was the general issue of housekeeping. During the course of gathering the communication material, some agencies were able to provide a list of their products immediately because they had previously been called upon to evidence their community engagement. In contrast, other agencies reported that they did not have ready access to the products contained in their inventory. The lack of version control in some of the communication products was further evidence that document and record management was suboptimal in some of the agencies and, again, demonstrates the usefulness of adopting a more formal knowledge management approach. The failure to adopt formal information management protocols may reflect the volunteerist spirit of the agencies as well as a lack of capacity. It does suggest that in its written form much bushfire preparedness communication is disjointed and not fully managed in a considered and optimally effective manner.

Saturation and Waste

One of the key problems that emerges with bushfire preparedness communication is the widespread view that simply distributing information to a wide audience is not enough to increase people's preparedness for bushfire (Robinson, 2003; Rhodes *et al.*, 2011; Frandsen, 2012). This fundamental problem of effectiveness is also evidenced by research more generally undertaken in the hazards field, which shows that provision of information is not directly related to the adoption of hazards adjustment (Brenkert-Smith, 2010). Many issues contribute to this problem. Alavi and Leidner (2001), for example, observe that creating new capacities for taking action is achieved when people are genuinely interested in participating in a continuous learning and knowledge sharing process.

As Barnard (1938) observed, motivation to act upon communication is a basic consideration of effectiveness.

The limitations of saturation campaigns are a recurrent theme in both the academic literature and was also evident in the interviews undertaken in 2010–11. Many elderly residents from the Yarra Ranges, for example, reported that they had found the paper-based information of preparedness 'excessive' (Yarra Ranges Council, 2010) and that they often had difficulty in interpreting the information and how it might apply to their own situation. Similarly, residents interviewed in the Southern Otways, including staff from the CFA who provide services to those areas, admitted that the Fire Ready information packs delivered to residents often remain sealed in their plastic packs, unopened and unused (Akama and Ivanka, 2010). The problem is often explained as one of distance – that the agencies are detached from the lived realities of residents:

> Actually, we look at it from an academic point of view, really, to see what are they sending out this time, because our experience is certainly at the higher end. But we look at it and think, is this likely to engage, are people – we actually look at it from that perspective rather than from ourselves. My experience – like last year, when all those great big heavy fire survival kits were sent out, that cost millions of dollars, I found even – because I was working for CFA at the time. I'd ask people about them and they'd say, 'yeah, we've had five in our house. I hope somebody opens one, I put them on the kitchen table, I hope somebody opens one, but they're still in their plastic. Just tragic.' So what we've received is what comes out from centralised government.
>
> (female, Vic, tree/sea change)

The main problem seems to be one of engagement. One participant, for example, received the information booklet, and felt it was important, but stored the information away without reading it:

> No, I don't think so. I mean I haven't – I'll be honest with you I haven't read that catalogue that came out – the brochure. I sort of thought yes, this is good material to have and I filed it away under a fire folder.
>
> (female, Vic, urban-rural interface)

Others respondents seem to have treated it as junk mail:

> There were just piles and piles of bins were overflowing and piles of these brochures together with the normal junk mail that you get but they were just heaped in there and it was just waste of a – gets through to a few people and that was an attempt to address

it but – yeah, a lot of people threw it away and it didn't even get to their kitchen table.

(male, WA, state FESA)

Another participant similarly expressed their opinion that the widespread distribution of the communication material had limited impact:

I think if we delivered a brochure to every house in Victoria, I think it would make very little difference. So I think, again, they have their place, and I think they can be helpful, but they're certainly not a tool in isolation. I think a mail dropout is a fairly useless endeavour and I think there's a lot – people probably rely too much on them. However, I would not like to see a world of education where we didn't have written materials.

(female, Vic, rural)

Perceiving communication principally as a kind of mass transmission can evidently lead not only to considerable waste but also to poor engagement.

Information Channels and Public Trust

It is not just printed materials that are at risk of being ignored or perceived as being ineffective, however. Interviews with residents in Kilmore East, after the 2009 Black Saturday tragedy, indicated that there was confusion and lack of trust particularly in the ability of websites to trigger or lead to the implementation of a resident's fire plan (Elliott and McLennan, 2011). Trust is a key issue in public policy studies and lack of trust in public agencies is a critical item in public communications.

In Elliot and McLennan's (2011) study, only 1 per cent of those interviewed described fire agency websites as the information source they used to decide to trigger their bushfire plans. In fact, around half of the residents interviewed (51 per cent) relied on environmental indications and phone calls from family and friends as cues for enacting their plans. Elliott and McLennan's study reveals that the slowness of information updates on websites, the ambiguity of information provided and a perceived absence of threat warnings through the official channels of communication were some of the reasons for not relying on the internet for information. Taken together with the lack of trust, Barnard's (1938) observation concerning successful communication seemed lacking here.

The need for consistency was also emphasised by some participants and a concern that too many changes would diminish the value of the messages by others. A number of local agency personnel who had seen the bushfire safety messages change over the succession of safety programs suggested that too much information could cause the public to become detached and that it was important to ensure that the public do not disengage themselves from the communication process:

> You need to be really mindful of what you're sending and it's a united message for you to hear. Not saying this is the message this year and then the following message next year – and we've sort of stuck on our guns for the last five years of the messages of what we're trying to send out there is the same. It might be just slightly modified but it's the same message. So you can be bombarded with too much information to the point where it gets thrown in the bin. We cannot ever let, as a community go down that path.
>
> (male, WA, tree/sea change)

Convergence to the 'Prepare. Act. Survive.' national framework was thought to be a positive step, but participants also spoke about the difficulties faced with conveying bushfire safety messages that keep changing:

> The big emphasis that we're trying to get across now is the 'Prepare, Act and Survive' because it was always the 'Stay and Go' type messages... With the media, with the material that I've been supplied with, it's assisting us greatly. There are changes, as I mentioned earlier, but the changes are a little bit frustrating because we've just put a package out and then you update it again, then you do something and then you update it again. That's getting a bit hard to get back to the public, that we've got the message out and trying to get all those people involved, and then you're going back again and changing it and changing it.
>
> (male, WA, tree/sea change)

The transmission view of communication can diminish empowerment, participation and capacity building for change by the community. A stronger belief in the fire agencies' abilities to manage the threat of bushfire can lead to the reduction of levels of personal bushfire mitigation (Paton *et al.*, 2006). Akama and Ivanka (2010) observed complacency for preparedness and dependency on the fire services to 'tell them what to do' in communities in Victoria and Tasmania. The changing demographic of these areas also compounds issues of dependency and false expectations. Urban dwellers who may be used to service delivery are moving into rural settings where self-reliance and locally based initiatives become more important. As a result, the influx of newcomers is changing the networks and groups within communities like the Southern Otways in Victoria (Akama and Ivanka, 2010).

There is evidence where the power dynamics between the 'expert' fire authorities and 'non- expert' community compounds the issue of people still expecting to be told what to do. It was noted, for example, by some interviewees that some of the audience still expected decisions to be made for them by the agencies:

> Then there was another group who was alarmingly waiting for someone to tell them what to do at a point when they should have been doing things already. So ... we've offered a suite of communications here, but to get people to actually accept them and understand them and engage with it is still tricky.
>
> (male, Vic, state other)

There was also an aspect of organisational change where community engagement and communication were not the traditional focus of emergency organisations. One participant described the situation as:

> [I]t's always a challenge for us to keep the fire fighters engaged ... A lot of the fire officers, they join thinking their job is to go out and put wet stuff on the red stuff, it's not. They spend 5 or 10 per cent of their time doing that. The other 95 per cent of their time, they've got to be out there in the community. To be talking up to prevent fires.
>
> (male, Vic, state other)

There is a danger when this false perception, reinforced by the authority of communication products, replaces the critical human-to-human engagement needed for behavioural change to occur. Informal social processes are important mechanisms for spreading information, yet the critical role of such processes often lacks recognition in bushfire communication. Brenkert-Smith's (2010) research on bushfire mitigation among rural communities in Colorado indicates the benefits of bridging relationships between neighbours and the importance of social interactions that can lead to better fire preparation. Brenkert-Smith's findings are echoed in the following statement:

> Yes, and we're a very close-knit community where we are so I'm pretty sure, even though we haven't discussed it with neighbours, neighbours would be coming and saying there's a fire up the road or there's a fire over the back of us or it's – apart from sort of seeing the smoke and smelling it I'm sure neighbours would be actively telling one another about it.
>
> (female, Tas, tree/sea change)

Knowledgeable neighbours, who share the same risk, are often more trusted, relied upon and become sources of vital information. Brenkert-Smith's study reveals that many of these permanent residents become interpreters and consolidators of information, tailoring and detailing the information to enable it to become immediately applicable to the neighbouring property and local environment.

Engagement and Understanding

Beyond the communication between agencies and citizens, communication can be enhanced by building on existing communication products and using them as triggers for further engagement. One example of such an approach is placing a precondition to giving out a planning booklet. An agency interviewee, for example, described how the local volunteer brigade would distribute survival planning information:

> The other thing that we do is that we only give people a bushfire survival plan if they commit to let us come back and talk to them about it. So annually the RFS has an open day, corporate, and go to your fire station and all this sort of stuff. Like many brigades we don't hold it at a fire station because our fire stations are remote and we just don't get people.
>
> (male, NSW, state RFS)

While this interactive method was made necessary because of the constraints of remoteness of the stations, the significant point was an acknowledgement of the commitment involved in preparing a survival plan.

Others reflected the same idea, where the bushfire planning booklet was of such complexity that agency personnel felt that they had to be prepared to provide a level of support in the form of 'hand-holding' or assisting some households to prepare their survival plans:

> I think just from handing this out and speaking with people, this is a document that needs to be explained. You need to go through it with someone rather than just hand it to them. You may ask them the question in the first instance, are you going to stay or are you going to go? Oh I'm staying, I'm staying, I'm staying. You go through this and you try to explain the different things that could happen. What you need. What you need to be prepared for. Some will change their mind by the end of the conversation. They haven't really – because they haven't experienced it they have no real concept of what could happen and what was expected of them. So it's definitely an explanation document.
>
> (male, NSW, state RFS)

Other experiences in the use of the communication products also captured other communication pathways in addition to direct mail-outs. Local events such as community market days were also mentioned as occasions where fire agencies could engage the public. The success of such events was determined in part by the proactive outreach of those attending, and one participant explained:

> My observation is that the success of those sessions, of having a stall at the market, depend very much on who's behind the desk ... if you have presenters there, either from the brigade or from the region, paid presenters, who sit at the stall and wait for people to come to them, they won't be very busy. But if you stand there with a handful of brochures, some balloons on a string and while people are walking past, you say, would you like a balloon, hello little child, whatever, they stop, they talk and before you know it, you're having really meaningful conversations. We could engage in 200 in-depth conversations in a day and come home exhausted, or you can sit back on your chair and wait for people to come to you and have 20 conversations.
>
> (female, Vic, tree/sea change)

Partnership with the community was also identified as an important factor in tailoring messages. Learning how to engage a diverse population has also been part of the communication program, but this may only be at the level of an individual jurisdiction:

> One of the gaps that was found, very much so in the rural areas, was the – engaging women, our rural women. So they've just launched a rural women's program up in the north-west because what happens in the small country towns – all the blokes go down to the shed and get on the trucks and the women just stay at home or get to face the fire alone or work out their own thing. So that there's different ways – they are different – very much a specific target audience, but we have a huge Diverse Populations Project happening at the moment where we're trying to access as many communities as we possibly can.
>
> (female, Vic, state CFA)

Clearly many of the problems with engagement of localities and their communities are currently being addressed via such programs but often only at the moment in an *ad hoc* manner – not, for example, in the interactive ways advocated by communications theorists proposing social marketing approaches (e.g. Smith, 2006).

Conclusion

The approach to developing and disseminating bushfire communication products was underdeveloped, with evidence of *ad hoc* and piecemeal approaches. Clearly there were differences between agencies across the four States, although, even when relatively sophisticated products had been developed, their dissemination was uneven.

To understand the potential for improvement it is necessary to remember that communication is always a two-way process, and this theme is picked up further with regard to diversity and gender in the next two chapters. It involves an understanding that an adequate understanding of communication requires a consideration of how, as individuals, we live in social settings which are complex, involve a range of dimensions (involving the public and private, system and individual, and macro and micro levels) and involve power inequalities. For communities, and the individuals who live in communities, it becomes important to understand the ways in which our social lives are networked with each other and tied into complex institutional arrangements, for example, agencies and related bodies.

In relation to bushfire and communication, two sets of relationships are noteworthy. First, communication is developed, produced and disseminated by agencies. Over time, as indicated, these agencies had evolved and had become central to the way bushfire preparedness was undertaken. Communication was and remains central to these processes, but in a number of ways it was deficient in monitoring and evaluating processes and products, the development of comprehensive and grounded knowledge management systems, and the commitment to a transmission approach to communications. Second, and complementing the first point, there was an inadequate understanding of the social complexity of communities, and the bases on which communication will be trusted, heard and acted upon.

7 Wildfire Safety, Communication and Diversity

Meagan Tyler, Bernard Mees and Peter Fairbrother

Communication about wildfire preparedness and wildfire safety is increasingly being seen by many fire agencies in Australia as an important part of day-to-day operations. This communication role is often shared between the main wildfire-fighting service in any given State and other relevant government departments. In this chapter we consider the changing nature of wildfire preparedness and safety communication, focussing in particular on the potential of a socially engaged approach to communication and the importance of recognising and engaging a variety of audiences. Insights from research in social marketing and public communications are used to analyse data collected from interviews with communication professionals working in the area of wildfire safety, in both fire agencies and government departments, across four different Australian States.

This chapter further demonstrates the significant variation in approaches to communication campaigns across different organisations and the differences in attitudes among professionals in this area. We highlight a number of areas of concern, including messaging development and evaluation, audience engagement and understandings of audience segmentation and diversity, as well as the ongoing and ineffective focus on a transmission model of communication that involves a top-down 'command and control' attitude and practice. It is imperative to recognise the power dynamics between state agencies and communities, as well as within communities themselves, and for agencies to understand and account for the complex circumstances in which people live, rather than bemoaning that residents in bushfire-prone localities 'don't listen' to existing messaging.

It should be noted that the accounts analysed in this chapter are based on the perceptions of the participants. Responses from participants provide evidence of existing attitudes, perceptions and understandings of how communication campaigns around wildfire operate rather than capturing how they are supposed to operate as per official guidelines or policy.

Public Communications and Social Marketing

Public communications campaigns, especially those that are intended for the greater good, such as health promotion campaigns, are now most commonly referred to as 'social marketing'. The term 'social marketing' (Kotler and Zaltman, 1971) implies an approach that draws on marketing and public relations rather than on more traditional, technologically-based communication theories. Traditional marketing approaches were originally more concerned with the study of delivering products as efficiently as possible to consumers (i.e. bringing them to the market). Subsequently, the development of market research and the analysis of marketing channels have brought together much of the social science literature concerning communication in a practical manner. The initial focus of marketing was to develop strategies to bring about change in buyer behaviour (Alderson, 1957) and increasingly involved sophisticated social demographic research (e.g. by age, occupation and gender) to help target particular populations. This approach recognises that effective communication is grounded in understanding a target audience and appropriately tailoring the communication medium as opposed to the technological metaphors of 'transmission' or 'feedback' (Shaw and Jones, 2005). These basic concepts of marketing are now frequently applied in the context of public communications.

At the heart of social marketing is the famous question: 'Why can't you sell brotherhood like you sell soap?' (quoted in Kotler and Zaltman, 1971). Much of the research on social marketing has since set about trying to determine effective methods for the design and dissemination of communication campaigns for the public good as well as outlining a multitude of reasons that make selling soap very different from selling abstract notions of community togetherness or social betterment (Hornik, 2013). Today, a social marketing approach is increasingly applied to social programs, particularly in areas like health promotion, community development and environmental education. Indeed, it has been suggested that disaster preparedness falls into this category and can be best viewed as a 'health promoting behaviour' (Eisenman *et al.*, 2009). Such an approach may therefore present a way of understanding wildfire safety campaigns, particularly the social elements of wildfire safety campaigns, by going beyond the more psychologically based analyses often found in risk communication literature. It may also indicate the limitations of such approaches in relation to the social and political relations that define communities as localities in wildfire-prone areas.

Acknowledging the Audience(s)

One of the most important elements of a social marketing approach is acknowledging and understanding the target audience, or more accurately, target audiences. Walsh and colleagues (1993) outline three of the essential elements that were taking shape as a social marketing approach was becoming more widespread in health promotion. These three elements are:

(1) The process is disciplined. Objectives are clearly stated. A variety of research and management techniques are applied to achieve identified goals, which often but not always include the mass media. A systematic tracking process monitors progress and guides midcourse corrections. (2) The consumer is heard. Target audiences are segmented along several dimensions (demographics, "psychographics," and "mediagraphics"). This formative research goes beyond using traditional epidemiological data; it adds measures of values, images, aspirations, and concerns of potential clients. Qualitative and quantitative data collection techniques are used to develop an in-depth profile of what reaches and motivates targeted subgroups. (3) The product is responsive, based on iterative research into consumers' wants and needs. Consumers' responses are solicited repeatedly for continuous refinement of the fit between product positionings and market reactions.

(Walsh *et al.*, 1993: 109).

Understanding the beliefs and world views of target audiences is deemed critical to being able to produce effective messaging. This condition essentially necessitates meeting the audience where they are, accepting their current behaviours and attitudes, and designing messages that will be effective in either raising awareness or motivating behavioural change within that context.

The social marketing approach is in sharp contrast to the older 'transmission model' of communication (Shannon and Weaver, 1949), prevalent in early public communication literature and occasionally still found today. In this linear model of mass communication, information from an active participant is simply viewed as being transmitted to a receiver or receivers (the audience). The general assumption of the transmission model is that, unless there is some interference between the sender and receiver, the message will be understood in the way the sender intended (Eadie, 2009). The starting point of many wildfire agencies in designing campaign materials does still seem to reflect elements of this model. This feature is perhaps most evident in the way that expertise is marshalled among fire agency specialists and disseminated to the public and the often militaristic 'command and control' approach taken within agencies themselves (Reynolds, 2017). The transmission model has been heavily criticised for a number of reasons, most prominently, for not taking into account the full complexities of human communication (Voltmer and Römmele, 2002; Mees *et al.*, 2009; Akama *et al.*, 2016). Instead, attempts at reconceptualising communication as the 'sharing of meaning' rather than the 'transmission of messages' have resulted in approaches, like social marketing, which focus much more heavily on audience perceptions and communication as a two-way process (Voltmer and Römmele, 2002; Akama *et al.*, 2016).

As is discussed in the later sections of this chapter, an audience-centred approach was often lacking in the narratives expressed by the communications professionals we interviewed about wildfire safety; instead there was a palatable frustration with 'the audience' not adequately receiving, understanding or acting on the existing messaging. While several participants mentioned evaluative processes to determine the effectiveness of campaigns once they were rolled out, there was little or no discussion of pre-design research on the target populations. Similarly, although a couple of the participants recognised that target audiences are segmented, there was only very limited acknowledgement that demographics, geographical location, values, or other factors may require the tailoring of campaign messages. This suggests that a traditional 'transmission model' of communication was still the dominant paradigm among some communications professionals working in the area of wildfire safety and preparedness at the time of our research (see also Mees *et al.*, 2013; Akama *et al.*, 2016).

Challenges of Diversity and Audience Segmentation

The recognition of audience segmentation in public communications and social marketing has led to an acceptance in contemporary communications theory that 'there is no such thing as the general public' (Maibach *et al.*, 2008: 493). As a result, any communications campaign aimed at the mass of a 'general public' is seen as likely to be ineffective. This position reflects an increasingly common view among public communications and social marketing practitioners that successful campaigns need to identify specific sections of the broader population that are 'at risk' or are likely to find particular messaging especially relevant to them (Atkin and Rice, 2013). Therefore, to reach audiences effectively, campaigns 'must be targeted on the basis of audiences' interests, values and current behavioural patterns' (Maibach *et al.*, 2008: 493).

Atkin and Rice (2013) outline two main reasons why this approach is important and why understanding and addressing a variety of segmented audiences is more useful than attempting a 'one size fits all' message:

> First, message efficiency can be improved if subsets of the audience are prioritised according to their centrality in attaining the campaigns objectives as well as receptivity to being influenced... Second, effectiveness can be increased if message content, form, style and channels are tailored to the attributes and abilities of subgroups.
>
> (Atkin and Rice, 2013: 5)

In this model, communications professionals need more than just multiple ways to distribute the message; they need to modify and adapt *the message itself* depending on the audience.

One of the great challenges now facing public communications campaigns is how to adapt messages for different demographic categories. So while the general aim may be to disseminate a message about say, disaster preparedness, to all citizens, there is increasing acknowledgement that the message will need to be adapted for different groups (Nepal *et al.*, 2012). The variation in messaging may be organised by a variety of factors, including (among others) age, occupation, location, ethnicity and gender. As we have discussed in previous chapters, it is important to see communities as fragmented and as potentially containing different, or even competing, interests rather than as a more simplistic homogenous mass. In countries like the United States, Canada, the United Kingdom and Australia, with significantly multicultural populations, the issues of cross-cultural communication are likely to be particularly pertinent (Banks, 2000). Again, this means that public communications campaigns need to be understood and analysed as sense-making processes:

> Where reality is negotiated and constructed in cultural contexts and situations, rather than distributed from a sender to a recipient.
> (Falkheimer and Heide, 2006: 180)

That is, it cannot be expected that the message will be received by diverse populations in the way that that the sender (usually public or government agencies in this context) intends.

However, in public communications literature, and in crisis communication and disaster preparedness literature, in particular, there has been a notable lack of engagement with the issues surrounding cross-cultural communication (Banks, 2000; Falkheimer and Heide, 2006). Many marginalised groups have been overlooked in public communication campaigns for disaster preparedness:

> Historically, the messengers and messages used for disaster preparedness have been best suited to mainstream and easy to target audiences. New immigrants, people who do not speak the dominant language, those who are transient or illiterate, and the poor who do not have internet access are often left out.
> (Eisenman *et al.*, 2009: 513)

Others come to a similar conclusion:

> Past experiences have shown that these generic prescriptions for preparedness remain beyond the reach of many low income residents, older residents, disable persons and others.
> (Nepal *et al.*, 2012: 266)

A range of groups are unlikely to receive the message unlikely to comprehend the message, unlikely to interpret the message as intended by the sender, unlikely to believe the message is relevant to them or unlikely to feel able to act on the message.

The diversity of groups within the larger target population therefore poses significant challenges to those engaging in public communications and social marketing. As Banks (2000) argues, one of the first hurdles in this area is getting communication professionals to recognise that diversity is actually an issue. He notes that in the early 2000s, it was still common to hear communication practitioners say things like 'Diversity isn't a problem for us. We don't have any diversity here', and, as discussed further later, this is certainly a narrative that appeared in a number of our interviews. This view is not uncommon, and there have been other public claims that demographic diversity is irrelevant in crisis communication in Australia. For example, in the State Emergency Service (SES) paper 'Developing a Risk Communication Model to Encourage Community Safety from Natural Hazards', it is claimed that:

> Though often discussed, demographic variables do not appear to be used as primary criteria for segmenting audiences in risk communication marketing campaigns… While intuitively it may make sense to link specific variables such as income and education standards to the willingness to accept and act on safety messages, there is little hard evidence to support these ascertains.
>
> (O'Neill, 2004: 16–17)

As Banks (2000) points out, however, there is substantial evidence to show that understanding demographic variables helps to explain why messages from public communications campaigns may not carry well to specific groups. Why crisis communication, or communication related to disaster preparedness, would be exempt from this is unclear. O'Neill (2004) suggests that social marketing campaigns dealing with natural hazards lack a sophisticated approach to audience segmentation because there is no hard evidence to support the need for it but there is now mounting evidence of the need to diversify messages related to disaster preparedness across a variety of demographic groups (e.g. Falkheimer and Heide, 2006; Andrulis *et al.*, 2007; Eisenman *et al.*, 2009; Nepal *et al.*, 2012). Again, this suggests an over-reliance on a transmission approach to communications, and outdated top-down models, where state agencies seek to blame citizens for failing to listen to the message rather than questioning why the message has either not been understood, accepted or acted upon.

Second, Banks (2000) argues that even when the importance of demographic diversity is recognised in a public communications context, this is often only at a very superficial level. Most often, the superficial acceptance of diversity manifests in a belief that the literal translation of messages from the dominant language (usually English) into other languages 'solves' the problem of cross-cultural communication but a reliance on translation misses the complexities of both cultural difference and of communication itself. As Banks (2000: 32) explains further, 'communication is interpreted within the cultural contexts of recipients, not sources...audiences cannot be expected automatically and always to take the cultural perspective of the practitioner'. Therefore, a much deeper understanding of cultural difference, and the segmentation of audiences by demographics, is required in order to reach minority groups, or simply groups that do not share the dominant culture of the message sender. These themes will be revisited in the analysis of the data from interviews (across the four states) with communication practitioners in the area of wildfire safety and preparedness.

Communication Approaches and Strategies

One of the most striking elements of the interviews analysed in this chapter is their marked variation. Some participants reported significant support for community engagement within their organisations while others noted ongoing resistance. Some participants detailed formal processes of message development and evaluation within their organisations while others confided that they had neither the resources nor the ability to carry out such activities. However, there were also notable similarities among some of the accounts provided by the participants. Three of the most common points of similarity found in these interviews were the lack of an 'audience-centred' approach to communication, the lack of discussion around audience segmentation and the equation of 'community diversity' with a limited understanding of cultural and linguistic diversity (and an associated lack of acknowledging the power dynamics within communities or between state agencies and minority groups within communities).

Changing Nature of Wildfire Safety Communication

At the outset, it should be noted that several participants mentioned the changing nature of bushfire safety communications in Australia. These practices were perceived, by a majority of the participants, to be in a period of adjustment and re-evaluation. As one interviewee stated, 'In terms of what's required in engagement, I think that's a question for the whole [wildfire agency] – and it's not just [my agency] it's for everybody in the fire services. I think there's a recognition that a new approach is required' (VIC 03).[1] Four of the participants specifically mentioned that they perceived the remit of bushfire agencies to be changing, especially with regard to communications and that, with varying degrees of success, community engagement was becoming part of the normal operation of the fire services. As stated:

> At the moment, all our brigades, or 98 per cent of our brigades, have a focus on fire-fighting. It's only a handful that also do community

engagement work. Those that do, their success rates are very high. So an early challenge for us is to encourage other brigades to take that approach too.

(TAS 01)

While communication engagement was recognised, it was not a core feature of activity at the level of brigades, those firefighting and preparation bodies in localities. Yet there was also an acknowledgement of change that was in process:

I think there's been a lot of improvement just in the last couple of years by recognising the fact that communication about fires is every bit as important as the actual, on ground, fighting the fires... I think there's been a big step forward but there's still some work to be done. It's still sometimes a bit of an afterthought.

(TAS 02)

Hence, while these practices were of recent origin, at least in Tasmania there was an attempt to centre such engagement as a core activity in relation to fire awareness and preparation. This shift in understanding was evolving in inclusive, albeit in limited ways:

We actually consider the media a part of the overall fire-fighting effort. Now while they're not jumping on trucks and rolling hoses and things like that, we consider them a part of the fire-fighting effort because part of the fire-fighting effort is ensuring that the community is informed.

(NSW 01)

The sentiments noted in the previous chapters about intervention and top-down engagement also informed the understandings of agency officials. Yet there also was recognition that the agencies had to move beyond such approaches and help facilitate the conditions for community engagement:

I suppose you've got the traditional media approach of just pushing information out which we tend to do quite well, to what I'm trying to bring about is more of engaging with communities and giving them meaningful information and entering into a dialogue with them, which is a much more difficult prospect.

(NSW 02)

Overall, some of the communication practitioners talked about what they saw as the successful integration of community engagement within wildfire agencies, while others spoke primarily of resistance to this change. There were significant differences in how well respondents felt their own organisation was addressing and engaging with the intended audiences for their wildfire safety materials. The last participant, who mentioned attempting to enter into a 'dialogue' with communities, specifically spoke of the tension in trying to adopt open communication with residents as a strategy within a bushfire agency that has traditionally used a 'command and control' approach to communication:

> I think the organisation is very response- and tactically-based anyway...when you start talking about resilience and engaging communities and building capacity and things like that, that a lot of the staff within the organisations [wildfire agencies] don't actually get that stuff. So it's very much a – I think, as much a cultural challenge as it is an organisational challenge.
>
> (NSW 02)

This is a critical point to take into account. Many of the fire agencies involved in promoting wildfire safety do not come from traditions of public communications. Rather, they were often based on military-like structures where communication is traditionally seen as very much embedded in the transmission model: a message is sent from the top of the hierarchy, received as intended by others and acted upon (generally without question). As discussed earlier, this is not a useful model on which to base effective public communication and social marketing campaigns. Taking into account the intended audience (or, better still, audiences), and attempting active engagement with the audience/s, is crucial. However, it is important to recognise that many of the agencies now involved in bushfire safety campaigns do not have a long history of this form of engagement and may face significant challenges in trying to adopt new and varied methods. Indeed, this process of transition may help to explain, in part, the variety of responses we received from some practitioners regarding the methods of message development and evaluation as well as the integration of methods (or lack thereof) for understanding and addressing audience segmentation and diversity.

Message Development and Evaluation

One of the most dominant themes across all nine interviews, in terms of public communication strategies, was the issue of message development and evaluation. These responses were often triggered after the interviewer asked questions regarding the development of key messages, evidence that the messaging was effective, or whether or not there were any formal procedures of evaluation for the relevant communications.

In terms of both message development and evaluation procedures, there were significant differences in responses across organisations and across the four States. Some participants mentioned that there were a variety of people involved in developing the relevant messaging for a particular campaign, while others noted a lack of any support for this element of the campaign process. The most extreme example of a lack of consultation in development came from one participant who, when asked if there was a process for message development within their organisation, responded by saying, 'No, the message development is me' (WA 01). Obviously such an approach is extremely problematic from both a traditional communication approach and a social marketing perspective. Without any prior understanding of how intended audiences respond to existing messages, or are likely to respond to proposed messages, the communication practitioner is, at best, playing a guessing game. The messages may work, they may not. In such a scenario it is almost impossible to know. Without feedback mechanisms, collaboration between colleagues or across agencies, or research into target audiences, campaign messaging is likely to be ineffective.

In contrast, there were also accounts of greater collaborative development of messaging. One practitioner described collaboration between agencies and government departments, as well as collaboration with a major newspaper, as part of the message development for a particular campaign:

> The key messaging that drove a lot of messaging for this year was generated in the [wildfire agency]…it was written by someone in the [government department] and there was a table of people from every agency that was sitting around the table at the [State-based newspaper office] going through every page.
>
> (VIC 03)

While collaboration between organisations can certainly be very useful in messaging design, it is important that this kind of expert knowledge does not displace attempts to engage target audiences. As Atkin and Freimuth (2013: 53) explain, that specialists and experts do not always recognise that they may 'differ substantially from their audiences in topical knowledge, values, priorities, and level of involvement'; they therefore lack an experiential understanding of their audience. Therefore, engagement with the intended audience during message development is still required.

Two other respondents noted the importance of taking into account 'the community' as the audience for the intended messages:

> So we got the [market research] to do key message research with groups from high risk areas and the general…population so that we

could get a lot more direction on what the key messages should be and which were resonating with the community.

(VIC 02)

And:

media and public affairs and community engagement would come up with some concepts that we would then sit down and say to the guys who are out on the ground, the volunteers, the operational services and largely the community engagement area who know how the messages are then interpreted or actioned by the community.

(WA 01)

These two accounts do at least mention 'the community', so there was some recognition of the importance of the audience, even if it was still treated as a relatively homogenous whole. In the first account the participant described using market research to determine which of the key messages would resonate best with 'the community', which precludes any understanding of significant audience segmentation. The second account assumes that volunteers from within the wildfire agency knew how the key messages were 'interpreted or actioned by the community'. Again, there was the homogenous sense of 'the community', but here it was coupled with an assumption that the volunteers within the agency did actually know how the messaging was interpreted by residents. Such a system relies on the perception of volunteers rather than actual responses from groups within the target audience. It also overlooks the fact that volunteers themselves were unlikely to represent a full cross section of residents in their locality, nor were they likely to come into contact with a full cross section of residents in their locality. As specialist operators in the area of wildfire they were not likely to be, in Akin and Freimuth's (2013: 53) words, 'the "average" person'.

Clearly, there is substantial variation in the way that communications professionals describe the message development process within their agencies and departments. Our research team found a similar breadth of variation in the descriptions provided of evaluative processes. Participants were asked whether or not there were formal systems in place to determine if messaging was reaching its intended audiences and having the desired effect. Again, there was a range of accounts, from formal embedded processes to a complete absence of formal evaluation procedures. One practitioner referred to funding:

We invest between 10–20 per cent of our campaign budget each year in pre- and post-campaign research to measure the impact that they are having.

(TAS 01)

Another referred to assessments that had been initiated in relation to advertising or communication:

> [S]o we do pre- and post-campaign research on all our annual advertising just by way of benchmarking and making sure that we are actually getting the cut through.
>
> (NSW 01)

Yet another practitioner noted that this agency did not conduct any planned assessment of communication activity:

> [W]e don't actually do any survey work or monitoring or research on before and after behavioural change type stuff.
>
> (NSW 02)

In a different State, this absence of assessment was a resource issue:

> Look, we don't do any sort of quantitative analysis...generally we find we're too busy getting the stuff out to be monitoring it in that way... That would be nice to be able to do it.
>
> (WA 02)

The first two participants viewed research on the effectiveness of the campaigns as a central part of the campaign itself and the first respondent mentions that the money required for this is specifically set aside in the initial budget. According to our interviewees, however, this was not a process replicated by all other organisations. Two participants recounted no support for evaluation programs, despite the final respondent noting that it would be 'nice' to have the resources available to determine effectiveness. Much like a lack of consultation and collaboration in the message development stage, a lack of evaluative processes deprives the communications professional of important feedback about the efficacy of their campaign. It is extremely difficult to design and implement more effective campaigns in future if there is no institutional support for formal evaluation procedures (Valente and Kwan, 2013).

These accounts raise several issues. First, they highlight the lack of consistency across organisations involved in bushfire safety campaigns. Some agencies and departments appeared to have well-resourced communications teams, while others were apparently left working mostly on their own with little support. It is not surprising then that there was also significant variation in attempts at audience engagement and campaign evaluation. This highlights the second important point, which is that some professionals reported they were running campaigns with no formal evaluation procedures whatsoever. Such a situation should be of serious concern to rural wildfire services and other professionals working in the area of wildfire safety. Without proper evaluation procedures, public communications campaigns can simply be a waste of resources (Valente and Kwan, 2013). Finally, when participants did speak of evaluation processes, these were generally taken to be testing before and after campaigns to determine whether or not residents in wildfire-prone areas had encountered particular messages and if they could recall them. There was much less sense of genuine consultation with a variety of groups or the need to understand the context in which different demographic groups may make sense of key messages.

Understandings of Diversity

When asked about the target audience for wildfire safety campaigns, several practitioners responded that the audience was essentially everyone living in wildfire-prone areas. Unless prompted by the researcher, participants generally did not talk about segmentation or diversity within this broad target audience. As a result, the following responses around the theme of diversity generally arose after the researcher asked if the participant knew of any strategies to deal with diverse audiences, or if there were any elements of their campaigns designed to address diverse audiences or 'community diversity'.

There were three main ways that communication practitioners responded to these questions about audience diversity. The first was to deny that diversity was relevant (two participants). The second was to interpret diversity as referring to culturally and linguistically diverse (CALD) populations (eight participants). The third was to interpret diversity as dealing with 'vulnerable groups', identified as older residents or people living with disabilities (two participants). The first two of these themes will be considered in the remainder of this chapter.

After the interviewer raised the issue of diversity within the target audience, two participants suggested that it was not an issue that required addressing as the localities they were responsible for were not diverse:

> I have to say…that around [this locality] it's pretty Anglo still. There are not large numbers of non-English people, non-English speaking background, for example.
>
> (VIC 01)

While the first practitioner referred to a bushfire-prone locality, another practitioner referred to the whole State:

> We haven't put much emphasis on it [community diversity] because I mean Tasmania is pretty – it's not all that diverse. It really isn't. It's a very decentralised…very small, small towns. Most of them aren't towns; you'd call them more villages. They're very – they're very much – they're not diverse communities.
>
> (TAS 02)

Both of these interviewees interpreted 'diversity' as relating only to cultural and linguistic diversity and then subsequently dismissed it. The example of Tasmania as not culturally or linguistically diverse is particularly interesting for analysis as so much of Tasmania is determined to be bushfire prone that the target audience is often considered to be most of the State. Indeed, one of the other participants (TAS 01) described 'the whole of Tassie' as bushfire prone with the exception of the inner metropolitan areas. This interviewee estimated that this translated to about '95 per cent of the land' and that '85 per cent of the population' of Tasmania were living in bushfire-prone areas and could therefore be deemed the target audience for wildfire safety communications (TAS 01). The 2011 Census data from the ABS, however, shows that almost 20 per cent of residents in Tasmania were born overseas and almost 10 per cent of residents had a language other than English spoken at home (ABS, 2013). Although this is relatively low compared to some other parts of Australia, there were still clearly differences on the basis of cultural and linguistic diversity to take into account.

Indeed, the primary way in which the term 'community diversity' was interpreted by participants was as an issue of cultural or linguistic diversity – something, it is worth noting, that interviewees themselves lacked (being almost exclusively Anglo/white, native English speakers). Only two respondents identified other demographic variables as part of addressing 'community diversity': one mentioned gender and another mentioned low-income earners.

When asked how their relevant agencies and departments were dealing with cultural or linguistic diversity, the most common response from participants was that bushfire safety communications materials are translated into multiple languages:

> We do advertising in different languages...we've had some core material translated into 18 different languages. The [wildfire agency] do 32 different languages. We also run – we have the press and radio translate it into about 10 different languages.
>
> (VIC 02)

And:

> So we have a culturally and linguistically diverse program which largely focuses on making sure all materials are translated into 22 different languages across the State. We also have community spokespeople, translators that can be called to come in.
>
> (VIC 03)

And:

> Well everything's broadcast in English. On our website you've got
> the capacity to translate into one of a zillion other languages. I've
> never tried it. It's something I should probably do.
>
> (WA 02)

For several participants, the only strategy for addressing diverse audiences
was the translation of pre-existing materials. As mentioned earlier, this is an
inadequate and relatively superficial way of attempting cross-cultural communication (Banks, 2000). Direct translations from the original language
may not be appropriate or accurately convey the intended meaning. This is
especially a concern with automatic or machine translation, as is implied by
the third respondent, where translations can be significantly different to the
intended meaning and may even be misleading (Aiken and Balan, 2011).

Three communication practitioners did mention taking further steps in
attempting to use different channels for disseminating the translated messages to CALD groups and developing different messaging for these groups:

> The cultural and linguistically diverse group, they have got connec-
> tions with most not-for-profits, most advocacy groups, the advocacy
> networks, and they give them all the literature.
>
> (VIC 03)

The focus here was on using specific groups to connect materials with
'diverse' groups. Others were more specific:

> [W]e particularly focus on culturally and linguistically diverse com-
> munities. We've done a lot of work with multicultural radio agencies
> here, the SBS [special broadcasting service], and we look at develop-
> ing key messages and information that targets those groups.
>
> (WA 01)

And:

> We've produced or we've assisted in the running of, I think it it's two
> sort of broad-based community events where it's targeted at multi-
> cultural communities. That's a little different. That's about actually
> overcoming some fears that multicultural communities have about
> people in uniform.
>
> (VIC 01)

The first respondent mentioned using specific channels to disseminate
the original or translated material to CALD groups, while the second

and third respondents actually spoke of the development of specific messaging targeting CALD groups. Although the second excerpt did not explain how the key messages were modified to be more appropriate for non-dominant cultural groups, the final quote does provide a concrete example of a more insightful understanding of potential cultural difference.

The third respondent mentioned that the agency had been involved in running programs to help introduce uniformed personnel to recent migrants who may have come from radically different backgrounds. This reference was the only indication given in our interviews of an example where the messaging, content and channel chosen were adapted specifically to a non-dominant group. In this instance, with the recognition that basic understandings of the role and symbolism of government agencies may differ cross-culturally and that this needs to be taken into account in order to establish trust between residents and formal organisations promoting bushfire safety. This example is undoubtedly a step in the right direction from a social marketing perspective, but it was unfortunately an example that stood out as an exception to the standard practice described by the other participants, which suggests there is still a long way to go before understanding cultural and linguistic diversity is seen as more fundamental to effective messaging.

Conclusions

Communications professionals working in the area of bushfire safety in Australia face a difficult task. Like any attempt at social marketing, or communication for the public good, there are significant challenges in attaining attitudinal and/or behavioural change among target populations. Indeed, international research shows that the effectiveness of public communications campaigns is generally 'modest at best' (Devin and Foreman-Werne, 2013). The effectiveness of campaigns can be limited by a variety of factors, from a lack of resources to an absence of theoretical frameworks and modelling or poorly conceived strategy (Atkin and Rice, 2013).

The task for communications practitioners working within bushfire agencies may be even more difficult given the quasi-military history and 'command and control' style operations of many rural fire services in Australia. Certainly, some of our participants noted that this history and organisational set-up could, at times, impede current attempts at community engagement and this research has identified several areas of concern.

There was clearly substantial variation in the way in which communications professionals approach bushfire preparedness and safety campaigns in Australia. Accounts from the practitioners suggest that different organisations sometimes had drastically different processes and procedures for message development and evaluation. In some instances, in fact, there were no formal processes in place for either message development or evaluation, leaving communications practitioners to simply guess at what would constitute effective messaging. It must be acknowledged by organisations working in this area that without processes in place for these critical elements of public communication, campaigns may simply be a waste of resources (Atkin and Freimuth, 2013; Valente and Kwan, 2013).

This research also shows that there are wide-ranging attitudes to incorporating audience diversity into wildfire safety campaigns. While almost all of the interviewees for this project interpreted the term 'diversity' in the same way – as differences in culture and language – very few could explain how this diversity might have had an impact upon their campaign strategy. It appears as though the translation of existing wildfire preparedness and safety materials was the most common strategy for addressing CALD groups, but this is unfortunately only a relatively superficial strategy and is unlikely to engage non-dominant cultural groups effectively (Banks, 2000). While there were isolated examples of more thorough engagement with CALD groups, overall, the data suggests that there is still a lot more that could be done to integrate approaches to audience segmentation and diversity in the area of wildfire safety and preparedness.

There appeared to be an underlying frustration expressed by a number of the participants about the ineffectiveness of current campaigns, particularly in terms of (a lack of) audience behaviour change. There is little doubt that achieving behaviour and attitude change is a very difficult task indeed (Devin and Foreman-Werne, 2013), and we do not wish to diminish the challenges that still lie ahead in terms of bushfire safety communications in the Australian context. However, some of the frustration from participants appeared to be directed at the perceived audience: that (some) residents in wildfire-prone localities were simply 'not listening' to the messages sent out by agencies. There was a sense that there was nothing wrong with the message itself, and that it was the responsibility of the audience/s to make the effort to interpret them as intended. It should be clear that any such approach will be doomed to fail. Blaming the audience for misusing, misinterpreting or ignoring messaging will not create better future programs and ignores the need for agencies to better tailor messages to different target audiences. It also fails to recognise the marginalisation of CALD groups within particular localities, and the power dynamics between bushfire agencies and CALD groups, particularly when agency personnel are generally unlikely to be drawn from CALD communities. In short, we must accept that the audience is always right. Attitudes that promote attempts to better understand audiences, and the social and political complexities of their lives, will be much more useful for developing effective wildfire safety campaigns than those that begin from a misdirected criticism of audiences.

Notes

1 The identifiers for this set of interviews have been altered to protect the anonymity of the participants.

8 Power within Households

Gender Inequality and Wildfire Preparedness

Meagan Tyler and Peter Fairbrother

In the Australian context, fire authorities have, for some decades, presented residents with a choice to evacuate or defend a property when threatened by wildfire[1] and the issue of why some people defer or delay this choice has become a crucial issue of research. The work of Proudley (2008a, 2008b, see also Goodman and Proudley, 2008) suggests that in terms of wildfire preparedness and decision-making, the gendered dynamics of households are an important but generally overlooked factor. While the gendered norms surrounding 'Prepare, Stay and Defend, or Leave Early' (PSDLE) have drawn some interest over the past ten years, they remain under-researched and under-recognised (Tyler and Fairbrother, 2013a, 2013b). There is a growing understanding, for example, that men are more likely to want to 'stay and defend' a property while women are more likely to want to evacuate. However, there is little recognition of the dynamics within households themselves and, in particular, between heterosexual couples that can make decision-making particularly complex.

Our proposition is that decision-making cannot be understood purely from a psychological perspective but must also been seen as shaped by social, political and economic circumstances (Johnson *et al.*, 2012). We suggest that disagreement about wildfire safety within households, especially between members of heterosexual couples, is common and, moreover, that such occurrences may be an impediment to the ability of individuals and families to develop adequate household-level preparedness and response strategies. These dynamics also raise sharp questions in relation to power and inequality in relation to wildfire events, and the relations between the state and communities. Like the previous chapter, this analysis highlights the ways in which agencies have often failed to adequately recognise the real-world social context in which messages about wildfire safety are taken up by residents.[2]

Why is Gender Important?

As the importance of the social sciences has increasingly become recognised in wildfire research in Australia, the areas of investigation regarding wildfire safety have expanded. Following the Royal Commission into the Black Saturday fires in Victoria, there has been significant public discussion about how best to understand the relationship between people, place and wildfires: how best to prepare for, communicate about, respond to and recover from these kinds of disaster events. There has also been discussion around the now substantial amount of wildfire-related research undertaken in Australia and debate over what areas are most in need of future exploration. We have argued elsewhere (Tyler *et al.*, 2012; Tyler and Fairbrother, 2013a, 2013b) that an understanding of the social construction of gender is both critically important and generally overlooked in wildfire research at this point in time, and that this area warrants further examination.

While the study of gender and associated questions about the social construction of masculinity and femininity have been established as important elements of social science research for decades, gendered analysis entered disaster studies relatively recently. It was not until the late 1990s, for example, that the first edited collection on gender and disaster was published (Enarson and Morrow, 1998). Since this time, there has been a steady increase in international literature dealing with the relationship between gender and disaster, and there has been some progress too, in Australia. In 2013, the *Australian Journal of Emergency Management* published its first special issue on gender, and in 2012, the annual conference of the Australasian Fire and Emergency Service Authorities Council (AFAC) included a special panel addressing gender and disaster. However, there is still a long way to go before gendered analysis is accepted as a valued part of wildfire research and policy in Australia.

It should be noted at the outset that the study of gender is not concerned with biological differences between men and women. Gender refers specifically to the 'socially learned behaviour and expectations that distinguish masculinity and femininity' (Peterson and Runyan, 1999: 5). For some decades, the social construction of gender has been a focus in disciplines such as sociology and anthropology, with gendered analyses evident in areas ranging from criminology to international political economy. The importance of gender is also recognised in the trend towards 'gender mainstreaming' evident in many national and international public policy discourses (Walby, 2005).

The integration of gendered analysis in the social sciences has led to a greater recognition of the role that the social construction of gender plays in affecting the attitudes and behaviours of individuals as well as social, political and economic institutions. There are few, if any, areas of social life where norms of masculinity and femininity, as well as inequalities between men and women, are not evident (Lorber, 1994). In terms of disaster, one of the more obvious ways in which the influence of gender norms has been recognised is through the masculinised and male-dominated structure of emergency services organisations (Tyler and Fairbrother, 2013b). There are, however, a number of more complex and subtle ways in which disasters have gendered consequences. For instance, there is evidence to suggest that, globally, women are at greater risk from the effects of disaster than men (Enarson and Morrow, 1998; Enarson and Chakrabarti, 2009). Gendered differences have also been documented in relation to disaster risk perception and exposure, preparedness behaviour, styles of and access to warning communication, response to warning communication (especially with regard to evacuation), physical and psychological impacts, recovery and reconstruction (Fothergill, 1998).

What emerges from this work on gender and disaster is that women are, in a number of different ways, more vulnerable to the effects of disaster than men. Again, this is not thought to be the result of some innate or biological differences between men and women; rather, these differences are understood to be the result of sociopolitical factors, including gender inequality. Marginalised groups are more likely to suffer from the effects of disaster; women are often disadvantaged because of their social and economic positions in society.

Various gendered social restrictions impact women's responses to disaster. For example, women are less likely than their male counterparts to have been taught how to swim. They are also more likely to wear restrictive or inappropriate clothing because of gendered expectations about dress (Enarson and Morrow, 1998; Enarson and Chakrabarti, 2009). It is therefore not surprising that women are over-represented in deaths from drowning during floods and tsunamis (Ariyabandu, 2009). In some instances, regardless of the type of natural hazard, women are hampered in their attempts to flee because they are more likely to experience restrictions on their outdoor or public movements (Ariyabandu, 2009; Chakrabarti and Walia, 2009). Women are also more likely to take on care-giving responsibilities for children, the elderly and the infirm, and it has been theorised that these responsibilities often impede a woman's ability to escape imminent danger (Enarson and Morrow, 1998). In terms of preparation and communication, in many developing countries, women are less likely to be literate and therefore the chances of women being able to read and understand preparedness information and disaster warnings are diminished (Enarson and Morrow, 1998).

Substantial gendered differences have also been found in disaster preparation and response in (post)industrialised states. One of the most prominent of these discrepancies is women's more common preference for evacuation (e.g. Scanlon *et al.*, 1996; Bolin *et al.*, 1998; Fothergill, 1998; Bateman and Edwards, 2002; Mozumder *et al.*, 2008). The evidence for this difference comes mostly from instances of floods, hurricanes and earthquakes but has also been noted in some case study research on forest fire (e.g. Mozumder *et al.*, 2008). This literature indicates that women are significantly more likely to favour preparation for evacuation, while men are more likely to want to stay in an area of danger (Scanlon *et al.*, 1996; Bolin *et al.*, 1998; Mozumder *et al.*, 2008). In some places around the world, women's preference for evacuation is actually portrayed in a positive light. Enarson (2009), for example, shows that women's more common preference for evacuation is seen by a number of emergency agencies internationally as a valuable asset in promoting risk aversion.

There is an understanding within many of these agencies that a preference for evacuation is often linked to gendered norms of responsibility (e.g. care-giving). This understanding, highlighting the social roots of gendered behavioural difference, is further supported by studies on risk perception which show that the most privileged groups – in particular, wealthy, white men – are much more likely to have low risk perception (Bateman and Edwards, 2002; e.g. Finucane *et al.*, 2000), while the poor, minority groups and women are more likely to have high risk perception. Finucane and others (2000) suggest that this stems from inequality, different environmental factors and life experience, that is, those who are the most privileged tend to experience the least fear in their everyday lives and, as a consequence, may underrate risks associated with events such as natural disasters.

Gender, Evacuation and Wildfire in Australia

As McLennan and colleagues (2012) note, there are relatively few studies exploring residents' readiness to evacuate for wildfire disasters. However, within the limited number of studies available regarding the Australian context, women's preference for evacuation during a wildfire threat has been noted by Proudley (2008) and is also mentioned in a report from the Office of the Emergency Services Commissioner in Victoria (OESC, 2010). These accounts have since been supported by a more comprehensive study by Whittaker and colleagues (2016), based on 'more than 600 interviews with survivors and a questionnaire of 1314 households in fire-affected areas' (p. 1), dealing with gendered responses to the Black Saturday fires. Again, this shows a marked gender difference in preferences for evacuation. In the surveyed sample, 23 per cent of women wanted to 'leave as soon as they knew a fire was threatening', while only 11 per cent of men intended this course of action. In comparison, 56 per cent of men intended to stay and defend throughout a fire, compared to 42 per cent of women (Wittaker *et al.*, 2016: 6).

We have written elsewhere (Tyler and Fairbrother, 2013b) that many fire agencies in Australia have, in the past, taken a notably different view of women's more likely preference for evacuation from their overseas counterparts. Indeed, there have been programs which have tried to 'educate' women out of their initially stated choice of evacuation (Tyler and Fairbrother, 2013b). What is also very different in the Australian context is the unusually gendered nature of wildfire death tolls. Unlike the trend in disasters internationally, where women are over-represented in death tolls (Enarson and Chakrabarti, 2009), in Australia, more men than women die in wildfires. Indeed, a survey of wildfire deaths has shown that almost three times more civilian men than women died in wildfire events in Australia between 1900 and 2008 (Haynes *et al.*, 2010), although this difference has narrowed in more recent fire events. Haynes and colleagues (2010) suggest that one of the reasons men may be over-represented in wildfire fatalities is that they are more likely to 'actively defend a house' during a fire while women are more likely to 'shelter passively'.

However, the issue is not only the intended or carried out course of action in response to a disaster event; it is also how that course of action is chosen. There is evidence to suggest that disagreements between men and women within a household, over the best course of action to take during a fire threat, are a significant issue. Proudley (2008a), for example, found in her study of couples in South Australia that there were noticeable differences in what husbands and wives believed was the best course of action to take when wildfire threatened. Similar Whittaker and others (2016) note disagreements being reported in their interview data. Furthermore, Handmer and colleagues (2010) have shown how the consequences of disagreement within a household can, in fact, be deadly. In a review of fatalities from the Black Saturday fires, they submitted the following to the Royal Commission:

> There is evidence of disagreements as the fire approached. In virtually all cases this was between women who wanted to leave and take the men with them and men who either wanted to stay and defend or who felt they had to support others in that role. In some cases it appears that the difference in opinion was long standing, in other cases it was only acknowledged at the last minute. This led to some people changing their plans at the last minute. This appears particularly the case for couples. There are instances where women who fled under these circumstances survived. Conversely, there is also evidence of such disagreements where males refused to leave, but relatives decided to stay, leading to additional fatalities.
>
> (Handmer *et al.*, 2010)

Our research, in part, picks up on this trend. Over the course of our research on residents' preparedness behaviours and responses to wildfire preparedness communication, participants often spoke about what they believed they would do if (and occasionally, what they had done when) a wildfire threatened their area or home. In all but one of the locality case studies, there were recorded instances of heterosexual couples preferring different courses of action. The most obvious pattern that emerged from these differences was couples or families who had agreed that the female partner would leave and, if there were children in the household, evacuate with them, while the male partner would stay with the property, either to make further preparations or with the intention of staying to defend. The research team also found several instances of stated disagreements between couples as to their wildfire preparation and response planning. It should be noted, however, that at no point did interviewers ask participants about gender, nor did we specifically have gender as a focal point of analysis at the outset of the project. The theme was so strong that we added it during the research process.

The focus here, therefore, is not so much to prove that women are more likely to favour evacuation, but rather to better contextualise the existing evidence that there are likely to be differences in the favoured method of wildfire preparation and response between men and women. Furthermore, we aim to explore the gendered dynamics that may be involved in determining a household wildfire plan, and the way in which gendered expectations may, in fact, impair a heterosexual couple's ability to communicate and negotiate effectively with regard to wildfire safety. This is a notably different approach to much existing research. Instead of adopting an individual-based psychology of decision-making approach (Johnson *et al.*, 2012), we have focussed on understanding the social (in this case, gendered) relations of intra-household communication. We also go further than Whittaker *et al.* (2016), in trying to explain the importance of gender inequality and the cultural construction of men's and women's roles in wildfire preparation and response as central to understanding how these disagreements play out.

Gendered Households

Our findings suggest a more complex understanding of household decision-making and gender norms than that put forward by others. Goodman and Cottrell (2012), for example, draw on a relatively small sample (17 interviews in one rural locality) to detail a common theme of men's 'burden' of decision-making within households with regard to wildfire preparedness and response. They also outline the stories of several women who were 'dependant' on advice from their husbands during a wildfire threat. Our data, however, shows a much more multi-faceted process of negotiation between members of heterosexual couples regarding wildfire safety. While some female respondents in our study did report deferring to their husbands on issues of wildfire preparation and response, we found it was much more common for there to be active disagreement within households, where men and women had substantially differing opinions about the best course of action to pursue. Many women were very vocal in their opposition to a male partner's plans to 'stay and defend', for example, but expressed difficulty convincing men that leaving early was a better option.

The most prevalent themes around gender and wildfire safety in the interview data were found to be a wildfire plan that involves a female partner evacuating and a male partner staying, disagreement between members of a heterosexual couple regarding an optimal wildfire plan, a lack of clarity between a heterosexual couple as to an agreed wildfire plan and gendered differences in motivations to 'stay and defend' or evacuate. The first two of these themes are the primary focus of the analysis in this chapter.

Men Stay, Women (and Children) Leave

Among those residents interviewed who did have a clear wildfire plan, and articulated this to the researcher, there was a noticeable trend among those who stated that 'stay and defend' was part of their wildfire response plan. While there were instances where both members of a heterosexual couple planned to stay, it was more common that the male partner planned to stay and the female partner planned to evacuate. This trend was often brought out in discussions with the researcher about wildfire planning for the household in response to questions such as 'Do you have a wildfire plan?', 'Are you preparing to evacuate?', 'Is there a trigger that would lead you to evacuate?' or 'Have you discussed this plan with anyone else in the household?'

One participant in Victoria stated, for example, 'I will not leave my property'. When asked if his wife was leaving, he responded, 'My wife know she's got to walk one property up to the school' (male, Vic, urban-rural interface). Another participant in New South Wales gave his 'general strategy' as:

> [M]y wife and daughter...they would vacate the area and then we'd [the participant and his son] make an assessment as to whether there was a need to stay.
>
> (male, NSW, urban-rural interface)

A woman in Western Australia talked about why she had concerns about staying to defend with her husband:

> [W]e have said if it's really, really imminent over there somewhere, Kathleen[3] and the girls and I will go in the safe time and you [her husband] and Andrew [her son] will stay. Because I don't think – I think I would be a bit useless quite frankly..
>
> (female, WA, tree/sea-change)

These are indicative examples of the kinds of ways in which residents explained an agreed difference in approach to wildfire response within the household. It is important to note that there were no instances found where women planned to stay while their male partners planned to evacuate. These kinds of plans, which involve the splitting up of the adult members of the household, were found to be present among older retirees and younger couples, both with and without children, although children were sometimes mentioned as a motivating factor for evacuation. So while there may be a connection to gendered norms of care-giving, as mentioned in the international literature on gender and disaster (e.g. Enarson and Morrow, 1998; Bateman and Edwards, 2002), this is not the only issue. There were, for example, several instances where children, or the care of others, were not factors in determining that a female partner would leave and a male partner would stay.

Indeed, it seemed that underlying gendered expectations of behaviour ran deeper than the norm of women's caregiving. Several men also expressed a belief that it was their role, as men, to stay. In at least one instance, a male partner could not articulate why he was not prepared to leave with his partner. When questioned as to why he had chosen to 'stay and defend', he responded by saying:

> I'm not sure why because I don't have a huge emotional tie to the whole place and it's insured...But I just think that's what I should do
> (male, WA, tree/sea change)

Other participants, when asked to explain the reasoning behind their current wildfire plans, gave examples of past experience where gender had been a defining factor:

> I went through Ash Wednesday and I could see that you could save your house by staying there, as long as you're well prepared. My wife wouldn't do that, she'd clear out.
> (male, Vic, tree/sea change)

Another commented on his agency:

> During the 2001 [wildfire] event, my wife and daughter were evacuated. It wasn't a compulsory evacuation at the time...I was determined to stay here and did so...
> (male, NSW, tree/sea change)

Yet another spoke of the evacuation of his partner and daughter as part of the preparation to defend the house:

> [B]ecause I'd just had my little girl when the last fire went through, so it was a case of getting them [his daughter and female partner] down to where they had to be so that I could stay with the house.
> (male, NSW, tree/sea change)

And another drew attention to the history of 'Stay or Go' in practice:

> [A]ll the guys stayed in '86 or '83. All the guys would and all the women left...back then they were saying evacuate women and children.
>
> (male, Vic, urban-rural interface)

Also drawing on past experience, one interviewee mentioned that he did not necessarily plan to 'stay and defend' but would stay longer than his wife in order to assess the situation:

> I know from experience that you get your wife and your children away from the danger and then you make a decision, how well you are prepared to either stand the fire against the house or whether to leave yourself. That's a judgment you make depending on the ferociousness or the velocity of the fire.
>
> (male, NSW, tree/sea change)

Another man in New South Wales described a similar plan:

> I would get my wife to leave with her photographs and the other stuff...I would have my car parked up the street, ready to leave, but I would stay as long as I could basically, and put the sprinkler system on and also have the grounds wet; make sure that we've got buckets of water around and all that sort of stuff.
>
> (male, NSW, urban-rural interface)

These plans should be of particular interest to agencies, which have focussed on trying to dissuade residents from late evacuation (Tibbits *et al.*, 2008; e.g. AFAC, 2005). In some ways this strategy of separation within a household can be seen as deferring a more concrete decision on whether to 'Stay or Go'. Women should remain 'safe' and prepare for early evacuation while these men believe they are better equipped to prepare the house and possibly stay and defend, but also possibly attempt late evacuation.

Furthermore, it appears from this research that such plans are not uncommon. Indeed, two participants commented on having noticed a more widespread practice of women leaving early and men staying to either defend or wait and see:

> The scary thing is most of them are probably half and half. So often it's the wife and kids are going to go and the husbands are going to stay.
>
> (female, Vic, urban-rural interface)

And:

> Well, I know most of the women here are planning to leave…All the
> women have said: 'We're just going. We're not going to be staying
> here. We're not risking our lives in it'.
>
> (female, Vic, urban-rural interface)

Taken together, the evidence from the residents we interviewed across
Victoria, New South Wales and Western Australia, as well as previous
research from Proudley (2008), the OESC (2010) and Whittaker *et al.*
(2016), does show there is a noticeable trend in planning for wildfire
that splits households along gender lines. The importance of considering
a 'split' plan, however, has often been overlooked. So, while others have
highlighted differences in intended wildfire responses there has been little analysis of split plans specifically, or why these plans seem to only
split one way. That is, while there are some women who choose to stay
and defend with their male partners, and some men who choose to evacuate with their female partners (Whittaker *et al.*, 2016), we found no
instances where men evacuated or planned to evacuate – either on their
own or with children – while leaving female partners to stay and defend.

This behavioural trend, combined with some participants' inability
to explain why men should stay and women should leave, confirms the
limited existing research on wildfire and gender in Australia, which has
shown that wildfires are largely seen as 'men's business' (Poiner, 1990;
Eriksen *et al.*, 2010; Tyler and Fairbrother, 2013a). As the next section
will explore in more depth, this assumption of appropriate gender roles,
which means that men are more likely to stay and fight a wildfire (and
much more likely to stay and fight a wildfire on their own), can cause
significant tension within a household and may limit a couple's ability to
effectively communicate and negotiate around wildfire safety.

Disagreement over a Wildfire Plan

While it is clear that some heterosexual couples had an agreed plan for
the woman to leave and the man to stay, there was also a group of participants who mentioned disagreement over a wildfire plan. Again, this
generally centred on whether or not the male partner or both members
of the couple would 'stay and defend'. The issue of disagreement was
often raised by participants after the researcher asked if a wildfire plan
had been discussed with all members of the household and, if so, if there
was any dispute. Some typical examples of the disagreements recounted
by participants are given in the following.

> RESEARCHER: Was there any disagreement?
> PARTICIPANT [FEMALE]: There was to an extent. I've been very clear.
>   I said: 'Ben, really you're much more important to me. I don't
>   want to have that fear of thinking you're not all right' (female,
>   Vic, tree/sea change).

And an observation after reflection of previous bushfire events:

> RESEARCHER: So there was more disagreement over the plan about you defending the property?
>
> PARTICIPANT [MALE]: That was probably the biggest disagreement, my macho defensive, protective thing. But I wouldn't have stuck to that if my life was at risk and I would change it a bit now anyway (male, Vic, tree/sea change).

And another refers to some of the ways people refer to property and landscape when making decisions:

> RESEARCHER: [W]ould you plan to evacuate early or would you stay and defend?
>
> PARTICIPANT [FEMALE]: I talked about this with [my husband] and he – I sort of think oh, grab [the animals] and run. He is more of the opinion that we'd stay because our property – we've got five acres...We haven't got any huge trees around the house. We keep things clear. So [he] is of the opinion that he'd stay, or we'd stay. I'm of the opinion, open the gates, let the [animals] go, grab the dogs and shove them in the car and go. But he's pretty gung-ho my husband (female, WA, rural).

In all of the occurrences of disagreement about a wildfire plan recounted to the research team, it was men who wanted to stay and women who wanted to leave. We found no examples of women trying to convince their male partners to stay, or of men trying to convince their female partners to evacuate.

In some instances, such as the previous one, the disagreement had still not been resolved at the time of the interview. Ongoing disagreement over a plan was mentioned by other participants as well and, in the following case, with reference to a previous experience when a wildfire had threatened:

> RESEARCHER: Okay. You're planning to go. Did you discuss that with your husband as a formal thing?
>
> PARTICIPANT [FEMALE]: [Simon] was more confident about being all right here. I never was. Perhaps I'm a scaredy cat. I don't know... I'm very cautious.
>
> RESEARCHER: He was saying: 'Well maybe we could stay'?
>
> PARTICIPANT [FEMALE]: I hate saying this – am I allowed to say it? He was saying it's not a worry. I was quite angry with him for a time...I did feel very slightly – I realised how on my own I was...I didn't want to be here, but I had no means of getting out on my own. This is going to sound a rather morbid thing to say, but I would probably rather perish with Simon...I don't know that I'd want to live and have him left behind to perish.
>
> RESEARCHER: [W]as there some kind of argument or conflict?

PARTICIPANT [FEMALE]: No argument, no. Just Simon making that statement. I know my husband very well, and I just thought: 'Right, maybe, but I don't want to do it' [stay and defend]. As it played out though, I ended up staying in this house... (female, Vic, urban-rural interface).

This woman became quite upset during the interview process and perhaps this should not be surprising; when asked about wildfire plans, many residents perceived this to be a serious life or death issue. This participant felt as though she had to face the possibility of staying with her husband to die or leaving him to risk death alone.

A number of women in our interviews explicitly spoke of their fear about having to choose between staying with their husbands, even when they wished to leave, or leaving their husbands to stay and defend on their own. As one woman in Western Australia commented, while being interviewed with her husband: 'But the other thing is, how would I go leaving you? I just don't know' (female, WA, tree/sea change). Her husband, perhaps in response to his wife's intimation that she felt uncomfortable with the idea of leaving him, suggested that they could stay together. He interrupted her at this point of the interview, quite authoritatively, by saying:

And this is where we do the defend and go...We can get everything prepared, turn the defences on, stay until the last minute.

(male, WA, tree/sea change)

Like many of the plans agreed by couples where there was a gender split (female partner leaves, male partner stays) in the previous section, it appears there may be a link here that results in a plan for late evacuation. It is possible that conflict within a household, or between a couple, may result in a preference for late evacuation as some sort of compromise.

It must also be acknowledged that these discussions on wildfire planning between couples may actually be extremely difficult and can create significant tension and emotional distress. This too may influence the way in which a couple determines their wildfire plan. Indeed, some women, rather than trying to resolve disagreement regarding a wildfire plan, simply hoped to convince their partners to come with them, quite literally in the heat of the moment. One participant stated that she thought her husband 'might change his mind' (female, Vic, rural) if there was a serious wildfire event, while another thought that:

If we were in that situation and we realised how close it can get, he would – I could convince him to go.

(female, Vic, urban-rural interface)

The following exchange is another typical example of how several female respondents believed they were going to deal with disparate views within the household:

> RESEARCHER: Now, in terms of your own household, what's your plan?
>
> PARTICIPANT [FEMALE]: My husband and I have talked about this... He says he would stay and I'm not okay with that. I would like to go. I would only go purely because of my children...So we have a little bit of a differing opinion about this. He would – he says he would stay for as long as he thought it was safe and then he would go. There's no way I would stay here with the kids.
>
> RESEARCHER: How do you think it's going to be resolved?
>
> PARTICIPANT [FEMALE]: I don't know. I think it would be resolved if it got scary and he said: 'Yeah, you're right. Let's get out of here' (female, WA, rural).

It is interesting to note that in this participant's story, a divergence of opinion on whether to 'Stay or Go' is minimised; she refers to it only as 'a little bit of a differing opinion' but it is possible to see from her account how such a 'differing opinion' may lead to serious problems. It is not just that this couple have not determined an agreed wildfire plan but that they fundamentally disagree on the type of action to take. It is not difficult to understand how such situations can lead to the kind of crisis within a household described by Handmer and colleagues (2010) during the Black Saturday fires. That is, disagreement at the time of a fire may lead to a delay or a lack of action that puts members of the household in danger.

That the ability to make the best decision and communicate effectively in a time of crisis is likely to be limited as conflict within the household seems self-evident. However, the data collected here points to something more than simply intra-household conflict; it shows that there are broader influences regarding the social construction of gender that are likely to lead men and women to believe that different courses of action are best. That is, it is important to consider why there were no recorded instances of men trying to convince their 'gung ho' female partners that early evacuation was the best option, and why we found no instances of women trying to convince reluctant male partners to 'stay and defend'. The relationship between dominant constructions of masculinity in Australia and staying to defend certainly warrant further examination. As staying to defend largely conforms to norms of Australian hegemonic masculinity (Tyler *et al.*, 2012; Tyler and Fairbrother, 2013a), there are likely to be forms of social pressure on men to choose this course of action. In comparison, leaving early is seen as more feminised and even weak (Griffiths, 2012; Tyler *et al.*, 2012; Tyler and Fairbrother, 2013a).

Taking this course of action, as one of the residents puts it, may mean that you are seen by others, or may even see yourself, as a 'scaredy cat' (female, VIC, urban-rural interface). Furthermore, the fact that these kinds of gendered expectations are prevalent, and yet are rarely mentioned in either policy or research, certainly lends support to the claim that such assumptions about gendered behaviour are deeply ingrained.

Conclusion

The difference in gendered expectations associated with wildfire response, coupled with the cultural construction of wildfires as 'men's business' in Australia, creates difficult conditions for compromise among couples with differing preferences for a household wildfire plan. It is likely to be especially difficult for women to voice their concerns about their husbands 'staying to defend' and have them taken seriously in a cultural environment which privileges men's knowledge of wildfire as innately more authoritative (Poiner, 1990). The husband from Western Australia who interrupts his wife to clarify their plan as 'defend and go' (male, WA, tree/sea change) is an illustrative example. His wife would prefer early evacuation but he takes over the discussion to explain that the better option for them is really late evacuation, even though late evacuation is inherently more risky and is actively discouraged by fire agencies (Tibbits *et al.*, 2008). The 'defend and go', as he puts it, is not a recognised option at all. It is, in fact, just late evacuation.

These examples, and our research more broadly, also suggest that many women are not 'dependant' on advice from their husbands, as has been put forward elsewhere (Goodman and Cottrell, 2012), but rather that they actively disagree with their husbands. Instead, it seems many women are involved in a process of negotiation within the household which they are likely to find challenging, given the social support for men's decision-making regarding wildfire safety. So, it is not that women are dependent on men but rather that men's plans and decisions in these situations – even when risky or ill-advised – are likely to be taken as more authoritative than women's plans and decisions. This is a result of not only gender inequality within households but also the broader social construction of men's natural authority, especially in areas of disaster preparedness and response. It therefore becomes important to name male power and privilege as a central issue, especially, as we note later, when this power of decision-making can contribute to carrying out ill-advised and risky responses to wildfire that put lives at risk.

The cultural support for men's decision-making regarding wildfire preparation and response, especially if their planned course of action is to 'stay and defend', also helps account for the theme of women in this study avoiding ongoing negotiation over a wildfire plan. Instead of confronting the issue with their male partner, several female participants reported gambling on being able to convince a male partner to leave once a fire actually threatens. This may have been perceived as an easier or less stressful option than having ongoing discussions about an issue that women are culturally deemed to know less about. Alternatively, it may have been seen as easier, or as less stressful, than having to challenge the dominant masculine norm of 'stay and defend', in trying to convince a male partner to adopt the 'feminised' plan of early evacuation. However, the decision to raise the issue again, only when a fire threatens, is obviously fraught with danger. If a woman succeeds in changing her partner's mind, then this process may lead to late evacuation; if she is unsuccessful, then she has to decide whether to leave him to defend the house alone, or reluctantly stay with him, against her own judgement.

More broadly speaking, these problems highlight the power dynamics and complexity of intra-household communication and decision-making around wildfire preparedness and response. Decision-making in disaster contexts has often been analysed at the level of the individual, with little consideration of the influence of sociocultural factors (Johnson *et al.*, 2012). This research highlights that the social construction of gender is a critical factor in determining what course of action may appeal to residents and how they determine, or attempt to determine, an agreed course of action within a household. Gendered expectations, particularly regarding hegemonic masculinity and the valorisation of 'stay and defend' for men, may play a role in inhibiting open discussion and negotiation between members of a heterosexual couple about the best course of action to take as a couple during a wildfire event.

The purpose of understanding that the construction of 'stay and defend' suits notions of Australian masculinity, while evacuation is feminised and seen by some as cowardly, is not to reinforce 'broad brush characterisations' (Whittaker *et al.*, 2016: 203) but rather to understand that the social pressures on men and women to undertake certain actions when wildfire threatens are different. Just because something is masculinised does not mean that men, exclusively, participate. but it can help to explain why men may feel pressured to participate in instances where women do not; that is, there are competing expectations for men and women (who are more likely to feel comfortable leaving early or feel responsible for the evacuation of others, especially children) which may make reaching agreement difficult. Even if couples do reach agreement on a split plan (where a male partner stays and a female partner leaves early), this brings with it a range of other problems. The emotional strain that some women expressed, for example, about leaving their husbands is a very real problem as is the possibility that when a fire threatens a couple become reluctant to separate.

Any ongoing disagreement within a household over a wildfire plan is therefore likely to create more risky outcomes for couples and families. Disagreement may result in a lack of preparation and delay or inhibit effective action when a wildfire event occurs. Evidence from the Black Saturday fires suggests that these kinds of disagreements may even have been a contributing factor in several deaths (Handmer *et al.*, 2010). What has not yet been widely recognised, however, is the important role that the social construction of gender, gender roles and gendered expectations play in defining these disagreements. While this research provides substantial evidence of 'split' household plans, where men leave and women stay, what is even more glaring is that not a single instance was found where these roles were reversed and women stayed while men left. This suggests an extremely gendered set of practices and expectations around wildfire preparation and response. In order for agencies and researchers to better understand intra-household communication and decision-making, it is clear that the social construction of gender and associated inequalities must be taken into account.

Notes

1 The options of 'Prepare, Stay and Defend, or Leave Early' only became the official policy of the AFAC in 2005, but the benefits of a 'stay and defend' approach had been more informally promoted by a number of fire services dating back to, at least, the 1970s (see Reynolds, 2017).

2 An earlier version of this chapter is published as:
Tyler, M. and Fairbrother, P. 2018. Gender, households and decision-making for wildfire safety, *Disasters*, First published: 13 March 2018. https://doi.org/10.1111/disa.12285
We would like to thank the journal editors for their kind permission to publish this chapter. The data in this chapter covers 3 States: New South Wales, Victoria and Western Australia. The reason for this selection is that a different set of interview questions were used by the researchers in Tasmania.

3 Please note that all names used in quotes from interview data are pseudonyms to protect participants' anonymity.

9   Challenges for Wildfire Policy and Practice

Peter Fairbrother and Meagan Tyler

The state, in its multilevel formation, is a key player in relation to wildfire events, in the preparation for, dealing with, and recovery from such events. Via state supported and promoted agencies, policy in relation to wildfire is formulated, elaborated and put into effect. These practices impact communities, where these events are experienced and dealt with in a myriad of ways. The question is: what are the constraints and opportunities for the elaboration and implementation of wildfire policies?

This concluding chapter returns to the challenging and rapidly changing context in which wildfire agencies are delivering services to residents in wildfire-prone localities. We argue that acknowledging the complexity of providing useful communication and facilitating active engagement regarding wildfire preparation is paramount. Understanding the diversity and inequality *within* communities that make up the intended audience for these communications is a first step towards democratic responsibility in relation to preparation for wildfire events. We also assert, more broadly, that, as a matter of priority, studies on wildfire in Australia, and research on disaster more generally, should be opened up to centre stage power and inequality in relation to disaster preparedness, response and recovery.

Power and Inequality

The state is a major actor in relation to disaster events and the preparation and recovery that may be invoked. Governments develop policies, establish authorities to prepare for and deal with such events and lay down guidelines for behaviour in and around these types of events. As illustrated earlier, government functions and related activity have been shaped and developed over time and in light of specific experiences with disaster events. In Australia, there is considerable variation in both provision and approach from State to State, although it should also be noted that these arrangements can mirror each other as well and connect across State borders. We argue that the governmental approaches to disaster events should be looked at in relation to interconnections from the municipality to the regional through the federal to the global (for the analytical underpinnings, see Clarkson, 2001: 504). Even so, such interconnected jurisdictions tend to be clustered around particular and specific State arrangements, which, for example, provide a sense of a Victorian approach to disaster events when compared with other States, such as New South Wales (NSW). The outcome is a degree of unevenness in State approaches to these events and the prospect of learning from each other over time.

The state operates at different levels in relation to disaster events, organising and operating over space and time. This multi-scalarity involves the state, via governments (Commonwealth, States and Territories, and local government), and it means engagement with communities in localities, communities of practice exemplified by networked relationships as well as complicated senses of belonging in these localities. The outcome is that there are a range of configurations in relation to state engagement in relation to the preparation for, involvement with and the recovery following disaster events. The question is, how can we make sense of this cacophony of layered relationships to embrace an approach to preparedness, the events, and their aftermath in engaged and participative ways?

The challenge to understanding these social relations is both theoretical and empirical. The theoretical challenge is to understand the nature and character of relations between the state on the one hand and the community on the other hand. This feature draws attention to authority and responsibility as policymakers and as citizens. Moreover, these dimensions play out in complicated narrative ways in liberal democracies, with challenges about the exercise of power, the subtle and not so subtle ways that power is exercised, often by the few rather than the many, by the active and often self-interested rather than the reflective and dispassionate. One outcome is that distended and distorted forms of accountability seem to prevail.

The first step in disentangling our understandings is to note at the outset that wildfires are episodic and very varied events in practice and increasing in their frequency (Climate Council, 2013). They range from wildfire in the bush away from populations to the peri-urban wildfire often adjacent to if not part of major urban centres. In these circumstances, there is a critical place for the exercise of responsibility in relation to both policy formulation and implementation, by and in the state, as well as by and within communities. Of note, the state has both the capabilities and the resources to address both the social and physical aspects of wildfire events; the question is how do they exercise such capacities, in directive ways, 'Stay or Go', or in engaged and participative ways, such as Strategic Conversations. This query draws attention back to the way in which we understand our democratic relations and the ways we put them into practice. Such aspects have already been addressed in theoretical terms, with the idea of state-synergy focussing on reciprocal engagement between state and civil society, in relation to a division of responsibility and in relation to personal networks within and between these spheres (Evans, 1996). And, as analysis almost always notes, this does not necessarily imply that the capacities within each sphere are equal, with commensurate capacities, and that they have similar understandings of the threats they face. It is critical that we consider the strengths and weaknesses of different interest groups that make up each sphere, how such interest groups relate to the populous more generally, and the ways these relations are expressed in practice (e.g. Kalinowski, 2008).

The second step is to locate these observations within the broader narratives of the modern liberal democratic state, where the focus has been on the interactions between the state and the social actors and institutions that make up civil society (Evans, 1977). Over the last three decades, the view of the ways various levels of government should intervene to regulate and organise social and economic life has been transformed. In the modern liberal democracy, there has been a paradigmatic shift towards multilevel governance, elaborated and underpinned via declarations that the state is committed to facilitating citizen engagement and participation in the formulation and implementation of a range of policy measures, such as regional, social and economic development (Clarkson, 2001). The parameters of this shift mean that wildfire agencies provide increased attention to the social arrangements for disaster preparation, although resting on a continued attachment to prevailing narratives about social behaviours and increasingly sophisticated technologically based practices of disaster mitigation and alleviation. We argue that while technological intervention and innovation are critical in relation to disaster events, democratic decision-making and participation are necessary features of the ways the state should relate to communities as localities and thus in relation to events such as wildfire occurrences.

The third point to note is in relation to localised communities. The evidence about belonging to different communities is both conceptually and empirically confused. If the argument is accepted that communities in part must be defined in relation to localities (Fairbrother *et al.*, 2013), then the opportunity is there to begin to discuss how a sense of identity based on material inequalities (gender, ethnicity, class and so forth) has a saliency in relation to the relationship with agencies and the dimensions of association and involvement within the 'community' (on cautionary views of this point, see Mowbray, 2005; Mulligan, 2013). It then becomes possible to discuss multiple and 'nested' communities, provided the sense of the local is retained, at least for the purposes of analysis.

The long-standing debates about the constituent features and parameters of communities as localities, aspects of subnational regions, draw attention to the multidimensionality of a region (Jessop *et al.*, 2008). As referred to earlier these dimensions identify questions relating to territoriality, scalarity and network-connectedness (Macleod and Jones, 2007; see also Goodwin, 2012 and Morgan, 2014). While we must begin to unpick the content of these ideas, in relation to wildfire events, as well as in relation to other aspects of sociopolitical life, the uneven and provisional nature of the exercise of political power in these circumstances must be noted. Empirically, the forms of disaster governance are often uneven, partial and relatively impermanent. These features would appear to be an aspect of the episodic character of disaster, and in particular wildfire events, as well as the underdeveloped relations between the state and localities as communities. Of consequence, the ways in which we understand these relations and their impact are often overlain by contested narratives about accountability and responsibility. Thus, the scalar politics that surround such events involve social and material interests that are both wide-ranging and fluid, with partial and varied, and at times catastrophic outcomes.

As noted earlier, the Australian state rests on two contradictory relationships in relation to disaster events. First, a distinction may be drawn between the administrative and representative structures that comprise the state apparatus in liberal democracies. Second, this distinction is underpinned with the complications between professional actors, the administrators, experts and full-time trained and skilled employees, on the one hand, and lay/voluntary relationships, exemplified by elected officials and volunteers, trained and skilled, although in different ways and often with varied outcomes, on the other hand. And, providing the constituent context for disaster events, the populous – residents, retirees, the young, visitors, waged workers and the self-employed, those in education and others engaged in caring activity, men and women, old and young, and so forth – may be involved, may be bystanders and may be marginalised and even excluded from the mainstream of disaster-related activity. The point is to note these features and then to stimulate reflective discussion and debate about them.

As demonstrated earlier, the state plays and should play a distinctive role in shaping policy and decision-making processes, promoting engagement by citizens within their communities. The reason for this observation is that it is the state that has the capabilities and resources to undertake this task. Moreover, ideally, democratic states are accountable to and responsible for the policies and practices that shape modern society. The problem is that form of accountability and responsibility increasingly promoted as 'shared responsibility' appear to be inadequate and wanting, in relation to a comprehensive engagement across all spheres of society, and in particular in relation to disaster events. The premise is spurious because 'shared responsibility' rests on inadequate conceptualisation of co-productive partnerships between the state *qua* agencies and the locality-based social groups within a disaster-prone area (cf., McLennan and Handmer, 2013). This form of 'responsibility' rests on an assumption relating to the mutuality of engagement that simply does not stand up in practice; it overlooks the heterogeneity and unevenness and inequalities that define many of the communities that constitute disaster prone communities (Tyler and Fairbrother, 2018). Hence, the starting point must be the communities in localities, not the state *per se*.

States and Disaster Events

A major and understandable challenge for governments and their agencies at all levels is to address the prospect of natural disaster and in this case the incidence and impacts of wildfire events. As noted earlier, promoting and achieving preparedness for wildfire is a complex process. It rests on the texture of relations between the state and civil society, and these relations are never stable and involve partial solutions which require forms of constant redress if the complexity of civil society is to be addressed. Specifically, it involves the production and dissemination of information by fire and safety agencies, and the success of such communication depends upon its reception by the public. In Australia, communication products for wildfire preparedness have been developed separately by public agencies in individual States with considerable collaboration and cross-pollination of ideas occurring between various state bodies. Agencies also develop and produce their own communication products and tailor delivery methods to local needs. Increasingly attempts are made to embed mutually reciprocal responsibilities into these activities, creating a sense of 'shared responsibility', which is somewhat undone by the ways that disaster agencies tend to focus on localities as a 'community', rather than on communities as such (see also Atkin and Rice, 2013).

Our research investigated the interactions between communication and behaviour through a study of the multiple relationships between communities, authorities and agencies engaged with fire prevention, preparedness and recovery. To open up these concerns, we developed a framework of analysis to examine communication practices, with the focus on bushfire. To explore this dimension, communication products from a range of agencies were collected and analysed, resulting in a snap shot of products used. These communication practices are often *ad hoc* and clumsy in their implementation. Knowledge management is underdeveloped and relatively unfocussed. The result is that while a general awareness of wildfire and its dangers and implications has been achieved, the mutuality of authentic democratic relations, in terms of accountability and responsibility, has not. This remains the challenge for all of us in the modern democratic society.

Communications professionals working in the area of wildfire safety in Australia face a difficult task (Chapter 7). As with any attempt at communications for the public good, the conditions for achieving proactive ways of dealing with the prospect of natural disaster challenges are difficult. From the point of view of the state the effectiveness of communication campaigns can be limited by a lack of resources, the absence of theoretical frameworks and modelling, and by poorly conceived strategies. Moreover, the hierarchical structures of disaster agencies, given the quasi-military history and 'command and control' style operations of many rural wildfire services, act as further inhibitors to engaged and participative engagements between the state and civil society.

For people to appreciate the risk of the 'hazards on their doorsteps', one claim is that they should be personally engaged with the messages coming from the emergency services organisations (King, 2000: 226; Prior and Paton, 2008). Another claim is that key messages should be consistent, easy to understand and relevant to the area where people live (Fairbrother *et al.*, 2010). As demonstrated, it is not enough just to send generic material and expect that people have the knowledge and skill to apply that information to their own situations (Prior and Paton, 2008). Achieving behaviour and attitude change through public communications is a very difficult task (Devin and Foreman-Werne, 2013). The frustrations that can arise in these types of situations mean that the audience is often blamed; people do not listen, they do not understand.

The challenge facing wildfire agencies is to develop communication strategies aimed at localities as evolving, changing and developing/declining communities. These localities may be long-established rural localities, with traditional and conventional forms of social organisation and practice. They may be areas that are undergoing social change, often involving inward migration, usually from urban areas, and in this context into fire-prone areas. Such localities may include regional-urban areas, sea-change/tree-change and peri-urban locales. Within such localities, there may be the movement of younger families to the urban fringe, complemented by middle age and older persons retiring to non-urban areas. Some areas attract tourists and in others holidaymakers may come and go. Alongside these more positive developments there are also localities within the wildfire-prone and wildfire-susceptible areas that are in socio-economic decline, often with the ending of traditional industries such as saw-milling, resource extraction, shifts in primary produce arrangements, the slow decline of services to smaller conurbations and so forth. Such changes often throw established relations and practices into sharp relief, and create challenges for newcomers to these natural environments, raising questions about wildfire preparedness and responses. In some cases there is evidence of tensions between different sections of the community about bush retention, cleaning up vegetation waste and related lifestyle preferences.

When developing strategies in relation to wildfire preparedness and response it is important to take into account the specificities of locality, such as peri-urban, sea-/tree-change and like features. One particular aspect that should be considered is the tension between everyday life and having time for local involvement and engagement, a feature that may be difficult to reconcile in practice. These dimensions are evident in other settings, where people may work outside a locality but live in a wildfire-prone area. It may also be the case that there is a disaggregation of such localities, in terms of work and employment, household engagement, and length or residency. These features are demanding and elicit varied ways to engagement; where agencies do not recognise such dimensions or do not make them an explicit reference, ineffective communication strategies are likely to result.

In preparing awareness materials, agencies and self-organised groups in localities should map divisions that characterise community populations and then develop strategies which take divisions into account in positive ways. One of the conditions for effective awareness materials is an understanding of the community populations in question. There was substantial variation in the way in which communications were promoted by agencies. In some instances, there were no formal processes in place for either message development or evaluation as well as for the incorporation of wide-ranging attitudes to the experience and implications of wildfire events. Even where such measures were in place, often they were relatively superficial and were unlikely to engage non-dominant cultural groups (Banks, 2000). While there were isolated examples of more thorough engagement with culturally and linguistically diverse (CALD) groups, overall, the data suggests that these approaches to audience segmentation and diversity in the area of wildfire safety and preparedness were underdeveloped. These deficiencies should be a serious concern for organisations involved in producing wildfire preparedness and safety messages. To illustrate, the absence of formal evaluation procedures meant that the opportunities for ongoing and cumulative learning, from both past and current experience, were limited. It meant that some of the repetition of recommendations seen in successive enquiries after disaster events becomes part of the problem rather than the solution. It also meant that governments of the day often make pyrrhic announcements about lessons learnt.

Wildfire-related communication, whether awareness or education, should engage individuals directly, be located within the communities that make up localities, provide relevant, tailored understandings and maintain preparedness and become a mutually reciprocal process between the state and citizens. The task is to better understand the audience, to focus messages in terms of audience understandings and engagement. In practice, this step would mean that the starting point for communication development and implementation must be the communities themselves as both audience and generator of topics and themes. Such an approach rests on mutual engagement and reciprocity in not only developing the message but also delivering it.

The populations that inhabit and are part of the locality-based communities learn about wildfire events in various ways. These processes include the formal (organised information sessions often led by emergency agency staff and members) and the informal (social media such as Twitter, Facebook, YouTube and more). Of note, given the importance of informal interactions and conversations in relation to locality awareness, it is important that not only should agencies take these matters into account when developing awareness strategies but that procedures are developed with citizens as the agents in the process (e.g. Blair *et al.*, 2010). We need to understand the ways in which informal relations, involving conversation, local meeting places and related social practices have a bearing on wildfire preparedness and response. Such practices, recognised and enhanced by disaster agencies may enable the elaboration and practice of forms of democratic engagement in relation to wildfire events.

Beyond Communication

Communities as localities are locked into relations with emergency and disaster agencies in complicated and often misunderstood ways, with negative implications for effective communication. Too often agencies are organised in complex ways, despite the seeming clarity of relations indicated by the militaristic model that characterises most emergency organisations internationally. The problem is that such organisational models lend themselves to linear and non-interactive approaches to communication. While expertise is paramount in the design, development and dissemination of messages, it also requires an open-minded and comprehensive involvement with so-called *audiences*, in particular the populations that comprise the communities in localities in wildfire-prone areas. Here the onus is on the agencies to be proactive, responsive and engaged. The examples of such practice are instructive, such as the 'Strategic Conversations' by the Department of Sustainability and Environment in Victoria or the self-organised locality groups, such as the various Community Fireguard initiatives. In these cases, the mark of organisation is engagement as a mutually interactive practice. But, as noted, they remain relatively isolated examples, they rested on particular relations between state agencies and the involved communities and they did not define the prevailing approaches to wildfire preparation and recovery.

Given that localities are undergoing change in various ways, with a range of outcomes, the question is: how can locality-based forms of engagement and preparation be achieved? We argue that network building is critical, within communities and between communities and agencies. First, a network perspective reveals the resourcefulness of communities and builds interdependence in ways that can build community resilience. Second, and linked to network building, some agencies have begun a process of promoting 'Strategic Conversations' and similar activities. Third, in a number of States, agencies have nurtured education awareness building practices, often under the rubric of Fireguard (Chapter 4). These steps also reinforce and embed the development of networks and awareness practices in relation to communities in and of localities. Fourth, complementing the process of network building, community-based wildfire education is a key strategy in the attempts to promote understandings (Chapter 5). Together these steps may lay the foundation of community engagement in and of localities.

It became evident that there are multifarious and cross-cutting understandings, both within and between agencies. On occasions, tensions were evident within agencies and between brigades and communities, particularly in relation to the role and nature of community engagement (Chapters 5 and 7). We claim that a less fragmented approach to community engagement should be adopted which focusses on community communication practices as a process and one that centre-stages participatory forms of involvement. Such approaches must rest on understandings of both the complexity and the sociopolitical environment of communities within and of localities.

Alongside communication strategies, social network building by those resident and active in communities is one way that the cross-cutting linkages that make up communities can be addressed in positive ways. One challenge for network building is to develop programs that recognise the ways in which particular individuals, their characteristics and interactions, and indeed their roles, are critical for wildfire preparation. Another challenge is to promote networks so that they have continuity within as well as a profile for the locality. Clearly, given the socio-demographic complexity of many locality populations, it may be necessary to encourage a range of networks. This step must involve the recognition of different capacities of a network population. It may also be necessary to facilitate capacities by providing support (e.g. information sessions, meetings with volunteer and professional agency staff), places to meet (e.g. homes, sports facilities, schools) and resources (e.g. finance, printed material). The important point to note is that network building is not likely to happen in the absence of such support.

Wildfire safety communications are at an elementary state of development, particularly in the Australian context. They tend to be from the agencies, down; those in the communities have to figure out what is being conveyed, to whom and for what purpose. These processes do not capture the prospects of democratic engagement as indicated by the recent debates about power and participatory engagement (e.g. Blair *et al.*, 2010; Timms and Heimans, 2018). While debate about these ideas is at the beginning, there are pointers to the ways in which communication strategies should be part of network building within and between communities that make up localities. These engagements can become the core of democratic responsibility in relation to wildfire events.

Communities in and of Localities

The complex composition of localities as communities requires an understanding of how communities are constructed, and an appreciation of the forces of cohesion and division that mark all communities. In so doing, relationships including gender, race and ethnicity, age and class must be emphasised. Communities as localities are defined by these relations of inequality. To explore the ways in which such relationships are structured, and the degree to which agency by the involved social actors becomes possible, we focussed on the form and complexity of gender relations in relation to wildfire events. Along with age, race and ethnicity, poverty and wealth, and the ability to act, gender constitutes a critical dimension in relation to the ways in which the capacities of women and men can be expressed (Tyler and Fairbrother, 2013a and Chapter 8).

The prevailing approaches to community interaction rest on premises that are often overlooked in the construction of interactive strategies between the state and communities and within communities themselves. To specify, gendered expectations, arising out of the social construction of gender, have not yet been well incorporated into understandings and then addressed through practice. Wildfire agencies need to be aware of these intra-household dynamics and we suggest that further research is required in order to understand the way in which the social construction of gender may affect the development of household wildfire plans. Unless agencies and researchers better understand intra-household communication and decision-making, there is little prospect of ever achieving inclusive humane and effective understandings to inform how we address and prepare for disaster events. Not only must the social construction of gender be mainstreamed into policy understandings, but also in other ways the inequalities associated with race, ethnicity and class must be centre-staged.

Generally, decisions about wildfire events are taken within the context of households. This focus raises the question of gender in relation to meeting the challenges posed by wildfire events. In particular, there are notable gender differences in preference for early evacuation or 'staying to defend' (or the various variations of the mantra 'Stay or Go'), and the way in which these differences are negotiated within couples. Even so, the evidence of different understandings about disaster threats by and within households is compelling; as we noted in Chapter 8, the existing gendered power dynamics give rise to 'split' household plans, where men stay and women leave. And to reinforce this pattern of behaviour, we could not find one example of the reverse response, namely women stayed while men left. There can be no dispute that heterosexual households display extremely gendered sets of practices and expectations around wildfire preparation and response. Our study suggests that disagreement about wildfire safety within households, especially between members of heterosexual couples, is common and that this impedes the ability of individuals and families to develop adequate wildfire preparedness and response strategies.

These household relations matter for firefighting units in particular, and for wildfire agencies in general. The particularity of gender must be recognised and acknowledged, and agencies should structure their internal practices as well as the texture and focus of policies, with questions relating to gender at the forefront. The evidence shows that recognition of gender relations is critical and long overdue. Issues around gender show up in relation to firefighting practices as well as in relation to how households address the prospect of disaster events. Moreover, there is evidence that these relations impact responses during a wildfire event. It is important, for example, that wildfire agencies are aware of the substantial gender differences in evacuation preference and how this can create difficulties in reaching an agreed wildfire plan (or plans) within a household.

It is incumbent on those concerned with awareness development in relation to wildfires to explore ways that populations can be encouraged to deliberate on these questions in positive ways. As illustrated and documented, communities as localities are socially constructed. In this process it is important to identify potential lines of division and misunderstanding; once done the task facing agencies is to promote practices that enable reflection and discussion about different experiences and understandings as well as agreement. These measures may open up challenging questions for network building as well as for education and communication.

The hegemonic narratives associated with the social construction of relationships often mask inequalities and are inhibitors to democratic responsibility. The social construction of gender, for example, and the material inequalities that support it mean that men and women may conclude that different courses of action are best. More specifically, in the case of gender, the relationship between dominant constructions of masculinity in Australia and staying to defend certainly warrant further examination, as do questions relating to ethnicity, class and age. For the elderly, it may be the case that they may resign themselves to fatalistic type decisions, on the grounds of social consideration and practicality. Or, in relation to class relations, many may not have the capacities to respond to materially challenging events, particularly in a recovery phase. The problem is that dominant expectations, reinforced by populist narratives – about age, racialisation and class (including the denial of many of these inequalities) – mean that these dimensions are rarely mentioned in either disaster policy or research on bushfire in Australia. The consequences can be devastating and horrific.

Challenging Power and Addressing Inequality

Over recent times, the ways that wildfire events are addressed by the state and civil society have involved the embrace of technological capacities, accompanied by gradual qualifications of a broadly based military-style approach. These steps were furthered with the promotion of shared responsibility in relation to wildfire events which rest on a set of assumptions about power and inequality. In particular, the approach rests on the possibility that all parties to the events can and will play an active and mutually responsible part in dealing with such events and the preparation for and recovery from them. Additionally, there is little recognition of the masculinist assumptions that underpin practice and inform almost all repertoires of action. An adequate approach should be based on an appreciation of the importance of the exercise of power and the narratives that reinforce this relatively restricted view of the relation between the state and civil society.

Wildfire agencies, at all levels, are critical players in dealing with wildfire events; they give content to state relations with communities as localities. Apart from fighting fires on the day and in the lead-up to such events, learning, practicing, deploying technologies and caring for and protecting the citizenry, they also play critical roles in preparing communities for the possible dangers of such events. Hence, the importance of complementing technique, technologies and the science of fire with a comprehensive appreciation of both the complexity of communities and an understanding of the social and natural environment which defines them as localities. Without an appreciation of the social in relation to the natural environment, the benefits of technologically-based approaches to such events is often immediate, on the day, and partial in their effect; it overlooks the centrality of the social in the lead up to and aftermath of such events underwrites, as well as during the course of the disaster event itself.

An alternative view begins from the premise that an inclusive and effective engagement would be based on the mutual and reciprocal recognition of capacities and accommodations that recognise diversity of interest and understanding. It would premise all practices within a socio-technical organisational approach to wildfire events, one that is informed and defined by diverse interests and understandings. This form of democratic engagement rests on the assumption that procedures and practices can be developed whereby the specificity of the social groups that make up communities as localities can play their parts in mutually accountable and responsible ways. Such engagement is not one way but is mutually beneficial, reciprocal and focussed.

Overall, awareness strategies should be grounded in relation to the detail and the socio-demographics of communities as localities. When developing awareness strategies for these types of communities the socio-demographics often associated with vulnerability must be taken into account, such as age, sex, language differences, lifestyle and financial well-being. Of particular importance, agencies must be encouraged to note the complexity of household decision-making in relation to wildfire events. This awareness may assist in making wildfire safety communication from agencies more effective if the possibility of disagreement within the household is openly acknowledged . As noted, these decisions can be momentous and consequential. Given the variety of households and the range of decision-making processes that are evident from the locality studies, it is critical that these households can express concerns and that agencies can develop in reciprocal ways appropriate advice and guidance, and ultimately engagement.

Enhancing Social and Political Capacities

Hence, wildfire incidents are social phenomena. As illustrated, wildfires become disaster events when they threaten the lives and well-being of people within their communities and in a community of practice as a locality. The challenge is how do we as a society prepare for, experience and recover from such events. As argued, the answer involves a disentanglement of the complex relationship between multilevel states and civil society. These themes call for a theory of disaster preparedness and response. Three touchstones open up such an analysis: communities within and as localities; the state, their agencies (professional and voluntary) and awareness strategies; and state-sponsored policies and approaches. The context in which these relationships will be worked out is a world subject to climate change and the increased frequency and intensity of a range of natural disaster events, such as, in Australia and many other parts of the world, wildfire.

Most policy and practice to date is informed by an approach to wildfire events that comprises a combination of technologically based practices supported by an assumption that a military-style form of social organisation is best equipped to deal with such events, particularly on the day (Reynolds, 2017). Of course, in practice this sharp view is qualified as the inadequacies of such an approach become evident. In event after event, in disaster after disaster, it has become apparent that the social dimension is critical, a problem for many and a frustration for others, especially the residents who experience wildfire events. Increasingly, there has been a recognition that there is a social dimension to wildfire and this has been taken on board by researchers and practitioners, particularly within the agencies, and in a more *ad hoc* way in localities. It is within this paradigm of evidence that the question of power and its exercise comes to the fore.

The first step is to demonstrate the ways in which power is a defining feature of these relationships. Underpinning the puzzle of how to address wildfire in the liberal democratic state is a recognition that it has a social basis to it. In general, and particularly since the Second World War, the relation between the state and civil society in relation to wildfire events has been one where the state via its agencies broadly defines and implements approaches to address wildfire events (e.g. see Reynolds, 2017). In Australia, such approaches come out of a rather contested history between locality-based firefighting units, comprised of volunteers and often concerned with retaining the decision-making autonomy that goes with such arrangements. The subsequent technological innovations and their promotion and use by states, coupled with economic arrangements to deal with the preparation for, conduct during and recovery from such events, meant that the state became the primary player in these practices. While enhancing the capacities to confront wildfire events, the social bases of these measures tended to be underplayed. Decision-making did not and does not rest in the communities as localities in the modern liberal democratic state; communities within and of localities have become more and more socially and politically complex and the social and natural environment of such localities is often fragile and uncertain. Nor is decision-making simply an issue of individualised psychology.

Power, the exercise of power and inequality can mean that specific social groups are misunderstood, marginalised and even ignored. This outcome is not necessarily deliberate, considered or even thought out; rather in a democratic state it is as likely to be an oversight, a result of the opaqueness of social relations, and an outcome of dominant and unquestioned narratives about people and their capacities or interests. The first point to note is that dominant and stereotyped narratives of various degrees of certainty can mask the capacities of many, evident in relation to gender relations, the racialisation of some social groups and the ongoing blindness about first nations peoples. Second, it is the case that many social actors, as individuals or as members of various communities of practice, may not have the capabilities and resources to address the divisive narratives that mark the social groups that comprise many localities, at least in ways that mitigate and allow adaptations to the prospect of wildfire events. Third, in these circumstances the exercise of power, by the state, by agencies and by those in politico-economic positions of prominence within localities, can be to the detriment of others, even when not intended. More to the point, these inequities can be the consequence of an narrowness in outlook, and simplistic understandings of the social and political complexity of the ways we live, work and conduct our lives.

What appears to be a sensible, a rational way of understanding such complexity is not the same for all. Of course in some cases inequality can be affirmed in vicious and tragic ways. Thus, the complex relations between the state, the economy and civil society can be marked by inclusiveness and closure; they may be structured so some can exercise agency, while others are more constrained. Hence, to address the social basis of disaster events it is necessary to understand the ways societies are organised and structured. Frequently, they are structured in terms of inequalities – wealth, social position, perceived capacities – and the exercise of power by dominant interests. This condition points to the proposition that those who have capability and resources matter, and those who are not in a position to exercise power are often forced to rely on others, evident in the case of many disaster events. The corollary to this proposition is that we should take steps, all of us, to reconstruct these relations so that accountability, responsibility and participations in mutually reinforcing ways become the mantra to address wildfire events.

If questions relating to power and inequality are placed at the forefront of analysis, the task is to consider and implement the ways of individuals and collectivities that make up communities in wildfire-prone localities may be enabled in relation to their vulnerability to such events. The challenge is that policymakers often lack comprehensive understandings of 'the vulnerable' and do not appreciate the social bases of vulnerability, the difficulties of access to resources or the impacts of unhelpful administrative and bureaucratic procedures. While not intentional, the neglect of this aspect of the exercise of power undermines the democratic ethos that should govern much of our social life in a liberal democracy. In this context, it becomes critical to identify who has power in any given social setting, trace out the ways power is exercised and define how and under what circumstances different social groupings can exercise agency in relation to wildfire events. Understanding wildfire events, therefore, should not be about creating technologically-based solutions enforced by traditional military-style organisations for wildfire events and then seeking to bring in the community in a variety of socially informed ways; rather it is about addressing from start to finish the social basis of wildfire occasions, recognising that these are social events. This requires acknowledging that the social, the need to better understand how people, in varied contexts, prepare for, react to and recover from disaster events, is axiomatic.

Disaster events bring power relations to the fore, whether that be at the very public level of the state or at the more private level of the household. With such recognition, it may be possible to develop practices whereby wildfire events can be addressed in ways that recognise the social costs of natural disaster. It requires a comprehensive understanding of our capacities, technically and in the communities as localities. It means that our technological experts, our environmental- and bioscientists have the capabilities and resources to address the threat of wildfire, and that our social scientists are empowered to put forward understandings of the social and political circumstances in which these threats play out. In this context, it requires policymakers at all levels to become the means and the medium for social exchange and mutual engagement, between the state and civil society. But, above all, to address wildfire events in a socially informed democratic way, communities as localities must be the starting point. After all, they also are the end point. Hence, wildfire studies can and should focus on inequalities and the exercise of power. The outcome will be the advocacy of an evolving and participative process of democratic engagement and responsibility that address some of the most horrific experiences we can imagine.

Bibliography

Adams, D. and Hess, M. 2001. Community in public policy: Fad or foundation? *Australian Journal of Public Administration,* 60 (2): 13–23.

AEMI (n.d.) Knowledge hub, http://www.emknowledge.gov.au/disaster-information/

AFAC 2005. *Position Paper on Wildfires and Community Safety.* AFAC: Melbourne. http://www.royalcommission.vic.gov.au/Documents/Document-files/Exhibits/TEN-001-001-0077

AFAC 2006. *The Stay and Defend Your Property or Go Early Policy.* Firenote, no. 7, http://www.bushfirecrc.com/sites/default/files/managed/resource/bcrcfirenote7staygo.pdf

AFAC 2013. *The Stay and Defend Your Property or Go Early Policy,* http://knowledgeweb.afac.com.au/research/community/plesd/The_Stay_and_Defend_Your_Property_or_Go_Early_Policy

AIC – Australian Institute of Criminology 2004. The cost of bushfires. *Bushfire Arson Bulletin* no. 2, https://aic.gov.au/publications/bfab/bfab002

Akama, Y. and Ivanka, T. 2010a. *Birds of a Feather: Emboldening community spirit and connectedness for bushfire resilience,* http://www.rmit.edu.au/browse;ID=tf3nrmdmr6tm1

Akama, Y. and Ivanka, T. 2010b. What community? Facilitating awareness of 'community' through playful triggers. *Proceedings of the Eleventh Conference on Participatory Design 2010,* ACM Digital Library, Sydney, Australia.

Akama, Y., Cooper, V. and Mees, B. 2016. Beyond transmission: An analysis of communication frameworks in Australian bushfire preparedness, *International Journal of Disaster Resilience in the Built Environment,* 7 (1): in press.

Alavi, M. and Leidner, D.E. 2001. Review: Knowledge Management and Knowledge Management Systems: Conceptual Foundations and Research Issues. *MIS Quarterly,* 25 (1): 107–136.

Alderson, W. 1957. *Marketing Behavior and Executive Action: A Functionalist Approach to Marketing Theory.* Irwin: Homewood, IL.

Anderson, B. 1983. *Imagined Communities: Reflections on the Origin and Spread of Nationalism.* Verso: London.

Andrulis, D., Siddiqui, N. and Ganter, J. 2007. Preparing racially and ethnically diverse communities for public health emergencies, *Health Affairs,* 26 (5): 1269–1279.

Argyle, M. 1987. *The Psychology of Happiness.* Methuen: London.

Argyris, C. and Schön, D. 1974. *Theory in Practice: Increasing Professional Effectiveness.* Jossey-Bass: San Francisco.

Atkin, C. and Freimuth, N. 2013. Guidelines for Formative Evaluation Research in Campaign design. In Rice, R. and Atkin, C. (eds) *Public Communications Campaigns*. 4th edition. Sage: Thousand Oaks, CA.

Atkin, C. and Rice, R. 2013. Theory and Principles of Public Communications Campaigns. In Rice, R. and Atkin, C. (eds) *Public Communications Campaigns*. 4th edition. Sage Publications: Thousand Oaks, CA.

Ariyabandu, M. 2009. Sex, Gender and Gender Relations in Disasters. In Enarson, E. and Chakrabarti, P.G. (eds) *Women, Gender and Disaster: Global Issues and Initiatives*. Sage Publications: London.

Australian Bureau of Statistics (ABS) 2011. Population by Age and Sex, Regions of Australia, 2010, 3235.0, released 4 August, www.abs.gov.au

Australian Bureau of Statistics 2012. Regional Population Growth, Australia 2010–11, Section Estimates by Local Government Area, 3218.0 www.abs.gov/AUSSTATS/abs@nsf/DetailsPage/3218.02010

Ayres, I. and Braithwaite, J. 1992. *Responsive Regulation: Transcending the Deregulation Debate*. Oxford University Press: New York.

Baber, W. and Bartlett, R. 2007. Problematic participants in deliberative democracy: Experts, social movements and environmental justice, *International Journal of Public Administration*, 30: 5–22.

Bainson, K.A. 1994. Integrating leprosy control into primary health care: The experience in Ghana, *Leprosy Review*, 65 (4): 376–384.

Banks, S. 2000. *Multicultural Public Relations: A Social Interpretive Approach*. 2nd edition. Iowa State University Press: Ames.

Banks, S. and Shenton, F. 2001. Regenerating neighbourhoods: A critical look at the role of community capacity building, *Local Economy*, 26 (4): 286–298.

Barnard, C.I. 1938. *The Functions of the Executive*. Harvard University Press: Cambridge, MA.

Bartholomew, D. 2008. *Building on Knowledge: Developing Expertise, Creativity and Intellectual Capital in the Construction Professions*. Blackwell: Oxford.

Bateman, J. and Edwards, B. 2002. Gender and evacuation: A closer look at why women are more likely to evacuate for hurricanes, *Natural Hazards Review*, 3 (3): 107–117.

Baum, F. 1999. Social capital: Is it good for your health? Issues for a public health agenda, *Journal of Epidemiology and Community Health*, 53 (4): 195–196.

Bayne, M. and Lazarus, M.E. 1940. *The Australian Community: A Critical Approach to Citizenship*. Longmans: London.

Beckingsale, D. 1994. Community fireguard and the rural–urban interface, *Fire Management Quarterly*, 10 (1): 1–8.

Bennett, J. 2012. Private and Public Provision of Firefighting Services in Rural Australia. In Lueck, D. and Bradshaw, K. (eds) *Wildfire Policy: Law and Economics Perspectives*. RFF Press: Hoboken, NJ.

Bentley, T., McCartney, H. and Mean, M. 2003. *Inside Out: Rethinking Inclusive Communities*. Demos: London.

Bird, D., Ling, M. and Haynes, K. 2012. Flooding Facebook – the use of social media during the Queensland and Victorian floods, *The Australian Journal of Emergency Management*, 27: 27–33.

Blackshaw, T. 2010. *Key Concepts in Community Studies*. Sage Publications: Los Angeles.

Blair, S., Campbell, C. and Campbell, M. 2010. *A Case Study of a Strategic Conversation about Fire in Victoria, Australia: Fire and Adaptive Management*, Report no. 79, Victorian Government Department of Sustainability and Environment, Melbourne, https://trove.nla.gov.au/work/37961015?selectedversion=NBD46006850Blair

Bohman, J. and Rehg, W. (eds) 1997. *Deliberative Democracy: Essays on Reason and Politics*. The MIT Press: Cambridge, MA.

Boin, A. and McConnell, A. 2007. Preparing for critical infrastructure breakdowns: The limits of crisis management and the need for resilience, *Journal of Contingencies and Crisis Management*, 15 (1): 50–59.

Bolin, R., Jackson, M. and Crist, A. 1998. Gender Inequality, Vulnerability and Disaster: Issues in Theory and Research. In Enarson, E. and Morrow, H. (eds) *The Gendered Terrain of Disaster: Through Women's Eyes*. Praeger: Santa Barbara.

Bond, W. and Keeley, J. 2005. Fire as a global 'herbivore'. The ecology and evolution of flammable ecosystems, *Trends in Ecology and Evolution*, 20: 387–394.

Boura, J. 1998. Community Fireguard: Creating partnerships with the community to minimise the impact of bushfire, *Australian Journal of Emergency Management*, 13 (3): 59–64.

Bourdieu, P. 1973. Cultural Reproduction and Social Reproduction. In Brown, R. (ed) *Knowledge, Education and Cultural Change*. Tavistock: London.

Bourdieu, P. 1985. The Forms of Capital. In Richardson, J.G. (ed) *Handbook of Theory and Research for the Sociology of Education*. Greenwood: New York.

Bourdieu, P. and Passeron, J.C. 1977. *Reproduction in Education, Society and Culture*. Trans. R. Nice. Sage Publications: Beverley Hills.

Bowman, D, and Murphy, B. 2011. Australia – a model system for the development of pyrogeography, *Fire Ecology*, 7 (1): 5–12.

Boyle, P. and Halfacree, K. (eds) 1997. *Migration to Rural Areas: Theories and Issues*. Wiley: Chichester.

Brackertz, N. and Meredyth, D. 2009. Community consultation in Victorian local government: A case of mixing metaphors? *Australian Journal of Public Administration*, 68 (2): 152–166.

Braun, V. and Clarke, V. 2006. Using thematic analysis in psychology, *Qualitative Research in Psychology*, 3 (2): 77–101.

Brenkert-Smith, H. 2010. Building bridges to fight fire: The role of informal social interactions in six Colorado wildland–urban interface communities, *International Journal of Wildland Fire*, 19: 689–697.

Brenner, N., Jessop, B., Jones, M. and MacLoed, G. 2003, *State/Space: A Reader*, Blackwell Publishing: Oxford.

Brent, J. 2004. The desire for community: Illusion, confusion and paradox, *Community Development Journal*, 39 (3): 213–223.

Brint, S. 2001. Gemeinschaft revisited: A critique and reconstruction of the community concept. *Sociological Theory*, 19 (1): 1–23.

Brummel, R. F., Nelson, K. C. and Jakes, P. J. 2012. Burning through organizational boundaries? Examining inter-organizational communication networks in policy-mandated collaborative bushfire planning groups, *Global Environmental Change,* 22, 516–528.

Bryant, C. 2008. *Understanding bushfire: Trends in deliberate vegetation fires in Australia,* Technical and Background Paper Series 27, Australian Institute of Criminology, Canberra.

Bryson, L. and Mowbray, M. 1981. Community: The spray-on solution, *Australian Journal of Social Issues,* 16 (4): 255–267.

Buergelt, P. and Smith R. 2015. Wildfires: An Australian Perspective. In Paton, D. and Shroder, J. (eds) *Wildfire Hazards, Risks and Disasters.* Elsevier: Amsterdam, pp. 101–121.

Buckle, P. 1999. Re-defining community and vulnerability in the context of emergency management, *Australian Journal of Emergency Management,* 13 (4): 21–26.

Bushnell, S., Balcombe, L. and Cottrell, A. 2007. Community and fire service perceptions of bushfire issues in Tamborine Mountain: What's the difference? *The Australian Journal of Emergency Management,* 22: 3–9.

Calhoun, C. 1980. Community: Toward a variable conceptualization for comparative research, *Social History,* 5 (1): 105–129.

Campbell, C. 2000. Social Capital and Health: Contextualizing Health Promotion within Local Community Networks. In Baron, S., Field, J., and Schuller, T. (eds) *Social Capital: Critical perspectives.* Oxford University Press: Oxford.

Campbell, C., Wood, R. and Kelly, M. 1999. *Social Capital and Health.* Health Education Authority: London.

Cass, B. and Brennan, D. 2002. Communities of support or communities of surveillance and enforcement in welfare reform debates, *Australian Journal of Social Issues,* 37 (3): 247–262.

Castells, M. 2001. *The Internet Galaxy: Reflections on the Internet, Business and Society.* Oxford University Press: Oxford.

Castells, M. 2009. *Communication Power.* Oxford University Press: Oxford.

Cattell, V. 2001. Poor people, poor places, and poor health: The mediating role of social networks and social capital, *Social Science and Medicine,* 52 (10): 1501–1516.

CFA 2012. *Annual Report 2011–12,* https://www.cfa.vic.gov.au/search?q=cfa+annual+report+2011

CFA 2016. *Annual Report 2015–16.*

CFA 2018. *Am I at risk?* Country Fire Authority, https://www.cfa.vic.gov.au/plan-prepare/am-i-at-risk

Chakrabarti, P.G. and A. Walia 2009. Toolkit for Mainstreaming Gender in Emergency Response. In Enarson, E. and Chakrabarti, P.G. (eds) *Women, Gender and Disaster: Global Issues and Initiatives.* Sage Publications: London.

Chase, R.A. 1993. Protecting People and Resources from Wildfire: Conflict in the Interface. In Ewert, A.W., Chavez, D.J. and Magill, A.W. (eds) *Culture, Conflict and Communication in the Wildland–Urban Interface.* Westview Press: Boulder, CO.

Chaskin, R.J. 2001. Building community capacity: A definitional framework and case studies from a comprehensive community initiative, *Urban Affairs Review,* 36 (3): 291–323.

Chia, J. 2010. Engaging communities before an emergency: Developing community capacity through social capital investment, *Australian Journal of Emergency Management*, 25 (1): 18–22.

City of Greater Bendigo 2016. *Community Engagement Guidelines and Toolkit*, https://www.bendigo.vic.gov.au/sites/default/files/2016-11/Community_Engagement_guidelines_and_toolkit_2016_ECM3377622.pdf

Clark, D. B. 1973. The concept of community: A re-examination, *The Sociological Review*, 21 (3): 397–416.

Clarkson, S. 2001. The multi-level state: Canada in the semi-periphery of both continentalism and globalization, *Review of International Political Economy*. 8 (3): 501–527.

Clay, S. 2008. *Here Comes Everybody: The Power of Organizing Without Organizations*. Penguin: New York.

Climate Council. 2013. *Angry Summer 2013/2014*, http://www.climatecouncil.org.au/angry- summer

COAG. 2011. *National Strategy for Disaster Resilience: Building our Nation's Resilience to Disasters*. COAG: Canberra.

Coates, L., Haynes, K., O'Brien, J., McAneney, K. and Dimer de Oliveira, F. 2014. A longitudinal examination of extreme heat events in Australia 1844–2010: Exploring 167 years of social vulnerability, *Environmental Science and Policy*, 42, 33–44.

Coates, T. 2007. *Building the Plane as You Fly It: Community Systems in New Orleans*. Unpublished Master's thesis, Harvard University.

Cohen, A. 1985. *The Symbolic Construction of Community*. Tavistock: London.

Coleman, J. 1988. Social capital in the creation of human capital, *American Journal of Sociology*, 94 (Supplement): s95–s120.

Cooke, P. and Morgan, K. 1998. *The Associational Economy: Firms, Regions and Innovation*. Oxford University Press: Oxford.

Cottrell, L. 1976. The Competent Community. In Kaplan, B., Wilson, B. and Leighton, A. (eds) *Further Explorations in Social Psychiatry*. Basic Books: New York.

Cottrell, A. 2005. Communities and bushfire hazard in Australia: More questions than answers, *Environmental Hazards*, 6 (2): 109–114.

Cottrell, A., Bushnell, S., Spillman, M., Newton, J., Lowe, D. and Balcombe, L. 2008. Community Perceptions of Bushfire Risk. In Handmer, J. and Hayes, K. (eds) *Community Bushfire Safety*. CSIRO Publishing: Melbourne.

Cox, H.M. and Holmes C.A. 2000. Loss, healing, and the power of place, *Human Studies*, 23 (1): 63–78.

Craig, G. 2007. Community capacity-building: Something old, something new...?. *Critical Social Policy*, 27 (3): 335–359.

Craig, G. and Taylor, M. 2002. Dangerous Liaisons. In Glendinning C., Powell, M. and Rummery, K. (eds) *Partnerships, New Labour and the Governance of Welfare*. Policy Press: Bristol.

Craig, R.T. 1999. Communication theory as a field, *Communication Theory*, 9 (2): 119–161.

Crisp, B.R., Swerissen, H. and Duckett, S.J. 2000. Four approaches to capacity building in health: Consequences for measurement and accountability, *Health Promotion International*, 15 (2): 99–107.

Crow, G. and Allen, G. 1994. *Community Life: An Introduction to Local Social Relations*. Harvester Wheatsheaf: Hemel Hempstead.

Cuthill, M. and Fien, J. 2005. Capacity building: Facilitating citizen participation in local governance, *Australian Journal of Public Administration*, 64 (4): 63–80.

DEC – FESA 2011. *Heads of Agreement for Partnership and Joint Bushfire Service Delivery Between the Department of Environment and Conservation (DEC) and the Fire and Emergency Services Authority (FESA)*. Government of Western Australia, http://www.ses-wa.asn.au/sites/default/files/FESA%20DEC%20agreement.pdf

DeFilippis, J. 2001. The myth of social capital in community development, *Housing Policy Debate*, 12 (4): 781–806.

Delanty, G. 2003. *Community*. Routledge: Abingdon.

Department of Police and Emergency Management 2015, *Tasmanian Emergency Management Plan, Issue 8*. Tasmania Government, http://www.ses.tas. gov.au/assets/files/Plans/State/Tasmanian%20Emergency%20Management %20Plan%20-%20Issue%208.pdf

Department of Sustainability and Environment 2012. *Guiding Principles: Facilitating Learning, Understanding and Change through Relationship*, Report no. 80, Victorian.

Devin, B. and Foreman-Wernet, L. 2013. Sense-Making Methodology as an Approach to Understanding and Designing for Campaign Audiences. In Rice, R. and Atkin, C. (eds) *Public Communications Campaigns*. 4th edition. Sage Publications: Thousand Oaks.

Dewey, J [1927]. The Search for the Great Community. In Boydston J (ed) 1987. *John Dewey the Later Works, 1925–1953, Volume 2: 1925–1927 Essays, Reviews Miscellany, and the Public and Its Problems*. Carbondale, IL: Southern Illinois Press, pp. 325–350.

DFES 2013. *Department of Fire and Emergency Services Inaugural Report 2012/13*, https://www.dfes.wa.gov.au/publications/Annual%20Reports/ DFES_Annual_Report_2012-2013.pdf

DFES – DPaW 2015. *Heads of Agreement for Partnership and Joint Bushfire Management Service Delivery between the Department of Parks and Wildlife and Department of Fire and Emergency Services*, https://www. dpaw.wa.gov.au/images/documents/fire/15570_head_of_agreement_ between_dfes_and_dpaw_-_signed_lr.pdf

DFES 2018. *Education: Building Disaster Resilience in Young People*, https:// www.dfes.wa.gov.au/schooleducation/Pages/default.aspx updated each year, since at least 2016.

DFES nd. *Bushfire Ready Groups*, http://www.dfes.wa.gov.au/safetyinformation/fire/bushfire/pages/bushfirereadygroups.aspx

Diprose, R. 2003. The hand that writes community in blood, *Cultural Studies Review*, 9 (1): 35–50.

Dufty, N. 2015. The use of social media in countrywide disaster risk reduction public awareness strategies, *Australian Journal of Emergency Management*, 30 (1): 12–16.

Duttan, R., Das, A. and Aryal, J. 2016. Big data integration shows Australian bushfire frequency is increasing significantly, *Royal Society Open Science*, 3: 150241. DOI: 10.1098/rsos.150241

Eadie, W. 2009. *21st Century Communication: A Reference Handbook*. Sage Publications: London.

Edwards, C. 2009. *Resilient Nation*. Demos: London.

Eisenman, D., Gilk, D., Gonzalez, L., Maranon, R., Zhou, Q., Tseng, C. and Asch, S. 2009. Improving Latino disaster preparedness using social networks, *American Journal of Preventative Medicine*, 37 (6): 512–517.

Elliott, G. and McLennan, J. 2011. *Civilian Decision Making Under Stress: Use of fire agency web-sites on Black Saturday*, http://www.bushfirecrc.com/resources/poster/civilian-decision-making-under-stress-use-fire-agency-web-sites-black-saturday

Elliott, G., Walker, M., Toh, K. and Fairbrother, P. 2013. *Developing and Evaluating Effective "Bushfire" Communication Pathways, Procedures and Products, Report Four—Localities and Bushfire Information: Findings and Recommendations*, Centre for Sustainable Organisation and Work, RMIT University, http://mams.rmit.edu.au/rmy3ncecm0ljz.pdf

Elsworth, G., Gilbert, J., Rhodes, A. and Goodman, H. 2009. Community safety programs for bushfire: What do they achieve and how? *Australian Journal of Emergency Management*, 24 (2): 17–25.

Emergency Management Victoria 2015. *Victorian Emergency Management Strategic Action Plan, 2015–2018*, State of Victoria.

Enarson, E. 2009. Gendering Disaster Risk Reduction: 57 Steps from Words to Action. In Enarson, E. and Chakrabarti, P.G. (eds) *Women, Gender and Disaster: Global Issues and Initiatives*. Sage Publications: London.

Enarson, E. and Chakrabarti, P.G. 2009. (eds) *Women, Gender and Disaster: Global Issues and Initiatives*. Sage Publications: London.

Enarson, E. and Morrow, H. 1998. (eds) *The Gendered Terrain of Disaster: Through Women's Eyes*. Praeger: Santa Barbara.

Eng, E. and Parker, E. 1994. Measuring community competence in the Mississippi Delta: The interface between program evaluation and empowerment, *Health Education Quarterly*, 21 (2): 199–220.

Eriksen, C., Gill, N. and Head, L. 2010. The gendered dimensions of wildfire in changing rural landscapes in Australia, *Journal of Rural Studies*, 26 (4): 332–342.

Evans, P. (ed) 1977. *State-Society Synergy: Government and Social Capital in Development*, Research Series no. 94, University of California at Berkeley.

Evans, P. 1996. Government action, social capital and development: Reviewing the evidence on synergy, *World Development*, 24 (6): 1119–1132.

Fairbrother, P. 2015. Rethinking trade unionism: Union renewal as transition, *The Economic and Labour Relations Review*, 26 (4), 561–576. DOI: 10.1177/1035304615616593

Fairbrother, P., Hart, A., Stratford, J. and Prokopiv, V. 2010. *CFA Community Fireguard Review: Improving Quality Control and Assurance*. RMIT University: Melbourne.

Fairbrother, P., Mees, B., Tyler, M., Phillips, R., Akama, Y., Chaplin, S., Toh, K. and Cooper, V. 2014. *Effective Communication: Communities and Bushfire Final Report*. Bushfire Cooperative Research Centre, East Melbourne, Victoria. http://www.bushfirecrc.com/publications/citation/bf-4519

Fairbrother, P., Tyler, M., Hart, A., Mees, B., Phillips, R., Stratford, J. and Toh, K. 2013. Creating 'Community'? Preparing for bushfire in rural Victoria, *Rural Sociology*, 78 (2): 186–209.

Falkheimer, J. and Heide, M. 2006. Multicultural crisis communication: Towards a social constructivist perspective. *Journal of Contingencies and Crisis Management,* 14 (4): 180–189.

FAO – Food and Agriculture Organisation 2010. Will help countries to detect fire hotspots in real time, https://www.fao.org/news/story/en/item/44613.

Fenna, A. 2012. Centralising dynamics in Australian federalism, *Australian Journal of Politics and History,* 58 (4): 580–590.

Ferguson, E. 2016. *Reframing Rural Fire Management,* Report of the Special Inquiry into the January 2016 Waroona Fire, Government of Western Australia, https://publicsector.wa.gov.au/sites/default/files/documents/waroona_fires_2016_-_volume_1_-_report_final.pdf; see also http://walga.asn.au/News,-Events-and-Publications/Media/Local-Knowledge,-Funding-Key-to-Fire-Improvements.aspx

Finn, J.L. and Checkoway, B. 1998. Young people as competent community builders: A challenge to social work. *Social Work,* 43 (4): 335–345.

Finucane, M., Slovic, P., Mertz, C.K., Flynn, J. and Satterfield, T. 2000. Gender, race and perceived risk: The 'white male' effect, *Health, Risk and Society,* 2 (2): 159–172.

Fire Services Commission (2013) *Bushfire Safety Policy Framework,* September 2013, http://files.em.vic.gov.au/EMV-web/Bushfire-Safety-Policy-Framework-Sept-2013.pdf

Forest Fire Management Group 2012. *National Bushfire Management Policy Statement for Forests and Rangelands.* COAG: Canberra.

Fothergill, A. 1998. The Neglect of Gender in Disaster Work: An Overview of the Literature. In Enarson, E. and Morrow, H. (eds) *The Gendered Terrain of Disaster: Through Women's Eyes.* Praeger: Santa Barbara.

Frandsen, M. 2012. *Promoting Community Bushfire Preparedness: Bridging the Theory –Practice Divide.* Unpublished doctoral dissertation, University of Tasmania.

FSC. 2013. *Bushfire Safety Policy Framework: September 2013.* FSC: Melbourne, http://fire-com-live-   wp.s3.amazonaws.com/wp-content/uploads/2013-Bushfire-Safety-Policy-Framework.pdf.

Geoscience Australia 2012. What Causes Bushfires? www.ga.gov.au/hazards/bushfires, August 24, 2012.

Gilbert, J. 2007. *Community education, awareness and engagement programs for bushfire: An initial assessment of practices across Australia,* Technical Report no. C0701, Bushfire Cooperative Research Centre.

Gilchrist, A. 2000. The well-connected community: Networking to the edge of chaos, *Community Development Journal,* 35(3): 264–275.

Gilchrist, A. 2003a. Community Development and Networking for Health. In Powell, J., Taylor, P., Grey, M., and Orme, J. (eds) *Public Health for the 21st Century: New Perspectives on Policy, Participation and Practice.* Open University Press: Buckingham.

Gilchrist, A. 2003b. Community development in the UK—possibilities and paradoxes, *Community Development Journal,* 38 (1): 16–25.

Gilchrist, A. 2009. *The Well-connected Community: A Networking Approach to Community Development,* 2nd edition. Policy Press: Bristol.

Gillies, P. 1998. Effectiveness of alliances and partnerships for health promotion, *Health Promotion International,* 13 (2): 99–120.

Glen, A. 1993. Methods and Themes in Community Practice. In Butcher, H. (ed) *Community and Public Policy*. Pluto Press: London.

Goodman, H. and Cottrell, A. 2012. Responding to a Fire Threat: Gender Roles, Dependency and Responsibility. In Paton, D. and Tedim, F. (eds) *Wildfire and Community: Facilitating Preparedness and Resilience*. Charles Thomas Publishing: Springfield.

Goodman, H. and Gawen, J. 2008. Glimpses of 'Community' through the lens of a small fire event, *Australian Journal of Emergency Management*, 23 (1): 30–36.

Goodman, H. and Proudley, M. 2008. The Social Contexts of Responses to Bushfire Threat: A Case Study of the Wangary Fire. In J. Handmer and K. Haynes (eds) *Community Bushfire Safety*. CSIRO Publishing: Collingwood, VIC, pp. 47–56

Goodman, R., Steckler, A., Hoover, S. and Schwartz, R. 1993. A critique of contemporary community health promotion approaches based on a qualitative review of six programs in Maine, *American Journal of Health Promotion*, 7 (3): 208–221.

Goodsell, T.L., Colling, M., Brown, R.B. and England, J.L. 2011. On past and future of community: A pragmatic analysis, *American Sociology*, 42: 277–287.

Goodwin, S. 2005. Community and Social Inclusion. In Smyth, P., Redell, T. and Jones, A. (eds) *Community and Local Governance in Australia*. University of NSW Press: Sydney.

Goodwin, M. 2012. Regions, territories and relationality: Exploring the regional dimensions of political practice, *Regional Studies*, 47: 1181–1190.

Government of Victoria. 2008. *Strengthening Community Organisations*. Government of Victoria: Melbourne.

Greeley, A.M. 1966. After secularity: The neo-Gemeinschaft society. *Sociological Analysis*, 27 (3): 119–127.

Griffiths, T. 2012. The language of catastrophe. *Griffith Review*, 30: np, https://griffithreview.com/edition-35-surviving/the-language-of-catastrophe

Habermas, J. 1984–87. [1981]. *The Theory of Communicative Action*. Trans. T. McCarthy. Polity: Cambridge.

Hackett, B. 2000. *Beyond Knowledge Management: New Ways to Work and Learn*. Conference Board: New York.

Hall, N. and Best, J. 1997. Health promotion practice and public health: Challenge for the 1990s, *Canadian Journal of Public Health*, 88: 409–415.

Handmer, J. and Haynes, K (ed) 2008. *Community Bushfire Safety*. CSIRO Publishing: Collingwood, VIC.

Handmer, J. and O'Neill, S. 2016. Examining bushfire policy in action: Preparedness and behaviour in the 2009 Black Saturday fires. *Environmental Science and Policy*, 63 (xx): 55–62.

Handmer, J., O'Neil, S. and Killalea, D. 2010. *Review of Fatalities in the February 7, 2009 Wildfires*. Report prepared for the Victorian Wildfires Royal Commission, www.wildfirecrc.com/managed/resource/review-fatalities-february-7.pdf

Hansen, C. and Griffiths, T. 2012. *Living with Fire: People, Nature and History in Steels Creek*. CSIRO Publishing: Melbourne.

Harpham, T. Grant, E. and Thomas, E. 2002. Measuring social capital within health surveys: Key issues, *Health Policy and Planning*, 17 (1): 106–111.

Hawe, P. 1994. Capturing the meaning of 'Community' in community intervention evaluation: Some contributions from community psychology, *Health Promotion International*, 9 (3): 199–210.

Haynes, K., Handmer, J., McAneney, J., Tibbits, A. and Coates, L. 2010. Australian wildfire fatalities 1900–2008: Exploring trends in relation to the "prepare, stay and defend or leave early" policy, *Environmental Science and Policy*, 13 (3): 185–194.

Hennessy, K., Lucas, C., Nicholls, N., Bathols, J., Suppiah, R., and Ricketts, J. 2006. *Climate Change Impacts on Fire-weather in South-east Australia*. CSIRO: Melbourne.

Hoggett, P. 1997. Contested Communities. In Hoggett, P. (ed), *Contested Communities: Experiences, Struggles, Policies*. Polity Press: Bristol.

Hornik, R. 2013. 'Why Can't We Sell Human Rights Like We Sell Soap?' In Rice, R. and Atkin, C. (eds) *Public Communications Campaigns*. 4th edition. Sage Publications: Thousand Oaks.

Hughes, P., Black, A. Kaldor, P., Bellamy, J. and Castle, K. 2007. *Building Stronger Communities*. UNSW Press: Sydney.

Ife, J. 2003. Community Development and Human Rights. Keynote address delivered at the People, Place, Partnership: Strengthening Communities Conference, 28–29 April, Sydney.

IPCC, 2014. *Climate Change 2014: Synthesis Report*. Contribution of Working Groups I, II and III to the Fifth Assessment Report of the Intergovernmental Panel on Climate Change [Core Writing Team, Pachauri R.K. and Meyer L.A. (eds)]. IPCC: Geneva, Switzerland.

Iscoe, I. 1974. Community psychology and the competent community, *American Psychologist*, 29 (8): 607–613.

Jakes, P., Kruger, L., Monroe, M., Nelson, K., and Sturtevant, V. 2007. Improving wildfire preparedness: Lessons from communities across the US, *Human Ecology Review*, 13 (2): 188–197.

Jessop, B. 1990. *State Theory: Putting the Capitalist State in its Place*. The Pennsylvania State Press: University Park, Pennsylvania..

Jessop, B., Brenner, N. and Jones, M. 2008. Theorizing sociospatial relations, *Environment and Planning D: Society and Space*, 26 (3): 389–401.

Jirasinghe, R. 2007. *The Rhythm of the Sea*. Hambantota Chamber of Commerce: Hambantota, Sri Lanka.

Johnson, B., Miller, G., Fogel, M., Magee, J., Gagan, M. and Chivas, A. 1999. 65,000 years of vegetation change in central Australia and the Australian summer monsoon, *Science*, 284: 1150–1152.

Johnson, P., Johnson, C. and Sutherland, C. 2012. Stay or Go? Human behaviour and decision making in wildfires and other emergencies, *Fire Technology*, 48 (1): 137–153.

Jones, R. 1987. Community Involvement: The Missing Link, *Bushfire Bulletin*, 9 (1 and 2): 14–15

Kalinowski, T. 2008. State-civil society synergy and cooptation: The case of the minority shareholder movement in Korea, *Korea Observer*, 39 (3): 339–367.

Kasperson, R. 1987. Public Perceptions of Risk and their Implications for Risk Communication and Management. In McColl, S.R. (ed), *Environmental Health Risks: Assessment and Management*. University of Waterloo Press: Waterloo.

Kawachi, I. 2001. Social capital for health and human development. *Development*, 44 (1): 31–35.

Kawachi, I., Kennedy, B.P., Lochner, K. and Prothrow-Stith, D. 1997. Social capital, income inequality and mortality, *American Journal of Public Health*, 87 (9): 1491–1498.

Keelty, M. 2011. *A Shared Responsibility: The Report of the Perth Hills Bushfire February 2011 Review*. Government of Western Australia: Perth, http://www.parliament.wa.gov.au/publications/tabledpapers.nsf/displaypaper/3813769afddf0dbf88c33147482578ef003031db/$file/3769.pdf

Keelty, M. 2012. *Appreciating the Risk: Report of the Special Inquiry into the November 2011 Margaret River Bushfire*, Government of Western Australia, https://publicsector.wa.gov.au/sites/default/files/documents/inquiry_-_margaret_river_bushfire_-_report_-_appreciating_the_risk_with_annexures.pdf

Kelly, D. 1999. The strategic-relational view of the state, *Politics*, 19 (2): 109–115.

Kenny, S. 2011. *Developing Community for the Future*. 4th edition. Cengage: Melbourne.

King, D. 2000. 'You're on Your Own': Community vulnerability and the need for awareness and education for predictable natural disasters, *Journal of Contingencies and Crisis Management*, 8 (4): 223–228.

Kotler, P. and Zaltman, G. 1971. Social marketing: An approach to planned social change, *Journal of Marketing*, 35 (3): 3–12.

Labonte, R. and Laverack, G. 2001a. Capacity building in health promotion: Part 1: For whom? And for what purpose? *Critical Public Health*, 11 (2): 111–127.

Labonte, R. and Laverack, G. 2001b. Capacity building in health promotion: Part 2: Whose use? And with what measurement? *Critical Public Health*, 11 (2): 129–138.

Lévesque, C. and Murray, G. 2010. Understanding union power: Resources and capabilities for renewing union capacity, *Transfer*, 16 (3): 333–350.

Lorber, J. 1994. *Paradoxes of Gender*. Yale University Press: New York.

Lyon, L. 1989. *The Community in Urban Society*. Lexington: Toronto.

MacDougall, C., Gibbs, L., and Clark, R. 2014. Community-based preparedness programmes and the 2009 Australian bushfires: Policy implications derived from applying theory, *Disasters*, 38 (2): 249–266.

MacKinnon, D. 2011. Reconstructing scale: Towards a new scalar politics, *Progress in Human Geography* 35, 21 –36. DOI:10.1177/ 0309132510367841

MacLeod, G. and Jones, M. (2007) Territorial, scalar, networked, connected: In what sense a regional world? *Regional Studies*, I41 (9): 1177–1191.

Magsino, S. 2009. *Applications of Social Network Analysis for Building Community Disaster Resilience*. National Academies Press: Washington, DC.

Maibach, E., Roser-Renouf, C. and Leiserowitz, A. 2008. Communication and marketing as climate change-intervention assets, *American Journal of Preventative Medicine*, 35 (5): 488–500.

Mansbridge, J., Bonham, J., Chambers, S., Estlund, D., Føllesdal, A., Fung, A., Lafont, C., Manin, B. and Martí, J.L. 2010. The place of self-interest and the role of power in deliberative democracy, *The Journal of Political Philosophy*, 18 (1): 64–100.

Marsh, G. and Buckle, P. 2001. Community: The concept of community in the risk and emergency management context, *Australian Journal of Emergency Management*, 16 (1): 5–7.

Marske, C. 1991. *Communities of Fate: Readings in the Social Organisation of Risk*. University Press of America: Lanham, MD.

Massey, D. 2004. Geographies of responsibility, *Geografiska Annaler*, 86B, 5 –18. DOI:10.1111/j.0435–3684.2004.00150.x

McClure, J. and Williams, S. 1996. Community Preparedness: Countering Helplessness and Optimism. In Paton, D. and Long, N. (eds) *Psychological Aspects of Disasters: Impact, Coping, and Intervention*. Dunmore Press: Palmerston North.

McDonald, C. and Marston, G. 2002. Patterns of governance: The curious case of non-profit community services in Australia. *Social Policy and Administration*, 36 (4): 376–391.

McGee, T.K. and Russell, S. 2003. 'It's Just a Natural Way of Life…': An investigation of wildfire preparedness in rural Australia, *Global Environmental Change, Part B: Environmental Hazards*, 5 (1–2): 1–12.

McLennan, B. 2016. Extending into community-led preparedness and planning just enough (but not too much?), *Australian Journal of Emergency Management*, 31 (1): 5–6.

McLennan, B. and Handmer, J. 2012. Reframing responsibility sharing for bushfire risk management in Australia after Black Saturday, *Environmental Hazards*, 11 (1): 1–15. DOI: 10.1080/17477891.2011.608835

McLennan, J., Elliott, G. and M. Omodei, M. 2012. Householder decision-making under imminent wildfire threat: Stay and defend or leave? *International Journal of Wildland Fire*, v21(3): 915–925.

McLuhan, M. 1967. *The Medium is the Massage: An Inventory of Effects*. Penguin: New York.

Mees, B., Fairbrother, P., Akama, Y., Phillips, R. and Tyler, M. 2013. Communication and Bushfire Preparedness. Unpublished discussion paper. Centre for Sustainable Organisations and Work, RMIT University: Melbourne.

Mees, B., and Ramsay, I. 2008. Corporate regulators in Australia (1961–2000): From companies' registrars to ASIC. *Australian Journal of Corporate Law*. 22: 212–254.

Melucci A. 1996. *Challenging Codes: Collective Action in the Information Age*. Cambridge University Press: Cambridge.

Montoya, D. 2010. *Bushfires in NSW: An Update*, NSW Parliamentary Briefing Paper No 10/2010, https://www.parliament.nsw.gov.au/researchpapers/Pages/research-papers.aspx

Moore, S., Daniel, M., Linnan, L. Campbell, M., Benedict, S. and Meier, A. 2004. After Hurricane Floyd passed: Investigating the social determinants of disaster preparedness and recovery, *Family & Community Health*, 27 (3): 204–217.

Morgan, K. 2007. The polycentric state: New spaces of empowerment and engagement?, *Regional Studies* 41: 1237–1251. doi:10.1080/00343400701543363

Morgan, K. 2014. The Rise of Metropolitics: Urban Governance in the Age of the City-Region. In Bradford, N. and Bramwell, A. (eds) *Governing Urban Economies: Innovation and Inclusion in Canadian City-Regions*. University of Toronto Press: Toronto.

Morley, D. 2005. Communication. In Bennett, T., Grossberg, L. and Morris, M. (eds) *New Keywords: A revised vocabulary of culture and society*. Blackwell: Oxford.

Mowbray, M. 2005. Community capacity building or state opportunism? *Community Development Journal*, 40 (3): 255–264.

Mozumder, P., Raheem, N., Talberth, J. and Berrens, R. 2008. Investigating intended evacuation from wildfires in the wildland–urban interface: Application of a bivariate probit model, *Forest Policy and Economics,* 10 (6): 415–423.

Mulligan, M. 2013. Rebuilding communities after disasters: Lessons from the Tsunami disaster in Sri Lanka, *Global Policy,* 4 (3): 278–287.

Murray, R. and White, K. 1995. *State of Fire: A History of Volunteer Fire Fighting and the Country Fire Authority in Victoria.* Hargreen: Melbourne.

Nabatchi, T., and C. Farrar. 2011. *Bridging the Gap between Public Officials and the Public.* In a Report of the Deliberative Democracy Consortium (DDC).

Narayan, D. 1999. *Bonds and Bridges: Social Capital and Poverty.* World Bank: Washington DC.

Neighbourhood Renewal Unit. 2002. *The National Strategy for Neighbourhood Renewal: Factsheet 2.* Neighbourhood Renewal Unit: Wetherby.

Nepal, V., Banerjee, D., Perry, M. and Scott, D. 2012. Disaster preparedness of linguistically isolated populations: Practical issues for planners, *Health Promotion Practice,* 13 (1): 265–271.

Nonaka, I. 1991. Creating the knowledge company, *Harvard Business Review,* 69 (6): 96–104.

Norris, F., Stevens, S., Pfefferbaum, B., Wyche, K. and Pfefferbaum, R. 2008. Community resilience as a metaphor, theory, set of capacities, and strategy for disaster readiness, *American Journal of Community Psychology,* 41 (1–2): 127–150. DOI: 10.1007/s10464-007-9156-6

NSW Rural Fire Service nd. *Translated Fact Sheets,* http://www.rfs.nsw.gov.au/resources/factsheets/translated-fact-sheets

Obach, B. 2004. *Labor and the Environmental Movement.* The MIT Press: Cambridge, MA.

O'Byrne, D. 2015. *Drawing a Line, Building Stronger Services,* Report of the Victorian Fire Services Review. 12, https://engage.vic.gov.au/application/files/1714/8608/1807/Report_of_the_Fire_Services_Review_2015_2.pdf

OESC – Office of the Emergency Services Commissioner 2010. '*Where Are They Going?' People Movement during Wildfires.* OESC: Melbourne. http://www.oesc.vic.gov.au/resources/d7e8b082-4488-4df7-b020-9340ff861ea6/people_movement_during_wildfires_research+-+final+report+march+2010.pdf

O'Neill, P. 2004. *Developing a Risk Communication Model to Encourage Community Safety from Natural Hazards.* State Emergency Service (SES): Sydney. http://citeseerx.ist.psu.edu/viewdoc/download?doi=10.1.1.466.108&rep=rep1&type=pdf

Papacharissi, Z. 2010. *The Networked Self: Identity, Community and Culture on Social Networking Sites.* Taylor & Francis: New York.

Pape, M. Fairbrother, P. & Snell, D. 2015. Beyond the state: Shaping governance and development policy in an Australian region, *Regional Studies,* 50 (5): 909–921.

Paton, D. and Jackson, D. 2002. Developing disaster management capability: An assessment centre approach, *Disaster Prevention and Management,* 11 (2): 115–122.

Paton, D., Kelly, G., Burgelt, P. and Doherty, M. 2006. Preparing for bushfires: Understanding intentions, *Disaster Prevention and Management: An International Journal,* 15 (4): 566–575. DOI: 10.1108/09653560610685893

Pearlin, L. 1985. Social Structure and Processes of Social Support. In Cohen, S. and Syme, S.L. (eds) *Social Support and Health.* Academic Press: New York.

Peters, B. 1996. *The Future of Governing: Four Emerging Models*, University Press of Kansas: Lawrence.

Peterson, V.S. and Runyan, A. (eds) 1999. *Global Gender Issues*. Westview Press: New York.

Phillips, R. 2007. *Community Capacity Building, Community Development and Health: A Case Study of Health Issues in the Community*. Doctoral dissertation, University of Edinburgh.

Pierides, D. and Woodman, D. 2012. Object-oriented sociology and organizing in the face of emergency: Bruno Latour, Graham Harman and the material turn, *British Journal of Sociology*, 63 (4): 662–679.

Pierson, C. 2005. *The Modern State*. Routledge: London and New York

Poiner, G. 1990. *The Good Old Rule: Gender and Other Power Relationships in a Rural Community*. Sydney University Press: Sydney.

Pope, J. and Zhang, W. 2010. *Indicators of Community Strength at the Local Government Level in Victoria 2008: Strategic Policy, Research and Forecasting*. Government of Victoria, Department of Planning and Community Development (DPCD): Melbourne.

Portes, A. 1998. Social capital: Its origins and applications in modern sociology, *Annual Review of Sociology*, 24: 1–24.

Postmann, Neil. 1985. *Amusing Ourselves to Death: Public Discourse in the Age of Show Business*. Penguin: New York.

Prior, T. and Paton, D. 2008. Understanding the context: The value of community engagement in bushfire risk communication and education. Observations following the East Coast Tasmania Bushfires of December 2006, *The Australasian Journal of Disaster and Trauma Studies* 2008-2. [n.p.]

Proudley, M. 2008a. Fire, families, decisions, *The Australian Journal of Emergency Management*, 23 (1): 37–43.

Proudley, M. 2008b. *Fire, Families and Decisions*. Unpublished Master's thesis, RMIT University.

Putnam, R. 1993. *Making Democracy Work*. Princeton University Press: Princeton.

Putnam, R. 2000. *Bowling Alone: The Collapse and Revival of American Community*. Simon & Schuster: New York.

Putnam, R. 2003. *Better Together: Restoring the American Community*. Simon & Schuster: New York.

Putt, J. (ed) 2010. *Community Policing in Australia*. AIC Reports, Research and Public Policy Series 111. Australian Institute of Criminology: Canberra.

Radford, W.C. 1939. *The Educational Needs of a Rural Community*. Melbourne University Press: Melbourne.

Ramphele, M. and Thornton, J. 1988. The Quest for Community. In Bouzaier, E. and Sharp, J. (eds) *The South African Keywords: The Uses and Abuses of Political Concepts*. David Philip: Cape Town.

Raphael, B. 1986. *When Disaster Strikes: How Communities and Individuals Cope with Catastrophe*. Basic Books: New York.

Reddel, T. 2002. Beyond participation, hierarchies, management and markets: 'New' governance and place policies, *Australian Journal of Public Administration*, 61 (1): 50–63.

Reddel, T. and Woolcock, G. 2004. From consultation to participatory governance? A critical review of citizen engagement strategies in Queensland, *Australian Journal of Public Administration*, 63(3): 75–87.

Reynolds, B. 2017. *A History of the Prepare, Stay and Defend or Leave Early Policy in Victoria*. Unpublished PhD thesis. RMIT University, Melbourne.

Reynolds, B. and Tyler, M. in press. Applying a gendered lens to the stay and defend approach to bushfire safety. *Australian Journal of Public Administration* (accepted 05/07/2017).

RFS. 2013. *End to One of the Worst Fire Seasons in Recent Times*, http://www.rfs.nsw.gov.au/file_system/attachments/State08/Attachment_20130403_04D06DD6.pdf

Rhodes, A., Gilbert, J., Nelsson, C. and Preece, E. 2011. *Evaluation Report 2010–2011 C2.10B Evaluation and Effectiveness Project*. CFA: Melbourne.

Rivera, F.G. and Erlich, J.L. 1981. Neo-Gemeinschaft minority communities: Implications for community organization in the United States, *Community Development Journal*, 16 (3): 189–200.

Robinson, L. 2003. *Education for Resilience: Community Safety Communication for Natural Hazards*, http://www.enablingchange.com.au/Resilience_and_risk.pdf

Rohrmann, B. 1999. Community-based fire preparedness programs: An empirical evaluation, *Australasian Journal of Disaster and Trauma Studies*, 9 (1): 1–21.

Rose, N. 1999. *Powers of Freedom: Reframing Political Thought*. Cambridge University Press: Cambridge.

Sassen, S. 2002. Toward a sociology of information technology, *Current Sociology*, 50 (3): 365–388.

Saussure, F. de. 1959. [1916]. *Course in General Linguistics*. Ed. C. Bally and A. Sechehaye; trans. W. Baskin. Philosophical Library: New York.

Scanlon, J., Osborne, G. and McClellan, S. 1996. *The 1992 Peace River Ice Jam and Evacuation: An Alberta Town Adapts to a Sudden Emergency*. Emergency Communications Unit: Ottawa.

Schramm, W. 1954. How Communication Works. In Schramm, W. (ed) *The Process and Effects of Communication*. University of Illinois Press: Urbana.

Schwartz, D. 2006. Aristotelian View of Knowledge Management. In Schwartz, D.G. (ed) *Encyclopedia of Knowledge Management*. Idea Group Reference: Hershey, PA.

Scillio, M. 2001–2002. Working with the community in emergency risk management. *Australian Journal of Emergency Management*, 16(4): 59–61.

Secomb, L. 2000. Fractured community. *Hypatia*, 15(2): 133–150.

Shannon, C. and Weaver, W. 1949. *The Mathematical Theory of Communication*. University of Illinois Press: Urbana, IL.

Shaw, E. and Jones, D. 2005. A history of schools of marketing thought, *Marketing Theory*, 5(3): 239–81.

Simpson, L. Wood, L. and Daws, L. 2003. Community capacity building: Starting with people not projects, *Community Development Journal*, 38 (4): 277–286.

Smith, M.K. 2001. *The Encyclopaedia of Informal Education*, Community, http://www.infed.org/community/community.htm

Smith, W.A. 2006. Social marketing: An overview of approach and effects. *Injury Prevention*, 12 (Suppl. 1): 38–43.

Smith, R. with Leask, J., Valenti, A. and Negreiros, A. 2012. *Report on – 'Investigation of house losses in the Margaret River bushfire, 23rd November 2011'*, Environmental Protection Branch, DFES, https://www.dfes.wa.gov.au/safetyinformation/fire/bushfire/BushfireResearch/Margaret%20River%20Fire%2023%20November%202011%20-%20House%20Loss%20Survey%20Final%20Report.pdf

Smyth, J. 2009. Critically engaged community capacity building and the 'community organizing' approach in disadvantaged contexts, *Critical Studies in Education*, 50 (1): 9–22.

Snell, D. & Fairbrother, P. 2010. Unions as environmental actors, *Transfer*, 6 (3): 411–24.

Snow, D.A., Burke Rochford Jr., E., Worden, S.K. and Benford, R.D. 1986. Frame alignment processes, micromobilization, and movement participation, *American Journal of Sociology*, 51: 464–481.

Stacey, M. 1969. The myth of community studies, *British Journal of Sociology*, 20 (2): 134–147.

State Fire Commission and Gill, T. 2009. 125 Years Hobart Fire Brigade 1883–2008, State Fure Cinnussuib, Hobart, Tasmania, ISBN 978-0-646-50684-5.

State of Victoria 2011. *Implementing the Government's Response to the 2009 Victorian Bushfires Royal Commission*, Government Printer, [Melbourne], http://trove.nla.gov.au/work/164151537

State of Victoria 2012. *Victorian Emergency Management Reform: White Paper*, Victorian Government, Melbourne

Stoker, G. and Bottom, K.A. 2003. Community Capacity Building: Notes for a talk given to MAV Conference. Lorne, 25–27 July.

Strange, S. 1996. *The Retreat of the State: The Diffusion of Power in the World Economy*, Cambridge University Press: Cambridge.

Sullivan, M. 2003. Communities and their experience of emergencies, *Australian Journal of Emergency Management*, 18 (1): 19–26.

Sydney Morning Herald. 2013. *Bushfire Disaster Reminds Us We Are One Community*. October 18, http://www.smh.com.au/comment/smh-editorial/bushfire-disaster-reminds-us-we-are-one-community-20131018-2vrs3.html

Taksa, L. 2000. Like a bicycle, forever teetering between individualism and collectivism: Considering community in relation to labour history, *Labour History*, 78: 7–32

Taylor, M. 2003. *Public Policy in the Community*. Palgrave MacMillan: Basingstoke.

Teague, B., McLeod, R., and Pascoe, S. 2009. *Victorian Bushfires Royal Commission: Interim Report*. Government Printer: State of Victoria, Melbourne.

Teague, B., McLeod, R., and Pascoe, S. 2010a. *2009 Victorian Bushfires Royal Commission: Final Report*. Government Printer: State of Victoria: Melbourne.

Teague, B., Mcleod, R. and Pascoe, S. 2010b. *2009 Victorian Bushfires Royal Commission, Vol. 2: Fire Preparation, Response and Recovery*. Parliament of Victoria, Melbourne

Tibbits, A., Handmer, J. Haynes, K., Lowe, T. and Wittaker, J. 2008. Prepare, Stay and Defend or Leave Early: Evidence for the Australian Approach. In Handmer, J. and Haynes, K. (eds) *Community Wildfire Safety*. CSIRO Publishing: Melbourne.

Tierney, K. 1999. Toward a critical sociology of risk, *Sociological Forum*. 14 (2): 215–241.

Tilly, C. 1995. Contentious Repertoires in Great Britain, 1758–1834. In Traugott M. (ed) *Repertoires and Cycles of Collective Action*. Duke University Press: Durham, NC, pp. 15–42.

Timms, H. and Heimans, J. 2018. *New Power: How Power Works in Our Hyperconnected World - and How to Make It Work for You*. Pan Macmillan Australia Pty Ltd: Sydney.

Toh, K., and Tyler, M. 2013. *Making Knowledge Visible: Collecting and Collating Bushfire Communications Products*. Firenote no. 102. Bushfire CRC: Melbourne.

Tönnies, F. 1887 [1957]. *Community and Society*. Trans. C.P. Loomis. Harper: New York.

Traugott, M. 1995. Recurrent Patterns of Collective Action. In M. Traugott (ed) *Repertoires and Cycles of Collective Action,* Duke University Press: Durham and London, pp. 1–14.

Trebilcock, M. and Daniels, R. 2006. Rationales and Instruments for Government Intervention in Natural Disasters. In Daniels, R., Kettl, D. and Kunreuther, H. (eds) *On Risk and Disaster: Lessons from Hurricane Katrina*. University of Pennsylvania Press: Philadelphia, pp. 89–108.

Turner, B. 2001. Outline of a General Theory of Cultural Citizenship. In Stevenson, N. (ed) *Culture and Citizenship*. Sage Publications: London.

Turner, V. 1985. *On the Edge of the Bush*. University of Arizona Press: Tucson, AZ.

Tyler, M. and Fairbrother P. 2013a. Bushfires are 'Men's Business': The importance of gender and rural hegemonic masculinity in Australian understandings of bushfire, *Rural Studies*, 30: 110–119.

Tyler, M. and Fairbrother, P. 2013b. Gender, masculinity and bushfire: Australia in an international context, *Australian Journal of Emergency Management*, 28 (2): 20–25.

Tyler, M. and Fairbrother, P. 2018. Gender, households and decision-making for wildfire safety, *Disasters*, First published: 13 March 2018. https://doi.org/10.1111/disa.12285

Tyler, M., Fairbrother P., Chaplin, S., Mees, B., Phillips, R. and Toh, K. 2012. *Gender Matters: Applying gendered analysis to wildfire research in Australia*. Working Paper No. 3. August. Centre for Sustainable Organisations and Work at RMIT University: Melbourne.

UNISDR 2007. *Hyogo Framework for Action 2005–2015: Building the resilience of nations and communities to disasters. Extract from the final report of the World Conference on Disaster Reduction*. United Nations: Geneva.

van Aalst, M. 2006. The impacts of climate change on the risk of natural disasters, *Disasters*, 30 (1): 5–18.

van den Honert, R', Coates, L., Haynes, K. and Crompton, R. 2014–15. A century of natural disasters—what are the costs, *Fire Australia*, Summer.

Varischetti, B. and Prendergast, J. 2016. WA volunteer bush firefighters will only support rural fire service independent of Department of Fire and Emergency Services. Posted 24 June 2016, https://www.dfes.wa.gov.au/safetyinformation/fire/bushfire/pages/bushfirereadygroups.aspx

Verity, F. 2007. *Community Capacity Building: A review of the literature*. South Australian Department of Health: Adelaide.

Vicary, J.R., Doebler, M.K., Bridger, J.C., Gurgevich, E.A. and Dieke, R.C. 1996. A community systems approach to substance abuse prevention in a rural setting, *Journal of Primary Prevention*, 16(3): 303–318.

Victorian Government 2012. *Bushfires Royal Commission Implementation Monitor Final Report*. State of Victoria. www.bushfiresmonitor.vic.gov.au in Adobe PDF. ISBN: 978-1-921627-66-8. See also www.igem.vic.gov.au/documents/CD/15/418771) 2012

Voltmer, K. and Römmele, A. 2002. Information and Communication Campaigns: Linking Theory to Practice. In Klingemann, H. and Römmele, A. (eds)

Public Information Campaigns and Opinion Research. Sage Publications: London.

Voss, K. and Sherman, R. 2003. You Just Can't Do It Automatically: The Transition to Social Movement Unionism in the Unites States. In Fairbrother, P. and Yates, C. (eds) *Trade Unions in Renewal: A Comparative Study.* Routledge: London.

Walby, S. 2005. Comparative gender mainstreaming in a global era. *International Feminist Journal of Politics,* 7 (4): 453–470.

Walsh, D., Rudd, R., Moeykens, B. and Moloney, T. 1993. Social marketing for public health, *Health Affairs,* 12 (2): 104–119.

Webber, R. and Jones, K. 2013. Implementing 'community development' in a post-disaster situation. *Community Development Journal,* 48(2): 248–263.

Wellman, B. 1999. The Network Community: An Introduction. In Wellman, B. (ed) *Networks in the Global Village: Life in Contemporary Communities.* Westview: Boulder, CO.

Western Australia State Government 2012. *2011 Keelty Report Recommendations Implemented or Substantively Addressed,* http://www.dpc.wa.gov.au/ Publications/Documents/Draft%20Bushfire%20Implementation%20Stakeholder%20Briefing%20-%20Thursday%2023%20March%202012.pdf

Wettenhall, R.L. 1975. *Bushfire Disaster: An Australian Community in Crisis.* Angus & Robertson: Sydney.

Whiteley, P.F. 1999. The Origins of Social Capital. In van Deth, J.W., Maraffi, M., Newton, K. and Whiteley, P.F. (eds) *Social Capital and European Democracy.* Routledge: London.

Whittaker, J., Eriksen, C., Haynes, K. 2016. Gendered responses to the 2009 Black Saturday bushfires, *Geographical Research* 54 (2): 203–215.

Wiener, N. 1948. *Cybernetics or Control and Communication in the Animal and the Machine.* Wiley: New York.

Williams, R. 1958 *Culture and Society, 1780–1950.* Penguin Books: Harmondsworth, Middlesex.

Willmott, P. 1987. *Friendship Networks and Social Support.* Policy Studies Institute: London.

Wiseman, J. 2006. Local Heroes? Learning from recent community strengthening initiatives in Victoria, *Australian Journal of Public Administration,* 65 (2): 95–107.

Wisner, B. and Luce, H. 1993. Disaster vulnerability: Scale, power and daily Life, *GeoJournal,* 30 (2): 127–140.

Wright, E.O. (ed) 1995. *Associations and Democracy.* Verso: London.

Yarra Ranges Council. 2010. *I Fought Two Wars, I Can Fight This: Bushfire Awareness and Preparedness of Frail Older and Vulnerable Residents in Yarra Ranges.* Project Report. Yarra Ranges Council: Melbourne.

Yen, I. and Syme, S. 1999. The social environment and health: A discussion of the epidemiological literature. *Annual Review of Public Health,* 20: 287–308.

Young, I.M. 1986. The ideal of community and the politics of difference. *Social Theory and Practice,* 12 (1): 1–26.

Young, I.M. 2001. *Inclusion and Democracy.* Oxford University Press: Oxford.

Index

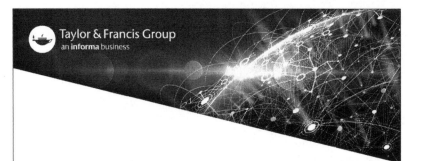